So Much More than the ABCs

The Early Phases of Reading and Writing

Judith A. Schickedanz and Molly F. Collins

National Association for the Education of Young Children
Washington, DC

National Association for the Education of Young Children
1313 L Street NW, Suite 500
Washington, DC 20005-4101
202-232-8777 • 800-424-2460
www.naeyc.org

NAEYC Books

Chief Publishing Officer
Derry Koralek

Editor-in-Chief
Kathy Charner

Director of Creative Services
Edwin C. Malstrom

Managing Editor
Mary Jaffe

Senior Editor
Holly Bohart

Design and Production
Malini Dominey

Associate Editor
Elizabeth Wegner

Editorial Assistant
Ryan Smith

Through its publications program, the National Association for the Education of Young Children (NAEYC) provides a forum for discussion of major issues and ideas in the early childhood field, with the hope of provoking thought and promoting professional growth. The views expressed or implied in this book are not necessarily those of the Association or its members.

Permissions

Figure 1-1 is from *Whistle for Willie*, by Ezra Jack Keats, copyright © 1964 by Ezra Jack Keats, renewed © 1992 by Martin Pope, Executor. Used by permission of Viking Penguin, a division of Penguin Group (USA) Inc.

Figures 3-2a and 3-2b are from *Max's Dragon Shirt*, by Rosemary Wells, copyright © 1991 by Rosemary Wells. Used by permission of Dial Books for Young Readers, a division of Penguin Group (USA) Inc.

Figure 4-1 is from *Raccoon on His Own*, by Jim Arnosky, copyright © 2001 by Jim Arnosky. Used by permission of G.P. Putnam's Sons, a division of Penguin Group (USA) Inc.

Figure 4-2 (left) is from *Daddy Longlegs*, by Catherine Anderson, copyright © 2003, 2008 by Heinemann Library. Used with permission.

Figure 4-2 (right) is from *Caterpillar*, by Karen Hartley, Chris Macro, & Philip Taylor, copyright © 1999, 2006 by Heinemann Library. Used with permission.

Figure 4-3 (left) is from *Bee*, by Karen Hartley & Chris Macro, copyright © 2006 by Heinemann Library. Used with permission.

Figure 4-3 (right) is from *Fly*, by Karen Hartley, Chris Macro, & Philip Taylor, copyright © 2008 by Heinemann Library. Used with permission.

Figure 5-9 is used by permission of Sesame Workshop. Sesame Street ® and associated characters, trademarks and design elements are owned and licensed by Sesame Workshop. © 2012 Sesame Workshop. All Rights Reserved.

Figure 5-10: Copyright © Bugbrained.com. Used with permission.

Figure 7-12: Copyright © Pinger, Inc. Used with permission.

Figure 7-13: Copyright © Tropisounds. Used with permission.

Figure 7-14: Copyright © Griffin Technology. Used with permission.

Figure 8-32: Copyright © Toca Boca. Used with permission.

Figure 8-33: Copyright © Launchpad Toys. Used with permission.

Figure 8-34: Copyright © Show Me. Used with permission.

Photo Credits

Courtesy of the authors: 80, 81, 84, 85; Courtesy of Annmarie Blaney: 130; Boston University Photography: iii (top); Copyright © Joel Goldman: 27; Copyright © Julia Luckenbill: cover, 5, 8, 73, 126, 139, 149; Copyright © NAEYC/Photo by Rich Graessle: 1; Copyright © Ellen B. Senisi: 7, 19, 30, 41, 47, 91, 117, 119, 127, 188; Courtesy of Vanderbilt University: iii (bottom)

Text Credits

Developmental editor: *Natalie Klein*

Indexer: *Sherri Emmons*

So Much More than the ABCs: The Early Phases of Reading and Writing

Library of Congress Control Number: 2012947839
ISBN: 978-1-928896-88-3

NAEYC Item #709

About the Authors

Judith A. Schickedanz, PhD (University of Illinois at Urbana-Champaign), professor emerita at Boston University, taught courses in child development, early literacy, and curriculum and instruction; served as director of the laboratory preschool; coordinated the early childhood program; and helped launch the Jumpstart volunteer program. She taught preschool and has worked extensively with early childhood teachers on funded projects, including Early Reading First. Her current interests include the study and support of story comprehension in preschoolers.

Schickedanz has authored numerous articles, book chapters, and books, including "For Young Children, Pictures in Storybooks Are Rarely Worth a Thousand Words" (*The Reading Teacher*, 2012); *Increasing the Power of Instruction* (NAEYC, 2008); *Writing in Preschool* (International Reading Association, 2009); and *Understanding Children and Adolescents* (Allyn & Bacon, 2000).

Molly F. Collins, EdD (Boston University), a lecturer in the Department of Teaching and Learning, Peabody College, Vanderbilt University, has taught graduate and undergraduate courses in cognitive development, language, and linguistics, and provided professional development on language and literacy for preschool teachers. She taught toddlers and preschoolers, and is past president of the Literacy Development in Young Children group within the International Reading Association. Current projects examine teachers' conversations and support of preschoolers' comprehension during storybook reading.

Collins' articles include "ELL Preschoolers' English Vocabulary Acquisition from Storybook Reading" (*Early Childhood Research Quarterly,* 2010); "Targeting Oral Language Development in High-Risk Preschoolers" (*Head Start Research Journal*, 2009); and "Sagacious, Sophisticated, and Sedulous: The Importance of Discussing 50-Cent Words with Young Children" (*Young Children*, 2012).

About the Contributors

Jessica L. Hoffman, PhD (University of Illinois at Chicago), is an assistant professor of teacher education at Miami University in Oxford, Ohio. She has worked with preschool children and teachers through research in two Early Reading First grants, was a teacher in early childhood classrooms, and now teaches preservice and practicing early childhood teachers. She is a member of the early literacy task force of the International Reading Association. Her current interests include read-aloud discussions in early childhood classrooms.

Hoffman's articles include "Coconstructing Meaning: Interactive Literary Discussions in Kindergarten Read Alouds" (*The Reading Teacher*, 2011); "Interactive and Coconstructive Discourse in Informational Text Read Alouds" (*Literacy Research Association Yearbook*, 2012); and "Looking Back and Looking Forward: Lessons Learned from Early Reading First" (*Childhood Education*, 2010).

Christina Cassano, MEd (University of Maine-Orono), a doctoral student at Boston University and an instructor at Salem State University, has taught courses in literacy and language, educational research, and literacy intervention. She taught kindergarten and worked with young English language learners in funded research. Her dissertation focuses on the relationship between vocabulary and phonological awareness in preschoolers. Current interests include the development of science literacy in preschool and kindergarten.

Cassano coauthored "Supporting Early (and Later) Literacy Development at Home and at School: The Long View," in the *Handbook of Reading Research, Volume IV* (2011); and *Effects of a Family Literacy Intervention on the Vocabulary and Literacy Growth of Children in Preschool to Grade Two: Final Report to the Nellie Mae Foundation* (2010).

Kathleen A. Paciga, PhD (University of Illinois at Chicago), is an assistant professor of elementary literacy education at Purdue University-Calumet. She started in the field more than 10 years ago as a kindergarten teacher and has worked with preschool children and teachers through research in two Early Reading First projects. Her research and service focus on several aspects of early literacy instruction, including the effective integration of technology in early childhood classrooms.

Paciga's articles include "The National Early Literacy Panel Report and Classroom Instruction: Green Lights, Caution Lights, and Red Lights" (*Young Children*, 2011); and "Examining Student Engagement in Preschool Read Alouds" (*58th Yearbook of the National Reading Conference,* 2009).

Acknowledgments

We thank the multitude of teachers and children from whom we have learned so much over the years and continue to draw inspiration. We also thank the many early literacy researchers whose work informed this book. We are also grateful to our invited contributors—Jessica L. Hoffman, Christina Cassano, and Kathleen A. Paciga—especially to Jessica for taking responsibility for Chapter 2. We are grateful, as well, for the editorial support that NAEYC provided, including Natalie Klein's excellent help in transforming our original manuscript into a coherent book, Elizabeth Wegner's final editing, the book design and page layout by Malini Dominey, and the photograph selection overseen by Ryan Smith. It's a gift to both authors and readers when a book's visual details are given such thoughtful attention.

Last, but certainly not least, we thank our families, immediate and extended, for their support and patience throughout.

Introduction:
A Time to Begin

If asked when children learn to read and write, the average person would probably say, "in first grade." Although this is indeed true for most children, success in first grade relies on more than just the instruction provided then; it also depends heavily on the knowledge and skills acquired long before. In fact, the experiences that build a foundation for learning to read and write have a history stretching all the way back to infancy.

Children who struggle in learning to read often enter first grade without the foundational knowledge they need. This situation is not easily overcome. Only about 25 percent of children who struggle in learning to read in first grade ever read within the typical range for their grade level! The other children in this group continue to experience major reading difficulties throughout all of their years of schooling (Juel 1988; Spira, Bracken, & Fischel 2005).

Some children succeed in *learning* to read in first grade but then begin to experience difficulties starting in the middle grades ("the fourth grade slump"), due to insufficient content knowledge, vocabulary, and overall language, and to difficulty in drawing inferences (Chall & Jacobs 2003; Lesaux & Kieffer 2010; Sweet & Snow 2002). Unfortunately, they struggle to comprehend the content in their subject area material, such as a biology or history book. This problem is found often among children from families with low incomes who attend urban schools, and is especially prevalent in children from families with lower incomes who are learning English as a second language (Crosson & Lesaux 2010).

It is essential to help children build strong foundations for both *learning to read* and *reading to learn* in the years *before* formal schooling. By engaging infants, toddlers, and preschoolers in experiences that foster oral language and content knowledge, literacy skills, and thinking, early childhood professionals help secure children's later academic success (NELP 2008; Sénéchal, Ouellette, & Rodney 2006; Storch & Whitehurst 2002). Maintaining children's interest and motivation is also crucial, as this also accounts for a significant portion of later reading achievement (Gambrell 2011).

We wrote this book to help early childhood professionals and families support young children in acquiring the understandings, knowledge, and skills needed for later success in learning to read and write. This book addresses four main points:

1. **What** children need to learn in these early years
2. The **strategies** that teachers can use to help children acquire these foundations
3. The **features** of emergent literacy and language understandings and skills
4. **How** to design materials and the physical environment in early childhood classrooms to support language and literacy learning

We stress throughout that a wide variety of interconnected factors are at play in each child's emergent literacy. One size does not fit all—appropriate teaching varies for each individual child's circumstance (Copple & Bredekamp 2009).

This book is for early childhood professionals and families who want to know what current research indicates young children should learn and what kinds of experiences best help them acquire these understandings and skills. We think seasoned teachers and caregivers will find information that both updates their current knowledge and validates much that they already do to support children's early language, literacy, and content knowledge acquisition. We also address a wide range of basics useful to preservice teachers and other students of early childhood education, as well as teachers and caregivers early in their careers. Families will also find this an informative resource for learning about the range of early literacy experiences provided by early childhood programs and ideas for literacy experiences at home.

Although this book is based on a great deal of research, we also drew on our own experiences with young children and early childhood professionals, as research has not yet addressed all important questions or provided sufficient information on all topics (Duke & Carlisle 2011). Throughout the book, we offer many samples of children's work and examples of their thinking. The names of children who are featured in the writing samples and other examples are a mixture of pseudonyms and actual names (used with permission).

Topics and their organization

This book is organized into two parts, discussing the following key topics.

Part I: Building a Foundation for Reading

▲ Chapter 1 provides an overview of two reading processes and two phases of reading development following the emergent literacy period. This overview offers a framework for understanding how experiences in the early years contribute to later success in conventional reading.

▲ Chapter 2 links motor, cognitive, language, and social development milestones from birth to 30 months to children's book interests and interactions.

▲ Chapter 3 discusses selecting picture storybooks, and goals and strategies for reading stories to preschoolers.

▲ Chapter 4 focuses on selecting informational books, and on goals and strategies for using these books with preschoolers.

▲ Chapter 5 details the literacy skills comprising early foundations for learning to read and write, and how to support their acquisition.

Part II: Building a Foundation for Writing

▲ Chapter 6 outlines phases of emergent writing and discusses conventional writing that follows after the emergent writing phase.

▲ Chapter 7 considers mark-making between 12 and 30 months, and toddlers' attributions of meaning to marks, and infant and toddler knowledge acquisition.

▲ Chapter 8 focuses on drawing and writing in children from about 30 months to 5 years and 9 months of age, specifically on the different organization used for picture and writing marks, and on word and picture creation, literacy skills, and language and content knowledge involved in drawing and writing.

Using this book

A reader interested in the entire span of the emergent literacy years will want to start at the beginning and read the book's chapters in order. But the book's layered organization by topic and age also makes it easy to find information of most interest without reading chapters in order. For example, if interested primarily in infants and toddlers, a reader might start with Chapters 1, 2, 6, and 7, and then turn to the other chapters to build an understanding of literacy development during the preschool years. A reader primarily interested in preschoolers might take a different path, reading Chapters 1, 3, 4, 5, 6, and 8 before examining the infant and toddler chapters.

In addition, lists of both children's books cited in the text and references for all other text citations are provided at the end of the book. Readers interested in learning more about the many topics we introduce are encouraged to read some of these studies, books, reports, and position statements.

This book's goals

It is not our goal to encourage early childhood professionals or families to teach children to read and write conventionally before kindergarten or first grade. Of course, some children will develop enough skill early on to do so. Most, however, will follow the more typical course, progressing to conventional reading and writing after the emergent literacy period on which this book focuses.

We also focus on more than just the understandings and skills that ensure success in learning to read. Instead, we take a long view: the early years are a launching pad for both *learning to read* and *reading to learn* (Paratore, Cassano, & Schickedanz 2011). We also stress learning from books right from the beginning, when adults read to children.

A stance on both of these issues is important, because these two phases of reading development depend on different factors (see Chapter 1). If teachers and family members emphasize one set of understandings and skills over the other, children's early literacy experiences will not help them reach their full potential in the long run.

Our goals also include keeping motivation to learn at the forefront. As a consequence of concern over insufficient early learning, early childhood professionals and family members sometimes rely on narrow and tedious lessons with little appeal and too few here-and-now applications. We encourage instructional approaches that support robust early language, literacy, and content knowledge learning, and are also playful, interesting, and useful.

With such a long road of school and learning stretching out before them, a primary goal of early literacy experiences is to build children's interest in reading- and writing-related activities and learning in general. Without interest, children will not be motivated to read or write; without motivation, children will read and write relatively little and only what and when they must. Children who read little are unlikely to become good readers. Children who write little are unlikely to become good writers. Therefore, promoting children's *desire* to read and write is as important as helping children develop the necessary understandings and skills essential for learning *how* to read and write (Gambrell 2011).

Teachers at all levels today recognize the importance of meaningful literacy experiences during early childhood. However, many children entering the early primary grades have not had the benefit of a full range of enriching literacy experiences at home, in preschool, or in other early childhood settings that foster not only *knowledge about* reading and writing, but *love for* them.

We have both the opportunity and the privilege to shape the progress young children make in acquiring the literacy skills, oral language, and background knowledge that are vital to their later success in learning to read and write. It is also an opportunity to shape children's basic emotional and social attachments to reading and writing. This book focuses on the range of considerations that help teachers and caregivers achieve these dual and complementary goals.

Building a Foundation for Reading

PART I

1 What's Involved in Learning to Read?

Meaningful, enriching early language and literacy experiences provide children with a crucial foundation for later conventional reading, which involves two processes and two phases of development. Basic information about these processes and phases is provided in this chapter to support the reader's understanding of how early emergent literacy experiences contribute to children's success in both learning to read and in long-term reading proficiency.

Reading processes and phases

There are two different, but simultaneous, processes in which readers engage: *decoding* and *comprehending*. Decoding involves translating printed words into their spoken counterparts. As a reader decodes, she also tries to understand—comprehend—what is read. Although both processes occur at once and constantly influence one another, they involve different sets of behaviors.

Conventional reading development occurs in two fairly distinct phases: *learning to read* (decoding words) and *reading to learn* (obtaining new information).

In the first phase, children must devote virtually all of their time and attention to decoding—to figuring out what the words say. Because reading is a meaning-making activity, it is important for children to understand what they read from the very beginning.

When decoding takes too much time, readers cannot comprehend what they are reading. This is why books for beginning readers are designed for easy comprehension, mostly containing words children already know, short sentences, and familiar content. These books also use relatively few words and repeat some of these numerous times. Similar sentences might also be repeated. If children can decode the words in these books, they usually can understand what they have read.

From kindergarten through second grade, children typically have access to simplified books in their school settings. After this period, most children can read many words at a glance, because they have encountered them repeatedly while reading, and can decode new words more quickly, using patterns of correspondence learned for individual letters (i.e., graphemes) and sounds (i.e., phonemes) (Adams 1990).

Of course, while children are learning to read, they still benefit from being read to aloud. They learn from books just as they did during their infant, toddler, and preschool years, and can comprehend material that is much richer than what they can read by themselves. Moreover, adults' comments and explanations continue to enhance children's comprehension, and children's motivation to engage with books is also likely to remain high when adults continue to read to them.

Once children can decode well, they enter a second phase of reading development; for most children this begins in third grade. In this phase the child reads to obtain new information—she reads to learn. Previously, reading to learn was a minor goal. However, the books children now read have a considerable amount of

unfamiliar content, new vocabulary, and longer and more complex sentences. As a consequence, comprehending becomes more difficult and increases in difficulty with each successive year of schooling.

It is important to keep reading aloud to children during all of the primary grade years, and even longer if a child still enjoys it, not just during the learning-to-read years (i.e., first and second grade) when decoding is the primary instructional goal (although it is especially important then). When children hear books above their own reading level, and adults discuss these books with them, they develop language, content knowledge, and skill in reasoning needed to comprehend texts they read on their own.

Reading in the content areas, such as early primary science, history, or geography textbooks, is especially challenging for many children. The textbook content is unfamiliar, the language is also more dense and abstract than in stories, and the vocabulary is more sophisticated and technical (Kelley et al. 2010; Nagy & Townsend 2012). Using bona fide informational texts at the preschool level, as we explore in Chapter 4, helps children build language and content that are related to later success in this arena.

Young children typically hear more narratives than informational text, because teachers and families tend to read stories most often; many books for beginning readers in kindergarten through second grade are also stories, not informational books (Duke 2000; Fang 2008). Moreover, many informational books for young children are written as stories or in verse, which differs from the more technical writing found in older children's textbooks. For all of these reasons, many children experience some difficulty later in school when reading content area texts.

Understandings and skills needed when learning to read

Decoding and comprehending require different understandings and skills. The two processes also differ in relationship to one another during the two phases of reading development. In this section, we discuss each of the major code-related skills necessary in learning to read. We also discuss how oral language and content knowledge provide some assistance in the final steps of the decoding process.

Print conventions

Print conventions specify how print is organized on a page and how words in print are designated. For example, in English and many other languages, print is organized on a page from left to right and from top to bottom, and clusters of letters are separated with spaces to indicate where one word stops and another begins. Other conventions specify usage of uppercase versus lowercase letters and punctuation.

Children begin to learn about the directionality of print during preschool, and consolidate this understanding during kindergarten and first grade. During preschool, children also notice that their names feature capital letters at the beginning, followed by lowercase letters; this awareness is a first step in learning that alphabet letters have a "big" or capital form and a "small" or lowercase form.

Children learn more about case use in the primary grades. Knowledge of other conventions is also acquired over an extended period of time. For example, although children might be interested in punctuation as early as preschool, learning about its use continues well into the intermediate grades and beyond.

The alphabet and phonological awareness

To decode words, a reader must translate individual letters or letter pairs (graphemes) into speech sounds (phonemes) and then blend these into the spoken form of the word. Decoding skill requires letter-name knowledge and ***phonological awareness,*** which involves knowing that each spoken word consists of a series of individual sounds (phonemes). Phonological awareness helps children understand that decoding involves translating letters in a printed word into sounds that comprise its spoken form. (See Chapter 5 for further discussion of phonemic and phonological awareness.)

Children must also learn many specific connections between individual letters or letter pairs and the phonemes they represent. For example, the letter B represents the /b/ sound, the letter T represents the /t/ sound, and C and H together represent the first sound heard in *ch*erry.

Of course, in English, some words begin with the same sound but are spelled with a different beginning letter or letter pair (city/silly; fun/phone), while others begin with different sounds but are spelled with the same first letter (eat/enter; Connie/Cindy). It takes several years to learn the basics of the English spelling system.

Oral language

Although oral vocabulary and grammatical understanding are not central to decoding, they do provide some support, both indirectly and directly. For example, oral vocabulary is thought to indirectly affect decoding skill (Dickinson, Golinkoff, & Hirsh-Pasek 2010). According to one explanation, words are first stored in the brain as holistic units. Then, as vocabulary increases and the phonological structures of some words overlap (e.g., cut/cat; mouse/house), words in these clusters are reorganized and stored as smaller units of sound. This finer-grained storage is thought to provide a foundation for phonological awareness (Metsala 1999; Metsala & Walley 1998).

A child's oral vocabulary also helps her reformulate an approximate pronunciation that she obtains after the initial steps of decoding a printed word (i.e., the pronunciation does not yet match the printed word). This happens somewhat frequently in the early stages of learning to read, when children's letter-sound knowledge is not yet secure and spelling irregularities still puzzle them.

Consider, for example, a beginning reader's difficulty decoding "peanut" and "butter" as he reads a new book to his mother at home:

1. 'p' (correctly translates to /p/; responds to 'e' correctly, but as if in *pediatric*)

2. 'a' (incorrectly responds to single letter, as 'a' in *ate*)

3. 'n' (correctly translates to /n/)

4. 'u' (incorrectly translates as 'u' in *chute*)

5. 't' (correctly translates to /t/)

6. Repeats the "word" with an extra syllable—'a' as in *ate*—and looks puzzled

7. Child then sounds out/reads "butter," but produces "beauter"

8. Child stops to think

9. Suddenly, child says, "peanut butter!"

How might such a sudden correction in pronunciation have happened? First, the child knew the story was about a picnic and that animals were making sandwiches, because he and his mother had discussed an illustration depicting a sandwich-making scene. Using knowledge of both this context and the kind of sandwich, the child suddenly transformed the sound approximations he had obtained into the actual words in the book. Had these words not been in his vocabulary, he might not have found his way past the approximations.

To be sure, oral vocabulary and background knowledge help only *after* a reader has engaged in basic decoding to arrive at a sound approximation (Adams 1990; Share 1999). But this assist is useful to a young child just learning to read, especially when he has interesting books at home that might not be simplified to the same degree as the beginning books he reads at school.

Additionally, linking the visual pattern of letters in a word to its pronunciation and meaning helps to anchor this pattern in the child's mind. As a consequence, he can read it much faster next time (Pikulski & Chard 2005).

Understandings and skills needed for reading to learn

In addition to good decoding skill, success in reading to learn requires good oral language, solid background knowledge, and reasoning skills. Here, we discuss each of these items, after explaining how decoding also affects comprehension.

Decoding skill

If children make serious errors in recognizing words, the meanings of sentences and passages are distorted. Additionally, if children struggle to sound out each word instead of recognizing some words automatically and decoding others relatively easily, they cannot think about meaning. In short, unless word recognition is fairly accurate and somewhat automatic, comprehension suffers (LaBerge & Samuels 1974; Pikulski 2006).

Oral vocabulary and other oral language skills

Oral vocabulary is very important to reading comprehension; readers need to know the meanings of individual words to understand the text as a whole. Syntactic and grammatical skills also matter, because word forms and meanings differ depending on the position and order of words in a sentence. Consider the difference between *wave* used as a noun and a verb:

1. *Wave* bye-bye to Grandma.
2. When we went to the beach, I saw a very large *wave*.

The position of a noun in a sentence differs from that of a verb, and the nearby words in each case also differ.

Skill with grammar and syntax helps children know whether a word is the name of something, stipulates an action, or modifies the meaning of another word. As sentences in books become more complex in later grades, the relationships they express increase in complexity as well. Good language skills become absolutely essential for good comprehension, especially of books that children read to study content areas, such as science, history, or geography (Nagy & Townsend 2012). A strong foundation of oral language skills in early childhood provides a framework for this later success.

Background knowledge

Background knowledge is everything a person knows about the physical, biological, and social worlds. Young children use background knowledge to comprehend books they hear read aloud, just as older children use it to comprehend books they read for themselves.

For instance, consider the effects of background knowledge (or lack thereof) on story interpretation in this preschool example from a reading of *Whistle for Willie* by Ezra Jack Keats (Schickedanz & Collins 2012). Immediately after the teacher read, "He jumped off his shadow but when he landed they were together again," (pp. 20–21) a child shouted, "He found another one!" (Figure 1-1).

Figure 1-1. Peter and two shadows.

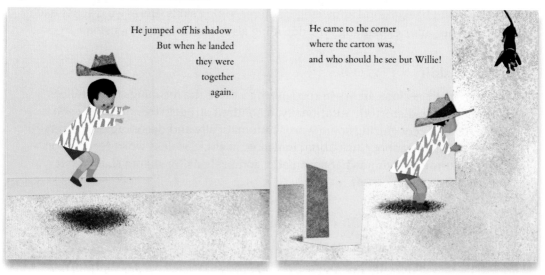

Adults understand "He jumped off his shadow" to mean that Peter's body made the shadows. But unless a child understands that shadows are nonmaterial objects—which many preschoolers do not (Carey 1985)—she could easily think a shadow stays where cast, and that someone coming along later might find it.

Background knowledge is also critically important for comprehending informational books. Although these books are designed to help children acquire information, when used in isolation children have difficulty understanding the concepts these books teach (Leung 2008). A child's science or geography text needs to be coupled with meaningful real-life experiences that use key words; otherwise children rarely know terms at the depth required to understand the book. Prior subject knowledge (including associated vocabulary) aids children's comprehension even when using books that teach about specific topics; good knowledge of grammar and syntax also helps.

Children also apply knowledge about different text structures. For example, informational books usually do not have characters, a problem, or a plot, while narratives (i.e., stories) do. Informational books are also denser with ideas than stories, and contain considerably more technical terminology (Kelley et al. 2010; Nagy & Townsend 2012). Knowledge about these differences in text structures helps children comprehend different kinds of books (Best, Floyd, & McNamara 2008).

Reasoning

Children must learn to use background knowledge in conjunction with information provided in a book's text and illustrations. This learning occurs as adults read books to children, model reasoning, and ask questions that prompt them to reason. Authors often leave gaps in stories, and expect readers or listeners to use reasoning to fill them in. For example, at the beginning of *One Dark Night*, by Hazel Hutchins, Jonathan (the main character) is awake in bed, looking out his window. The text tells us that a storm is approaching; lightning flashes and thunder booms. Although the text does not state that Jonathan was kept awake by the storm, our background knowledge helps us to infer this.

Table 1-1 "Examples of Thinking Needed to Fill in Gaps in *One Dark Night*" lists other events from *One Dark Night*, as well as gaps in the story that must be inferred. This filling in requires reasoning based on the integration of information from the book's text and illustrations and the reader's or listener's background knowledge.

Let's consider a classroom example that occurred as the teacher finished reading aloud the story *The Snowy Day* by Ezra Jack Keats. Peter, the main character, is going out to play in the snow with a friend who is not named in the text. One child suggested that Peter's friend was Gilberto, a character the children knew well from *Gilberto and the Wind* by Marie Hall Ets. Like Peter, Gilberto had also played outside by himself. Apparently, the child thought that Peter and Gilberto would make good friends, even though Peter lived in the city and Gilberto lived in the country.

Although it is unlikely that Peter's friend here is Gilberto, which the teacher commented about in her response, this is an example of a child's engagement in reasoning. Over time, preschoolers' reasoning becomes more accurate, because

Table 1-1 Examples of Thinking Needed to Fill in Gaps in *One Dark Night*

Event	Inference
Jonathan is in pajamas in bed, looking through the window. The text tells us it is night-time, and that Jonathan sees lightning and hears thunder. We can infer that Jonathan should be asleep or trying to sleep.	We use background knowledge about lightning and thunder to help understand why instead he's awake and looking out his window. He looks concerned. Our experiences with thunderstorms help us understand why Jonathan is a bit frightened.
The text says that Jonathan sees something small outside, and that it is looking back at him. We see the outline of a cat's head in the darkness, and its two green eyes.	We can infer that Jonathan might not know what the animal is; the text only says he sees "something small." Perhaps it's an owl, dog, or cat. We can use background knowledge to infer that it is an animal because of the eyes. We can also guess that it is a cat, given the shape of the head.
The text says Jonathan runs downstairs, opens the door, and lets a stray cat in. He's depicted near the door, as a cat runs in. Jonathan tells his grandparents the cat is afraid of thunder. Grandfather says stray cats are not afraid of thunder. Grandmother says she thinks the cat has a mouse in its mouth.	Jonathan's grandparents are introduced here; we might infer that he lives with them, or was sleeping over. We might also infer that the grandparents were awakened by the storm and heard Jonathan get out of bed and run downstairs. Perhaps they wondered what was going on and got out of bed to find out. Grandfather may have said something, such as, "Hey! Why are you opening the door?" which prompted Jonathan to say the cat was afraid of thunder. Finally, Grandmother might have thought the cat had a mouse because cats catch mice and like to show what they have caught.
We see a kitten on a rug. Jonathan is not shown, but the text says he announces, "It's a kitten!"	We can infer that the large cat is the kitten's mother. We don't see Jonathan with the kitten, but we can infer that he's there because he identifies it. We can also infer that his grandparents had not joined him, because he calls to them as if they are in another part of the house. Finally, we might infer from Jonathan's announcement that he is excited, and also wants Grandmother to know there is no mouse.

they learn to take account of more information (Duke & Carlisle 2011). They also learn to reason when teachers ask higher-level questions both during the story reading and in following discussions (Collins 2011).

Different learning from different experiences

Different experiences in the early years yield different kinds of learning. Some things children learn strongly influence decoding, while other learning mostly influences comprehending (NICHD 2005; Sénéchal 1997). Moreover, because books for beginning readers are simplified, we do not see the full effect of the understandings and skills that primarily affect comprehension until a reader moves past the first phase of reading development and encounters more challenging texts.

The first column of Table 1-2 "Selected Early Practices and Their Contributions to a Foundation for Reading" lists a selection of early literacy practices similar to typical preschool standards for language and literacy. Additional standards (such as science and social studies) also impact reading development, as background knowledge provides critical support for comprehension. The most important contributions that each experience makes are featured in the second column of Table 1-2. Columns 3 and 4 indicate whether a contribution is very important (e.g., strong) for either decoding or comprehension or less so (e.g., weak). Early childhood experiences that support oral vocabulary development and background knowledge significantly aid comprehension, but make some contribution to decoding skill as well. Good decoding skill is necessary (though not sufficient) to support good comprehension, as noted for the decoding items listed in column 3.

Adopting a long view

Children benefit more when teachers and families emphasize language development, background knowledge, and comprehension strategies rather than overly focus on code-related skills such as alphabet learning. Likewise, encouraging deep levels of word understanding with a rich language and content knowledge curriculum benefits children's comprehension more than teaching simple labels for words to increase vocabulary (Kelley et al. 2010; Ouellette 2006). These issues matter because the reading comprehension levels of school-age children in the United States are quite low in most national assessments (NCES 2011). We encourage early childhood programs to reach beyond the most basic practices to provide a balanced language and literacy approach that will benefit children for the long term.

Looking beyond code-related skills

Sometimes early childhood educators adopt a code-related focus without realizing that different sets of understandings and skills affect decoding and comprehending, or that young children must start building both sets before formal schooling begins. This results in overemphasis on decoding skills, because these are needed when children *learn to* read.

Table 1-2 **Selected Early Practices and Their Contributions to a Foundation for Reading**

Teaching Practice	Contributions	Importance in Decoding/Learning to Read	Importance in Comprehension/ Reading to Learn
Reading Storybooks	Print Conventions	Strong	Weak
	Oral Language/Vocabulary	Weak	Strong
	Reasoning	Weak	Strong
Reading Informational Books	Print Conventions	Strong	Weak
	Oral Language/Vocabulary	Weak	Strong
	Background Knowledge	Weak	Strong
	Reasoning	Weak	Weak
Reciting Songs and Nursery Rhymes	Phonological Awareness	Strong	Weak
	Oral Language/Vocabulary	Weak	Strong
Explaining Word Meanings	Oral Language/Vocabulary	Weak	Strong
Playing with the Sounds in Words	Phonological Awareness	Strong	Weak
Teaching Alphabet Letters	Alphabet Letter Identification	Strong	Weak
	Print Conventions (uppercase and lowercase letter forms)	Strong	Weak
Underlining Book and Poem Titles	Print Conventions	Strong	Weak
Field Trips	Background Knowledge	Weak	Strong
	Oral Language/Vocabulary	Weak	Strong

Oral Language/Vocabulary includes grammatical and syntactic skill, plus oral vocabulary support. *Background Knowledge* is information about the physical, biological, and social worlds. *Print Conventions* include left-to-right scanning of print and spaces in between words.

Some kindergarten and first grade teachers also may request that children know the alphabet and how to write their names when they leave preschool. These appeals will no doubt change, as current recommendations actually suggest that kindergarten and primary grade teachers address code-related understandings and skills and comprehension-related skills with more balance (Stahl 2012).

In fact, for years, research has shown the need for balance between code-related and language-related instruction in the early elementary grades. As one of the first longitudinal studies spanning preschool through fourth grade notes:

> Importantly, we must be careful not to focus on promoting decoding skills to the exclusion of comprehension skills. . . . Though improving code-related skills, such as phonological awareness and print knowledge, may necessarily be the focus of intervention in those children who have not yet acquired sufficient skill in reading words, we must not wait until children have solved the decoding puzzle to begin instruction in oral language skills, such as vocabulary and syntax. These oral language skills should be an integral part of reading instruction beginning in preschool and throughout elementary school. (Storch & Whitehurst 2002, 944)

We would only add that strong support for oral language must begin during infancy and the toddler years (Hart & Risley 1995; Huttenlocher et al. 1991). It must continue during preschool, and *forever* after that.

Looking beyond a narrow focus on recognition-level oral vocabulary

The oral language focus in curricula used in some early childhood programs is also sometimes too narrow. Merely providing the names of things develops oral vocabulary at only a simple recognition level; a deeper focus that provides children with information about words is of more benefit to their comprehension (Ouellette 2006).

To know words as more than mere labels, children must encounter them not only in books, but also in authentic contexts such as hands-on science experiences (Gelman & Brenneman 2004). They must also have multiple encounters with a word, in a variety of contexts (Nagy & Townsend 2012). In short, meaningful firsthand experiences (historically a mainstay in preschool programs) are part and parcel of good emergent literacy programs, with long-term effects.

Concluding thoughts about early childhood experiences

The truth is, early childhood professionals must keep many balls in the air, right from the beginning. The alphabet is not *the* place to start, nor is oral language or content knowledge. Early childhood teachers must start on many fronts simultaneously, which is why early educational standards include literacy skills, language, science, social studies, and more, and why curriculum frameworks suggest a wide range of experiences.

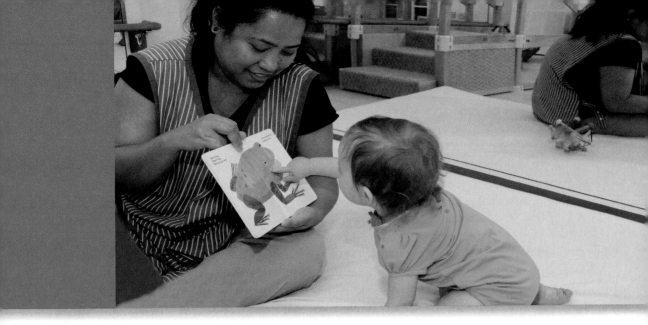

2

The Beginning:
Reading with Babies
and Toddlers

Jessica L. Hoffman with Christina Cassano

A young boy sits on his mother's lap, listening to her read a well-loved book, *Goodnight Moon* by Margaret Wise Brown. As she reads, "Goodnight light," the boy's eyes brighten. He smiles and slowly points up to the ceiling light. This one small gesture demonstrates his understanding that the purpose of reading is to make meaning.

Long before they can read—even before they can talk—children learn a multitude of skills, concepts, and values from reading. For example, they learn to attend to language, and, through this attention, learn new words and language structures, as well as something about the concepts they represent (Blake et al. 2006; Karrass & Braungart-Rieker 2005). Babies also come to understand that book language differs from oral language (Armbruster, Lehr, & Osborn 2003) and that stories communicate human experiences (Armbruster, Lehr, & Osborn 2003; Birckmayer, Kennedy, & Stonehouse 2008). They learn some physical things about books, too, such as how to orient them and turn their pages. Perhaps most importantly, babies and toddlers become acquainted with learning from others through books and begin to acquire cultural practices and values, such as seeking answers to questions and choosing reading as a pleasurable activity (Heath 1983).

This chapter provides information about infant and toddler development, books of interest to them, and ways to engage them in reading experiences. Reading with babies and toddlers is distinct from reading aloud to older children, because it requires a highly individualized approach that allows for adult responsiveness to the baby or toddler's unique needs. Therefore, this chapter focuses primarily on ways of reading to individual children, not to groups. A short discussion about reading to three or four older toddlers is provided later in the chapter.

Although this chapter's recommendations are based on decades of research, caregivers should consider this information in combination with their own deep knowledge. This chapter's age ranges, developmental milestones, and suggested books and reading practices are based on averages and approximations. Thus, readers should use the descriptions of children's behaviors and their interests when choosing books for a particular child, rather than rely strictly on our references to age.

Our goal is for adults to act both as interested followers and knowledgeable guides when sharing books with young children. In this balanced approach to shared reading, the child is given ample opportunity to guide what and how books are shared, while the caregiver creates engaging learning experiences with books that scaffold the child's use of language and texts.

Engaging babies and toddlers with reading

This part of the chapter is organized into six specific infant and toddler age groups. Within each grouping, we discuss what most children can do, choosing books for the children, and engaging children with books.

Birth to 3 months

What the baby can do. Physically, infants' heads must be supported when they are held upright. Over the first few months, babies become able to raise their heads for longer periods when lying on their stomachs. They also will begin to grasp objects reflexively when they are put into their hands and become more skilled in directing their hands to their mouths.

Babies this age do not yet have fully developed visual acuity, and therefore prefer images with high contrast and large shapes and patterns (Fantz 1963; Salapatek & Kessen 1966). They also attend more closely to images of human faces than to other objects (Johnson et al. 1991; Simion et al. 2001).

Young babies attend best to child-directed speech, with its high pitch and exaggerated intonation. Young babies' speech perception is keen, although they do not yet understand any of the words that people say. Newborns communicate through sounds, most notably, crying; within a few months, babies can also gurgle and coo.

Choosing texts for the baby. Books targeting the visual abilities and interests of young infants include Tana Hoban's black and white books (e.g., *Black on White* and *White on Black*) and others similarly crafted. Because babies also prefer faces, books with close-up photographs of human faces are other good choices (e.g., *Baby Faces* by Margaret Miller, *Mrs. Mustard's Baby Faces* by Jane Wattenberg, *Hugs & Kisses* by Roberta Grobel Intrater). Caregivers can also purchase books with transparent plastic sleeves into which they can place photographs of faces familiar to the baby.

All of a baby's reading material need not focus on visual and cognitive skills. Precisely because very young infants do not yet see illustrations well, understand the meanings of words, have keen interests, or grab and tear pages, it does not matter so much what is read to them, as simply that they are read to. Adults can read from storybooks or other young children's literature, or they can recite poems and nursery rhymes, or sing songs to babies this young without using any book at all. These vocal experiences are appealing to most babies. As early literacy researchers Zambo and Hansen noted, "Being held, feeling good, and hearing a familiar, comforting voice are more important than the kind of book or the content of a story" (2007, 33). At this young age shared reading is, at its core, about the social experience of connecting with others through language.

Engaging the baby. Much of a young baby's daily life is consumed by meeting basic needs for feeding, sleeping, and diaper changing. As a consequence, books and reading will not feature prominently in a very young baby's life. However, parents and adults in family or child care settings can weave experiences with books into the fabric of a young baby's day.

Even though books for young infants, such as the black and white or human faces books mentioned above, do not typically include much text to read, caregivers can create language to accompany the images when sharing these books. Talking about the images promotes language development, because it connects the sounds of our language with the objects, actions, or attributes to which the language refers (Hollich et al. 2000; Werker & Curtin 2005).

Because young infants cannot yet support their heads when held upright, adults usually cradle a baby in their arms while reading. As babies develop more head control, they will explore books like these more independently during "tummy time." (See Box 2-1 "Making Books Available to Babies Younger than 4 Months.")

The adult should let the baby's reaction guide what, how, and for how long they read together. Some babies are calmed and quieted when read to, some may even coo differently, as if imitating the rise and fall of the reader's voice, and when a bit older, will gurgle with delight (Holland 2008; Whitehead 2002). But, sometimes, babies indicate that they are overstimulated, disinterested, or otherwise not enjoying the experience. When a baby's behavior suggests a lack of interest, the reading should simply be discontinued until another time.

Four to 6 months

What the baby can do. Infants at this age grab, grasp, and mouth just about everything, including books. They are also learning how things work and how to move their bodies. The baby can now support her own head and sit upright comfortably when held in a lap, with support. Some babies may begin to sit up independently by 6 months of age.

Although babies this age are still prelinguistic—are not yet uttering meaningful words— they can communicate a lot through ***paralinguistic communications***. Paralinguistic communications include other vocalizations (cooing, laughing, crying), gazing, body language, gestures, and facial expressions. Adults and older children interpret babies' communicative efforts, and vary their own speech to engage babies' attention using ***child-directed speech*** (CDS) (formerly known as *motherese* [Snow 1972; Snow et al. 1991], or colloquially, "baby talk").

Compared to normal speech, CDS has higher pitch, exaggerated intonation, slower rate, clearer enunciation, simpler and shorter phrases (with emphasis on important words), more gestures and facial expressions, greater repetition, and, later, use of a child's own vocabulary (e.g., "go bye-bye" instead of "leave") (Cooper & Aslin 1990; Fernald & Simon 1984; Makin 2006; Ninio & Wheeler 1984). Research suggests that the main characteristics of CDS are relatively stable across languages and cultures (Bryant & Barrett 2007; Grieser & Kuhl 1988; Lieven 1994; Liu, Tsao, & Kuhl 2007).

Choosing texts for the baby. Because babies now grasp objects and take them to their mouths to explore, adults can select board books or books with fabric or plastic pages that can withstand crumpling, chewing, and drooling.

Books with high contrast and simple illustrations or photos are still good options, although caregivers can now include books with more colorful illustrations, because babies' color vision is more developed. Simple concept books, and books with a topic and image (and maybe a word or two) on each page, are good options (e.g., *The Baby EyeLike* series by PlayBac).

Choosing books with textures or other physical features, such as touch and feel, capitalizes on a baby's budding manual exploration. For example, *Little Feet Love* by Anthony Nex includes a variety of textures—terrycloth, sandpaper, and stringy grass—for little hands to explore.

Engaging the baby. Babies can now sit upright with support when held, which frees an adult's hands to hold a book in front of them for shared viewing. Because the baby will likely grasp and physically explore the book, durable books are good options. Provide the baby with a toy or teether to manipulate while reading to satisfy and also distract the baby from physical exploration, and perhaps increase the baby's engagement in shared reading. There is nothing wrong, however, with allowing a baby to physically manipulate books that are shared.

Items pictured can be named amid the baby's manipulation and the adult can even comment about the baby's physical actions on the book. Babies this age are usually out of their cribs more than younger babies, but are not yet walking. Thus, adults still need to take books to them.

When reading with infants this age, caregivers can use CDS to support babies' engagement by reading with expression. Reading with expression incorporates strategies such as exaggerated intonation, emphasis on important words, and use of facial expressions, gestures, and pointing. By reading with expression, the adult communicates meaning through the sounds and words of the language and also through the visuals of facial expressions, gestures, and images in the book.

Seven to 9 months

What the baby can do. During this period, the infant's large motor skills are developing rapidly. Babies this age sit up independently, begin to crawl or become otherwise mobile (e.g., scooting, creeping), and begin to pull themselves up to stand soon after that. With these new motor skills, babies enjoy being on the move.

While sitting, they manipulate objects with their hands, often holding an object in one, while patting, poking, or pulling on it with the other. Of course, babies still explore objects with their mouths. The difference now is that their visual inspection and manual manipulation of objects decreases the amount of exploration that takes place with their mouth. By the end of this period, most babies will have developed their ability to use a thumb and index finger in opposition (i.e., a pincer grasp) to pick up small objects. A pincer grasp dramatically increases dexterity and the baby's ability to manipulate objects, including books. Babies this age begin to develop an interest in **deformation manipulations**. In other words, they like to crumple or tear paper, intentionally, to explore what happens (Karniol 1989).

Babies might now understand a few words, even though they will not speak any meaningful words for several more months. If adults establish joint attention with babies (i.e., focus on the same objects as the baby) and comment about the objects of this joint attention, vocabulary growth is usually increased (Nagell 1995; Tomasello & Farrar 1986). Babies are also beginning to point with the index finger, which aids in establishing joint attention.

Choosing texts for the baby. With a pincer grasp, babies now begin to turn pages. But because a baby's pincer grasp and overall fine motor skills are still developing, board books with their thick stiff pages are good options. Board books are also good choices at this time because they can withstand a baby's attempts to crumple, chew, or tear. Adults can support lap board books, a fairly large and heavy kind of board book, when sharing one with a baby this age, but smaller board books are better suited for babies' small hands, when the baby is exploring a book independently.

Books with clear photos or illustrations of recognizable objects, people, and actions with simple labels can facilitate word learning at this age. For example, books like *Go* by Dwell Studio, *Peek-a Who?* by Nina Laden, or *In My Pond* by Sara Gillingham include clear illustrations of familiar objects, easy for adults to label and describe.

Engaging the baby. Babies this age are busy! Because they are beginning to crawl, their interest in sitting very long in one spot to read with an adult might decrease. This is perfectly okay. Reading should be an enjoyable experience for the baby, not a chore. There are, however, ways to encourage book engagement in even the busiest baby. For those who do still sit for brief periods, adults can share books in short segments. A few minutes here and there add up to a significant amount of time over the course of the day. While reading, the adult can follow the baby's lead by allowing the baby to manipulate the book—turn it around, turn pages, or open and close it. If the baby looks at or points to particular objects, the adult can name them.

Even babies who do not spontaneously express interest in books can be engaged in book reading if allowed to participate in meaningful ways, such as by turning the pages. Other babies who will not sit to share book reading with an adult often still enjoy listening to the adult read the book while they move about and play.

The two key developmental achievements of understanding words and learning to point are closely related. As the baby begins to understand that words refer to particular people, objects, and actions, the ability to point provides a new and highly effective tool for requesting words. Pointing facilitates ***joint attention***, which is established when the child and adult look at the same object or event (Colonnesi et al. 2010). For babies who are not yet pointing, gaze facilitates joint attention (Brooks & Meltzoff 2008) and word learning (Hollich et al. 2000). When babies point to or gaze more intently at illustrations in books, they call the adult's attention to the object, and the adult can reply with a label (Fletcher et al. 2005).

To support babies' developmental interests, adults can adapt their book-sharing strategies by shifting away from reading extended selections of printed text, which simply sounded interesting to a younger baby, to more labeling and talking about illustrations. "Reading" to babies this age can feel like an ongoing series of pointing and labeling, which makes the language of the text less important to consider when choosing books. For example, although a book written for preschoolers might include lengthy and complex text that is far beyond the comprehension of a 9-month-old, a baby can still enjoy the book if the topic and illustrations are of interest. When the caregiver uses the book as an opportunity for joint attention and talk about the illustrations (instead of reading the book as one would with a preschooler), the experience can be a perfectly engaging one for the baby.

Ten to 12 months

What the baby can do. As their fine motor skills continue to develop, babies are now more intentional in manipulating objects. For example, they may press buttons on toys and lift flaps in books. They are also becoming ever more mobile: crawling, cruising furniture, and possibly even taking their first wobbly steps. With increased mobility, babies are sometimes less interested in sitting with an adult for extended periods to read books.

Babies' language development is also accelerating. They understand about 50 words and might utter their first. Babies' receptive language continues to exceed their expressive language—they can understand more than they can speak. This pattern is true for all phases of language development and for all speakers of any language.

Choosing texts for the baby. Because the baby now expresses his individuality and shows budding interests and preferences for toys, play, and books, caregivers now begin to rely more on content than physical characteristics when choosing books. That is to say, the book will probably only be engaging if the content is familiar to and of interest to the baby. For some babies, an interest is in forms of transportation; for others, it is animals or babies.

Lift-the-flap books also become of interest because they allow a baby to actively engage in manipulating the book. Examples of baby-oriented lift-the-flap books include those by Karen Katz, such as *Toes, Ears, & Nose!*, whose bright, simple illustrations engage babies in exploring familiar concepts.

Board books are still good options, although damage inflicted at this age is more related to developing fine motor skills than the purposeful exploratory tearing of pages seen in babies a few months younger. A wide range of books is available in a board book format, some of which are more engaging than others. Board books with relatively simple language and clear connections to illustrations are the best because these features help the baby understand the language of the book, when supported with adult talk, gestures, and expressions. Some examples are

- ▲ Concept books with a focused topic and representative examples on each page, such as Byron Barton's series of transportation books (e.g., *Trucks, Boats*), *My Big Animal Book* by Roger Priddy, and *Go Baby!* by Richard and Michele Steckel

- ▲ Rhythmic/rhyming texts with familiar themes and concepts, such as *The Going to Bed Book* by Sandra Boynton, *Ten Little Fingers and Ten Little Toes* by Mem Fox, *Dog* by Matthew Van Fleet, and *Baby Dance* by Ann Taylor

Engaging the baby. Babies this age now begin to bring toys or books to a caregiver, as a way to ask, "Play this with me" or "Read this with me." Children who experience consistently warm and responsive support in play usually have better social and cognitive outcomes (Landry et al. 2001) and later literacy achievement (Taylor et al. 2008). Therefore, adults should follow babies' leads in play. For example, they can share a book when the baby is interested, allowing her to return to other play when her interest wanes.

Adults can also sustain active babies' engagement in reading by making reading itself active. For example, when reading rhythmic or rhyming texts, adults can emphasize the cadence and word play, vary the pace, sing the words, or create movement or dance to accompany the words. Adults can also share lift-the-flap books to provide opportunities for babies to manipulate books.

Now that babies are beginning to understand and use more language, shared reading becomes a context for more purposeful language interactions between adult and child. To support babies in understanding language, adults can use **comprehensible input** (Krashen 1985; 2003). Comprehensible input is best supported when the adult and child share a common context for language use. For example, in a non-book context, an adult and child might play with a ball, using words like *ball*, *throw*, and *roll*, which allows the child to link words to the objects and actions she observes.

Similarly, the adult and child share a context when reading a book. The adult makes book language more understandable by pointing to relevant illustrations, acting out actions, and making facial expressions. This behavior links words to concrete meanings. The adult also makes connections between concepts in the book and a baby's familiar experiences. For example, the adult says, "This is a dog [pointing to illustration], just like your dog [pointing to the animal curled up at their feet]." Making connections between books and real-life experiences is correlated with language development (Blake et al. 2006).

Adults support babies' abilities to produce language by encouraging expressive language attempts (i.e., **output**) (Swain 2005; Whitehurst et al. 1988). When reading to babies and prompting language from them, adults often follow this sequence:

1. Get the baby's attention

2. Ask the baby a labeling question

3. Wait for the baby to respond, or if necessary provide the answer yourself

4. Provide feedback (Ninio & Bruner 1978)

For example, first, the adult gets the baby's attention, by saying, for example, "Oh, look!" while pointing to a book's illustration. Then, the adult asks the child, "What do you see?" (seeking output). After the baby replies with a word, or just a smile of recognition, the adult then replies, "Yes, that's a monkey." If the baby stares blankly, indicating he has no idea what the object is, or incorrectly labels the object, the adult supplies the language, such as, "Well, it is brown like a dog, but this is a monkey. Monkeys have l-o-n-g tails."

This kind of adult language interaction supports or **scaffolds** (Mercer 1995; Wood, Bruner, & Ross 1976) a child's language development and leads babies toward more independent use of language. After several months of responding to requests for labels during book reading, toddlers begin initiating responses. For instance, a toddler may label objects while turning the pages of a book. Independent labeling behaviors represent the baby's first steps toward emergent reading of books, which is a precursor to conventional reading (Sulzby 1985; Teale & Sulzby 1986).

Toward the end of this age range, babies begin to associate objects with routines and events. For example, when an adult reaches for keys, the baby might say, "Bye-bye" or upon seeing her plate, ask, "Eat?" The baby's ability to make connections between objects and events can be used to establish routines for reading. In many homes, reading is part of the bedtime routine, but book reading can occur in any part of the day. For example, many babies like to wake up with reading or share books after a meal. No matter when reading occurs, a daily routine helps engage the baby in reading experiences as a predictable part of her day.

Thirteen to 18 months

What the toddler can do. Toddlers are now increasingly steady on their feet. For example, they can bend down to pick up objects from the floor when standing, and they also begin to climb onto furniture or into the lap of a caregiver. In the fine motor arena, toddlers become more and more able to manipulate objects. For example, they can turn the pages of a book independently.

Early in this time period, toddlers use single words to name familiar objects and people. Within a few months, their language expands to include two-word phrases or sentences (e.g., "more milk" or "doggie run"). Toddlers now also use

nonsense jabber that includes intonation, stress, pausing, and even gestures resembling actual speech. This is called **expressive jargon**. Sometimes, when looking at books, toddlers jabber in a way that resembles the overall sound of reading, called book babble. **Book babble** is another early form of emergent reading and indicates the understanding that book language differs from conversational language.

Choosing texts for the toddler. Toddlers are developing preferences in all aspects of their lives: foods, toys, activities, and books. They may express likes and dislikes for texts by bringing books they like to an adult or by reaching for or pushing away books during shared reading. If the toddler pushes a book away, or even protests with an adamant, "No!" the adult should offer other choices for their shared reading, because protests may be due to lack of interest in the book, not with the activity itself.

As the toddler's capacity for language develops, she enjoys slightly more complex books and is fascinated by more detailed illustrations. Some toddlers can now transition back to some books with paper pages, especially for supervised use, because they are increasingly able to turn pages and lift flaps without tearing or crumpling the paper.

Theme books are good choices for toddlers this age. As opposed to concept books with a topic and examples, theme books feature a series of sequentially related events and illustrations. A common theme for toddlers features a child's daily activities, for example, a child waking up, getting dressed, eating meals, playing, and going to bed. Theme books offer a transition from concept books to actual stories because they have a limited number of characters, familiar settings, simple events, but lack an actual plot (no problem and resolution). Good examples of theme books include *"More More More," Said the Baby* by Vera B. Williams, *Toddler Two/Dos Años* by Anastasia Suen, and *Freight Train* by Donald Crews. (See Box 2-2 "Placement of Books in the Toddler Classroom" for a discussion on how to set up the book nook.)

Engaging the toddler. Now that the toddler understands that words represent real things, he is usually interested in labeling and describing objects pictured in books and less interested in listening to extended readings of the printed text. The toddler points to things he recognizes and things he does not, often labeling those he knows and asking for labels for objects he does not know. With simple books, a

Box 2-2 Placement of Books in the Toddler Classroom

A book nook for toddlers in a group care setting differs from the typical upright book-display racks found in preschool classrooms, which are not functional or safe in a toddler room. First, toddlers are not tall enough to reach the higher shelves. Second, unseasoned walkers may lose their balance as they reach to obtain materials. Third, and more serious, the bookshelf itself can topple over if toddlers try to climb on it. (Furniture should, of course, be bolted or otherwise secured to walls or the floor.)

A book nook for toddlers can be made by standing some books up on the floor and laying others flat nearby. Because the opened and standing books can be seen from a distance, they catch a toddler's attention. A few additional books can be placed in shallow tubs or baskets.

A corner of the room serves best for a book nook, as traffic will not go through the area. The area should be covered with carpeting or a rug to make sitting comfortable. Pillows are not necessary or safe, because toddlers might trip over them. Moreover, because a book is easiest for a toddler to handle in his lap, leaning against a pillow or sitting halfway on top of one often positions a toddler in a way that makes it harder for her to manipulate it.

Although a special place in the older toddlers' room is provided for books, books need not stay there. Toddlers often get a book, look at it briefly, and then carry it as they go to another area of the room. Of course, no matter where books are placed, a toddler will probably take a book picked up in one place to other places, as she moves about. A book nook can be thought of not so much as where books belong but as a place to find toddler might fly through the pages labeling objects quickly as if expressing, "Yep, that's a chicken [turn page], ok, that's a pig [turn page]." Complex illustrations take much longer to "read," and the toddler may spend an extraordinary amount of time pouring over every detail, sometimes repeatedly. Repetition is important to toddlers' learning from book reading (Fletcher & Jean-Francois 1998; Simcock & DeLoache 2008). Caregivers provide repetition by reading the same book repeatedly and by sharing books that have highly repetitive language.

At this age, the caregiver and toddler can engage in more extended discussion about illustrations. Discussion may include descriptions of details in illustrations (rather than simple labels) and connections between the book and the child's world. For example, if the child points and says, "Airplane!" the adult can reply, "That is an airplane. It is flying high in the sky. We saw an airplane when we went to the park today, didn't we? What else do you see?"

Adults also might simplify a book's language by substituting language that is more comprehensible to an individual child (Martin 1998). For instance, an adult might say "nanna" in place of "grandma" if that is what the child calls his grandmother. Adults who scaffold reading experiences in this way have been described as using a *storytelling* or *interactive* approach. Interactive reading encourages the child's participation, by asking questions and making connections. Interactive reading that includes talk occurring outside of reading the written text is highly effective at promoting language development (Blake et al. 2006; Britto, Brooks-Gunn, & Griffin 2006).

them. If sturdy books are provided (i.e., thick cardboard, rather than paper, pages), they will withstand the wear and tear of traveling with a toddler throughout the room.

Once truly mobile, by about 14 months, toddlers can get to books that are provided in one area of the classroom (a book nook), although it is a good idea to put books in a variety of places. First of all, because toddlers between 14 and 18 months old like to be up and about, placing books in various places with collections of other toys helps to ensure that babies will have the option of looking at a book no matter where they wander.

Second, placement of a few books throughout the play space makes adults more available for interacting if only for a brief period, than if books are placed only in just one area and babies must take a book to an adult who is in a different area. Third, adults are likely to spot a child who is mouthing or chewing on a book, if books are distributed throughout the play space rather than only in a book nook. Although toddlers between 14 and 18 months of age mouth and chew books far less than younger babies, some still put books in their mouths. When adults are close by they can remove a book from the environment quickly after a baby has mouthed it, and disinfect it before another baby explores it. Some books should be set aside for just this age group. The books should be wiped with disinfectant solution after one child's use, before giving them to another toddler to explore.

Additionally, although it's perfectly okay for babies to mouth and suck on books, interactions with adults can prompt other book-related behavior that competes with mouthing and chewing. Even a brief interaction with only eye contact and a smile from a nearby adult, and perhaps a question (e.g., "Oh, what do you see in your book?"), can tilt the balance from the mouthing and chewing of books to more visual inspection.

Interactive reading also supports the toddler's engagement. Of course, children do differ in their engagement and interest in book reading (Fletcher & Reese 2005); however, there is research that suggests that promoting interaction positively affects a child's engagement (Ortiz, Stowe, & Arnold 2001). Some toddlers simply require interaction to be engaged at all in book reading. If an adult resorts to merely reading extended lengths of text to such a child, her attention quickly fades, as if to say, "If you're going to make it so I can't understand and participate, then I'm not interested." Yet, the same toddler might become highly engaged when an adult uses interactive reading strategies to support the toddler's comprehension and participation.

Nineteen to 30 months

What the toddler can do. At this age, motor development becomes less pertinent to caregivers' choices in books and their ways of reading. However, the toddler's language and cognitive development remain highly significant.

Toddlers now speak with more extended and complex language structures, and even use real sentences. They are also learning as many as six to ten new words a day, most acquired through language interactions involving real-life experiences. Book reading experience, however, is related to a toddler's expressive language development (Richman & Colombo 2007). If frequently engaged in book reading, toddlers may learn up to one-third of the new words they speak from books read aloud to them (Hepburn, Egan, & Flynn 2010).

Toddlers now are also capable of thinking and acting in more abstract ways. For instance, they might pretend to feed a doll or to read to a toy animal. Around 18 to 24 months, toddlers begin actively to respond with prosocial behavior to show empathy toward others (Zahn-Waxler et al. 1992). Toddlers' growing understanding of emotions, coupled with their new representational abilities (e.g., pretend play, attributing meaning to their scribbles), helps them to understand better the concepts in books that are shared with them. Toddlers also attend longer now, and may be able to engage in shared reading for slightly longer periods of time as they enjoy stories and concept books.

Also during this period, toddlers join more in conversations that involve recalling and talking about recent events in their lives (Fivush 1991; Sperry & Sperry 1996). For example, when asked, "What did you do today at child care?" a toddler between 24 and 28 months might reply, "Play balls Benji," to indicate she played with balls with her friend, Benji. Recounting life events in this fashion is an emergent form of one type of story, the **personal narrative**. Personal narratives share characteristics with the **fictional narratives** found in storybooks. For example, both have characters, a setting, and a series of events. When adults help toddlers include the important people, places, and actions when relating their own immediate past events, they are better able later to understand these key features in fictional narratives in books, and to include them in stories they write (Peterson, Jesso, & McCabe 1999).

Choosing texts for the toddler. Caregivers should continue using books with clear illustrations and direct connections to the text on each page. This structure supports the toddler in making connections between language and images, and allows the adult to point to illustrations of words as they read to the toddler.

Through their second year, toddlers' life experiences affect their book interests. The adult uses his knowledge of toddlers' recent and upcoming experiences to choose books of interest to them. Concept books and theme books, such as those already described, remain good choices. With the vast array of children's literature available, adults can find concept and theme books about almost any topic. Books about seasonal or holiday activities (e.g., *Pumpkin Day, Pumpkin Night* by Anne Rockwell, *The Snowy Day* by Ezra Jack Keats) or special family events (e.g., *Fiesta Babies* by Carmen Tafolla) allow the toddler to make connections to her own experiences.

Toddlers now also enjoy predictable books, because their repetitive nature helps them anticipate words and begin to chime in with the reading. For toddlers, predictable books also aid vocabulary development, because they provide repeated exposures to words that are unknown, and opportunities to chime in with the text supports language use. Examples include songs like *The Wheels on the Bus* by Raffi and repetitive texts like *Hush! A Thai Lullaby* by Minfong Ho and *Peekaboo Morning* by Rachel Isadora. Some predictable texts involve familiar concepts (e.g., *In the Tall, Tall Grass* by Denise Fleming, *How Do Dinosaurs Say Goodnight?* by Jane Yolen). Even wordless picture books, or books with very little text (e.g., *Oh, David!* by David Shannon), can promote toddlers' "reading."

As toddlers develop their ability to recount events from their own lives, they begin to understand and enjoy books with actual stories—a true plot with a problem and resolution. When choosing stories for toddlers, caregivers look for simple story problems and events familiar to the toddler because familiarity makes it more likely that a toddler will engage with and understand a story. Examples of stories with simple, familiar problems include a new baby at home (e.g., *On Mother's Lap* by Ann Herbert Scott) or losing a favorite possession (e.g., *Gossie* by Olivier Dunrea).

Older toddlers (i.e., 24 to 30 months) might now occasionally watch television programs or movies. Books related to TV programs fall roughly into two categories: (1) original books that were made into shows (e.g., *Max and Ruby* series by Rosemary Wells) and (2) original shows that were made into books (e.g., *Dora the Explorer* or *Bob the Builder* books) (all of these examples are written for older children). Original books usually have higher-quality writing and illustrations than books based on shows. Adults should offer selections of high-quality books from which the toddler can choose.

Engaging the toddler. Because the toddler is now capable of understanding and generating more complex language, conversations around books become even more integral to the reading experience. As before, the adult assumes dual roles during shared reading. First, he provides comprehensible input to help the child understand the book by commenting about the text and illustrations to fill in background knowledge, make connections to the child's life, and label and explain unknown objects and concepts. Second, he promotes the child's expressive language by welcoming the child's comments and questions and by asking questions, too.

As toddlers grow in life experiences and language ability, they can both understand and make increasingly complex connections between their lives and books read aloud to them. Toddlers are more likely to make these connections when adults consistently model connections as they read (e.g., "She has a teddy bear she sleeps with, just like you sleep with your bear"). Before long, the toddler makes connections herself. The toddler often begins by expressing connections physically, such as showing the adult her teddy bear, or pointing to his ceiling light as the boy did in the opening scenario of this chapter. Older toddlers voice their connections, "I sleep with my teddy, too!"

As toddlers become able to talk about the immediate past, they make connections to events in books that mirror their experiences (e.g., "We see elephants at the zoo"). As they develop empathy, they begin connecting the emotions portrayed in books with their own emotions or those observed in family members. As caregivers recognize toddlers' growing ability to think about emotions, they begin to include discussion about **narrative intangibles**, such as characters' feelings and motivations, in shared reading (McArthur, Adamson, & Deckner 2005). For example, the adult might explain, "Oh, I think the little girl [in the story] is feeling sad now. See? She's crying. She misses her mommy, just like you miss your mommy sometimes." With age and experience, children also begin to ask more questions about these intangibles (McArthur, Adamson, & Deckner 2005).

Questioning toddlers during shared reading supports language development by encouraging expressive language use (Blake et al. 2006; Deckner, Adamson, & Bakeman 2006; Whitehurst et al. 1988). Many caregivers naturally shift toward more questioning as a child develops (Deloache & DeMendoza 1987; Sénéchal, Cornell, & Broda 1995) and also becomes more familiar with a particular text through repeated readings (McArthur, Adamson, & Deckner 2005). As caregivers ask more questions, children assume a more active role in the reading experience (McArthur, Adamson, & Deckner 2005). Children's interest in book reading is also associated with caregivers' use of questioning and other language interactions around the text (Deckner, Adamson, & Bakeman 2006).

Toddlers this age also begin displaying some **emergent reading** or "pretend reading." For example, they chime in with particular words in well-known or repetitive texts or describe illustrations when browsing through books on their own. Caregivers encourage emergent reading by pausing to prompt the child to complete a well-known phrase. Or, if an older toddler is narrating a book by describing illustrations in succession, the adult can ask the child to "read" the book to her. Emergent reading behaviors such as these build a foundation for learning to read independently, which will develop more over the next several years.

All of these research-based suggestions might seem like a lot to manage with a toddler, but they become a natural part of interacting with a toddler around books when the adult's goal is to make a book meaningful to the child. The example provided in Box 2-3 "Engaging Toddlers in Shared Reading: Putting It All Together" illustrates how one parent wove specific support strategies into a very natural interactive conversation with an older toddler, while reading *The Mitten* by Jan Brett.

Reading daily to older toddlers in groups

Sometimes, programs schedule a daily read-aloud for toddlers who are 2 years and older, to help ensure that all toddlers benefit from book experiences. When caregivers read to a whole group of toddlers at once, however, it is difficult for all of the children to see the book's pictures, which decreases their attention. When reading to the whole group it is also difficult to encourage responses from children and to respond adequately; therefore, research suggests reading to toddlers in groups of four children or fewer (Phillips & Twardosz 2003). In doing this, one adult might read to rotating small groups of children during free play, while a second caregiver supervises children in other areas. Of course, appropriate staff-child ratios must be kept in mind.

Adults might also try reading to a different small group each day for only the first 10 minutes of free play, to ensure that every child in a group of 12 toddlers benefits from a small-group story experience at least every three days. Less might be more, in this case.

Because of the benefits of reading to individual or very small groups of toddlers, and the difficulty of managing this level of attention in groups of 10 or more toddlers, programs might enlist the help of volunteers and encourage visits by parents. Parents and other family members can also be encouraged to share books at home. Child care staff can help families learn about resources for obtaining books for infants and toddlers and provide workshops that focus on strategies for reading to very young children.

Early reading-related behaviors

Young children differ significantly in all aspects of early reading-related behaviors. While some snuggle right up to listen, others only pause briefly in the midst of their

---

Box 2-3 **Engaging Toddlers in Shared Reading: Putting It All Together**

In this very brief excerpt of a reading experience, we see a parent connecting a book (*The Mitten* by Jan Brett) to her child's experiences with yarn and knitting at his grandmother's. She warmly accepted the child's contributions, clarified or extended his language attempts, and asked questions that prompted his language use. She also explained the cause-and-effect relationship between Nicki's intrusions on the animals' homes and their fear and flight away to the mitten.

Adult: [reading text] "But Nicki wanted snow-white mittens so much that grandma [substituted for Baba] made them for him." Oh, look at all that yarn. See the yarn balls? [pointing] His grandma is going to knit some mittens. See here? She knits yarn just like your grandma does.

Child: Balls yarn mitten.

Adult: Yes, those are balls of yarn, and his grandma is going to knit and make mittens out of that yarn, just like grandma does . . . [continued reading and discussing next few pages]

Child: Rabbit coming!

Adult: Oh, yes, there's the rabbit. See here. Nicki is stepping on top of the rabbit's house? I don't think the rabbit likes that. He's scared, and he's going to run away. [discussing for a moment] Where is he going? [turning page]

Child: Coming in mitten.

Adult: Yup, here comes the rabbit to snuggle in the mitten. [reading text] "A rabbit came hopping by. He wiggled in [adult snuggling in closer to child] next to the mole." He's snuggling in [pointing to illustration]. . . . [continued reading and discussing next few pages] Oh, look. Nicki is stepping on another animal's house and scaring him. Who is that?

Child: Doggie. Where Sadie go? [looking for own dog]

Adult: I don't know where Sadie is. [pointing back to book] This does look like a dog, but it's a fox. Remember fox with the pointy ears?

Child: Fox.

Adult: Mm hmm, there's the fox, and looks like he's going to run to the mitten, too. . . .

This excerpt illustrates that intentional support of babies' and toddlers' language and literacy development does not require highly structured, lesson-like formats, but rather comfortable and genuine conversations about books.

---

active play to listen. Some children are provided with baskets of books designed for infants and toddlers, while others have less opportunity to engage in book reading. These variations in experience greatly influence how babies and toddlers interact with a particular book.

Reading-related behaviors, including book handling, language, comprehension, and emergent reading, are developmental precursors to more conventional forms of reading (e.g., NELP 2008; Paciga, Hoffman, & Teale 2011; Teale, Hoffman, & Paciga 2010). These behaviors result from the accumulated experience of babies and toddlers with texts and reading, as well as from their motor, cognitive, language, and social development.

Although most children exhibit early reading-related behaviors within about the same age range, the child (i.e., interests, interaction style, etc.) and her cumulative book-reading experience affect their emergence. For example, a 12-month-old with intense interest in and extensive experience with book reading may exhibit the behaviors typical of slightly older toddlers, while a 3-year-old with limited book reading experience may exhibit behaviors typical of a younger toddler.

See Table 2-1 "Early Reading-Related Behaviors" for information about reading-related behavior in babies and toddlers (book handling, language, comprehension, and emergent reading). Babies and toddlers exhibit the behaviors listed while both sharing books with adults and when exploring books independently.

Book handling describes children's physical manipulations and uses of texts, in both traditional print and digital forms. (Digital book experiences are appropriate only for children 2 years of age and older; see Box 2-4 "Sharing Digital Texts with Older Toddlers.") A baby's book handling depends not solely on her age, motor skill, and previous book experience, but also on book characteristics. For example, a very young baby typically maintains eye contact best with simple, bright, and high contrast pictures, and the size and composition of a book's pages (i.e., cardboard vs. paper) influence a toddler's ability to turn pages independently.

Language understanding and use while engaged with books includes both verbal and nonverbal communications with adults during book reading. This behavior includes the older toddler's use of story language to interact playfully with others (e.g., asks, "Mommy, Mommy, what do you see?" after reading *Brown Bear, Brown Bear, What Do You See?* by Bill Martin Jr.).

Comprehension behaviors indicate the baby and toddler's developing skill, both verbal and nonverbal, to construct meaning from the pictures and content of the texts that adults share. Opportunities for language and social interaction help very young children understand both fictional (i.e., narratives) and informational genres, and young children can express their comprehension of both kinds of texts.

Emergent reading behaviors indicate children's developing understanding of how reading works, and their desire to engage in it. For example, a young toddler who chants some of the phrases in *Brown Bear, Brown Bear, What Do You See?* demonstrates understanding that the language of the text remains constant (i.e., readers do not "make up" unique language to go with pictures each time they read a book). Or a toddler might express a developing love of reading by insisting that his favorite book be read again and again (and again) (i.e., reading is an enjoyable act).

Some items in the emergent reading behavior list overlap items in the language and comprehension lists, although the majority of emergent reading items focus on the child's active initiation of book reading, participation in the book reading (i.e., by chiming in on repetitive text), and interest in assuming the role of reader.

Box 2-4 **Sharing Digital Texts with Older Toddlers**

The American Academy of Pediatrics (2011) recommends that digital media of any form **not be used with children younger than 2 years**, because their extensive review of the research indicates that real-life experiences—free play, hands-on experiences, and traditional book reading—provide better support for language development than do experiences with digital media. Even after age 2, which includes the older toddler range (24 months to 30 months) included in this chapter, **children's total exposure** to all forms of digital media (games, television, computers) **should be limited** to relatively brief periods that total **no more than about one hour per day.**

When choosing digital texts for toddlers, caregivers look for books that do not just play continuously, but allow pacing control. They should also look for texts that allow the narration to be turned off so that the adult can read the text aloud (Labbo 2009).

Rather than rely on the sellers of digital books for information about digital texts, guidance and ebooks can be obtained from independent sources, such as:

- http://en.childrenslibrary.org. This online site offers thousands of free digital books in dozens of languages.

- www.childrensbooksonline.org. This online library features scanned historical children's books, many translated into several languages.

- http://digital-storytime.com. This site provides a searchable and browsable database of highly informative reviews.

- www.tumblebooks.com/library. This online collection of animated, narrated picture books is available by subscription, which many public library systems offer for their members. Includes English and Spanish titles.

Although many digital texts are designed for older toddlers to use themselves, children benefit more when adults interact with them during the experience (AAP 2011; NAEYC & Fred Rogers Center for Early Learning and Children's Media 2012). Adults can use the same practices that have been discussed throughout this chapter, such as labeling illustrations and animations, and referencing them to the story. Adults can also scaffold the use of digital media (scrolling, swiping, clicking), using verbal descriptions as they model and prompt children's use of interactive features (Labbo 2009; Smith 2001).

Table 2-1 Early Reading-Related Behaviors

Behaviors	Early	Later
Book Handling	• Makes eye contact with a book's pictures, but no attempt to handle a book (2–4 months) • Explores a book by grasping and bringing it to the mouth to suck and chew (5–10 months) • Shakes, crumples, and waves the book (5–10 months) • Holds cardboard books with both hands and explores how the book works by making the pages open and close (6–8 months) • Deliberately tears paper pages (7–15 months) • Helps the adult turn the pages, pressing the left-hand page after the adult has pressed it (7–8 months) • Shows a notable increase in visual attention to books and decrease in physical manipulation of books (8–12 months)	• Might accidentally tear pages due to difficulty in handling books, but intentional tearing of pages to explore decreases (12–14 months) • Turns pages awkwardly because of difficulty in separating pages (8–12 months) • Turns pages well (11–15 months) • Flips through a book by gathering clumps of pages and letting them fly past (14–15 months) • Turns an inverted book right side up, or tilts head as if trying to see the picture right side up (11–15 months) • Operates the basic functions of digital texts (e.g., opens applications, turns pages, clicks animations) (24–30 months)
Language Understanding and Use	• Looks intensely at pictures for several minutes, with wide-open eyes and thoughtful expression (2–4 months) • Coos and gurgles while adult reads (4–6 months) • Might understand words for familiar objects in pictures (7–9 months) • Laughs or smiles when a picture is recognized (8–12 months) • Points to individual pictures (8–12 months)	• Chimes in during reading of predictable song or story (16–30 months) • Points to a picture and asks, "What's that?" or requests a label in another way (e.g., "Dat?" or questioning intonation) (13–20 months) • Begins to use two- to four-word sentences (i.e., telegraphic sentences). For instance, describing pictures or events in books (e.g., "baby crying") (18–24 months)

(Continued on p. 38)

Behaviors	Early	Later
	• Makes animal or other appropriate sounds (e.g., "beep beep" in *Little Blue Truck* by Alice Schertle) (10–13 months) • Points correctly to familiar objects when asked, "Where is the . . . ?" (11–14 months) • Names objects pictured, although articulation may not be accurate (11–14 months) • Uses book babble (i.e., jabbering that captures the overall sound of reading) (13–18 months)	• Uses more complex sentences when talking about the book or favorite characters (e.g., "That not Dora backpack, that *my* backpack") (24–30 months) • Asks and answers simple questions during the story reading (e.g., "Where Momma go?" when listening to *Owl Babies* by Martin Waddell). Might ask the same question each time the story is read (27–30 months) • Plays with the story language outside of the story reading context (e.g., "Mommy, mommy, what do you see?" after reading *Brown Bear, Brown Bear, What Do You See?* by Bill Martin Jr.) (27–30 months)
Comprehension	• Understands words for familiar objects in pictures (7–9 months) • Relates an object or action in a book to the real world (e.g., retrieves a teddy after adult has read *That's Not My Teddy* by Fiona Watt) (10–14 months) • Selects texts on the basis of content, thus demonstrating some understanding of what some individual books are about (e.g., picks up a book with a picture of a duck after playing with a toy duck; selects a book about a doctor's visit after a check-up) (10–15 months)	• Shows preference for a favorite page by searching for it or holding the book open at that page, as if that part is particularly well understood or appreciated (11–14 months) • Performs an action shown or mentioned in a text (e.g., pretends to throw a ball when book mentions playing baseball) (12–23 months) • Shows empathy for characters or situations depicted in texts (e.g., repeats distress type—"hurt," "boo-boo," "miss mommy," while looking at pictures, and displays sad or concerned facial expression; pretends to cry after hearing that a child in the book is sad) (18–24 months)

Behaviors	Early	Later
		• Makes associations across texts (e.g., gets two books and shows the caregiver similar pictures or events in each one) (20–24 months)
		• Talks about the characters and events during the reading in ways suggesting understanding of what has been read or said (e.g., saying "Shhh! Bunny sleeping" at end of *Goodnight Moon* by Margaret Wise Brown) (20–26 months)
		• Relates events in texts to own experiences during shared reading (e.g., saying, "I play freight train," referring to own toy trains when reading *Freight Train* by Donald Crews) (20–26 months)
		• Links situations from a book to situations outside of the book-sharing context (e.g., reenacting events and reciting lines from *The Snowy Day* by Ezra Jack Keats when playing in the snow) (20–30 months)
Emergent Reading	• Coos or gurgles when read to (3–6 months) • Gazes at (7 months) and/or points (9 months) to illustrations while adult is reading and looking at a page (7–9 months) • Vocalizes (unintelligibly) while pointing at pictures (7–10 months) • Points to the pictures and vocalizes (more intelligibly), such as with rising intonation, to indicate "What's that?" (10–12 months)	• Imitates adult's hand-finger behaviors by pointing to the words or pictures when sharing the book (15–20 months) • Describes illustrations or familiar parts of text in own words (e.g., says "piggy's dancing" when adult reads *Moo, Baa, La La La!* by Sandra Boynton) (16–20 months) • Fills in the next word in the text when the adult pauses, says the next word when the adult reads it, or reads along with the adult when the text is highly predictable (16–24 months) *(Continued on p. 40)*

Behaviors	Early	Later
	• Makes animal or other appropriate sounds (e.g., "beep beep" in *Little Blue Truck* by Alice Schertle) (10–13 months) • Names objects pictured, although articulation may not be accurate (11–14 months) • Brings books to an adult to read, and after one reading hands a book back, suggesting the adult should read it again (12–16 months) • Uses book babble (to mimic the sound of reading) (13–18 months) • Begins to search more thoroughly through books on shelf or in baskets to find preferred books for adult to read (16–20 months)	• "Reads" to self and pretends to read to dolls or stuffed animals, holding the book so that they can see (17–25 months) • Recites entire phrases from a favorite story if the adult pauses at the opportune time (that is, cloze reading) (20–30 months) • Protests when an adult misreads or skips a word in a familiar, and usually predictable, text. Typically offers the correction (28–30 months) • Asks to read books or digital texts to the adult and may be able to recite several texts quite accurately, especially if simple and predictable (28–30 months)

Concluding thoughts about reading with babies and toddlers

Each baby and toddler is unique, and each reading experience with a baby or toddler occurs at a unique point in the child's development. Adults consider the motor, cognitive, language, and social development of each child, along with his interests and experiences, to choose books and ways of reading that will engage each baby or toddler. Moreover, because children are continuously growing and changing, the books or digital texts that are read, and the ways the books are shared, must continuously adapt to the child. Adults who make careful, intentional, and flexible decisions about reading with their babies and toddlers create experiences with reading that engage and enthrall, and begin a lifelong passion for reading and learning.

3 Reading Storybooks with Preschoolers

In this chapter, we discuss criteria for selecting storybooks, goals for storybook reading, and strategies for reading stories in ways that support meaning and language development. Much of this chapter is devoted to a discussion of storybook reading strategies, because *how* books are shared determines in large part what young children actually learn from them (Cunningham & Zibulsky 2011).

Selecting storybooks

The goal for a teacher or child care provider is to select high-quality stories suitable for a specific group of children. Three-year-olds need somewhat different stories than 4-year-olds, and a group with mixed ages needs yet a different selection. Book selection also depends on the topics children are studying, family experiences, and community characteristics, including local customs and celebrations.

It is helpful to keep several criteria in mind when selecting storybooks: (1) a book's complexity and its potential interest to young children; (2) the richness of a book's language; (3) the values it conveys, and the extent to which it represents diversity; and (4) the appropriateness of a storybook's illustrations and size.

Box 3-1   Kinds of Books

Familiarity with various book genres aids a teacher's book selection and influences the range of understandings and skills the teacher can support through book reading. Four different kinds of books are described here: narrative, informational, predictable, and concept.

Narratives

Narratives are fictional stories that have at least one character, a problem, and a plot that leads toward the resolution of the problem. Stories are usually written in the past tense, because they relate events that have already occurred. In narratives, characters try to resolve the story's problem by taking action. Through these actions, characters reveal their knowledge, points of view, and motivations to the reader or listener (Applebee 1978; Stein 1988). Unlike informational books that sometimes focus on physical cause and effect (e.g., what makes thunder), stories involve mostly psychological causation (e.g., why a character is sad or surprised).

Fictional narratives are the most common book genre available for young children (Duke 2000). Most storybooks for preschoolers are picture books in which words (i.e., text) and creative illustrations work together to provide information about the story's characters, settings, and events.

Informational books

Informational books are a type of nonfiction. Topics found in these books include animals and plants; natural habitats (e.g., deserts, swamps); human-made places (e.g., zoos, construction sites); natural events (e.g., water freezing into ice, tornadoes); customs and celebrations (clothing worn and food eaten; holidays and other special occasions); and transportation and commerce (e.g., airports, highways, grocery stores). The common feature of these texts is a focus on factual content or a process that pertains to the social, physical, or biological worlds.

Because informational books convey factual information that applies all the time, they are commonly written in the present tense (Duke & Bennett-Armistead 2003). Like picture

Interest, cognitive engagement, and story complexity

Preschoolers enjoy books with humor and imagination, and a surprise or two. They also like genuine, unique, and endearing characters through which they can see or imagine themselves. And while a good story must not be over the children's heads, it should provide new information and a lot to think and wonder about, across several readings.

Both younger and older preschoolers enjoy stories that vary in complexity, although older preschoolers can engage better than younger ones with stories that are more complex. A story's complexity depends on a number of things, but the main difference between simple and complex stories is that complex stories have a plot, while simple stories do not.

For example, in the simple stories *The Snowy Day* by Ezra Jack Keats, *Gilberto and the Wind* by Marie Hall Ets, and *Dog's Colorful Day* by Emma Dodd, each main character has multiple experiences of a specific kind—with snow, wind, and color stains, respectively. Yet, without a central problem, a story's events are not interrelated. Instead, a simple story has a series of events whose order could be altered considerably without harming it.

storybooks, informational books use both illustrations and text to convey meaning. But unlike a storybook's creative art, an informational book's illustrations are realistic (e.g., diagrams, charts, graphs, photographs). (See Chapter 4.)

Predictable text books

All predictable text books use one or more literary devices that make a text easy for young children to remember, and thus easy to anticipate and recall after hearing it just a few times. Young children enjoy the flow and rhythm of the language in predictable text books. They also enjoy these books because they can begin to chime in as the teacher reads them, and can soon "read" the books independently in the classroom book area.

Various literary devices make books predictable (i.e., easy for a child to learn and recall). These include (1) rhyming and alliteration; (2) repetition of a basic sentence frame with only one or two words varied each time; (3) use of a refrain; (4) cumulative text (one new sentence is added on each page, and text introduced previously is repeated on each successive page); (5) a close relationship between illustrations and text (every item or action mentioned in the text is pictured); and (6) placing on each page text covering only one idea or thought. *Goodnight Moon* by Margaret Wise Brown and *The Very Hungry Caterpillar* by Eric Carle are examples of classic predictable text books.

Concept books

These picture books introduce and teach a concept or skill, such as the alphabet, shapes, colors, numbers, body parts, feelings, opposites, or object names (i.e., word books). Concept books typically explore a concept in enjoyable ways (e.g., *Alphabet Under Construction* by Denise Fleming and *One Gorilla* by Atsuko Morozumi).

Most concept books lack main characters, a problem, and a plot. Instead, the concept of focus provides the book's framework. Some concept books, however, convey information and events in chronological order, with a hint of a problem to solve. This makes some concept books resemble a simple story (e.g., *Feast for 10* by Cathryn Falwell and *The Very Hungry Caterpillar*).

Characters in complex stories learn quite a lot throughout the story, and usually change remarkably in their understanding of self and others, as a consequence. For example, in *Peter's Chair* by Ezra Jack Keats, Peter has a "change of heart" after realizing that he can no longer use his little blue chair and that his parents still love him. As the plot unfolds in *Peter's Chair*, Peter expresses his thoughts and concerns, and experiences complex emotions. In contrast, although Peter (in *The Snowy Day*) and Gilberto (in *Gilberto and the Wind*) learn something about snow and wind, respectively, the range of their emotions is more limited, and neither has major insights about self or others. Peter and Gilberto are very much the same little boys at the end as those we met at the start of these stories.

Compared to simple stories, complex stories typically have richer language and more sophisticated vocabulary, including words that describe mental states (e.g., thought, surprised, knew, decided, wondered). Complex stories also have a main theme, such as friendship, perseverance, or parent-child relationships, not just a central topic focus (e.g., snow, wind, color stains).

Complex stories also prompt reasoning. For example, to understand *Henry's Happy Birthday* by Holly Keller, children must reason about how sacrificing his candy cup and discovering an oddly-shaped present affects Henry, and also how his reactions lead to an unconventional birthday wish (i.e., that it were someone else's birthday). Because the author does not state explicitly that Henry felt slighted or disappointed, children must draw inferences about Henry's emotions, and integrate story events to understand how they work together to motivate Henry's tearful wish.

Vocabulary and language structures

High-quality stories also have many words that are not yet in most preschoolers' vocabularies. Complex stories typically have an abundance of new words, while simple stories usually have only a few. For example, the complex story *Some Smug Slug* by Pamela Duncan Edwards has sophisticated words, such as *strolled, antennae, slope, shrieked, strand, slumbered, summit, sapphire, sauntered, skink,* and *sinister*, while the simple story *Dog's Colorful Day* has only *stains, pollen, trots, patch, splatters,* and *smudge.*

Complex stories also expose children to diverse sentence structures, which supports overall language development. For example, they convey characters' thoughts through dialogue, relate events in past tense, and say things efficiently (e.g., "Afraid to jump into the dark water, he stared back at the mud bank" in *Raccoon on His Own* by Jim Arnosky [p. 9]). The language in high-quality stories is also crafted differently—is more literary—than language used in everyday conversation.

For example, in *Duck in the Truck* by Jez Alborough, which is written in verse, we find the lines, "These are the feet that jumped the duck down into the muck all yucky and brown" (p. 5) and "This is the ear that hears the shout . . . " (p. 18). In ordinary conversation, we would likely say, "The duck jumped feet first into the mud" and "The goat heard the duck shout." Part of the pleasure experienced from reading or listening to stories comes from the beautifully crafted language that differs from the ordinary. But children must hear book language in order to understand and learn to enjoy it.

Values and diversity of characters, cultures, and family structures

The values in good storybooks apply to all people, everywhere (i.e., are universal). Universal values include concern and consideration for others, friendship, patience, courage, personal fortitude, perseverance, belonging, love, and responsibility.

The best stories have genuine characters from diverse cultures, races, linguistic backgrounds, and family structures. These characters display a full range of complex behaviors, as they deal with universal problems and themes in the roles they occupy. Although diversity of every kind cannot be present in a single book, all aspects of diversity can be addressed in the collection of books used over a year (Smith, Brady, & Anastasopoulos 2008).

Goals for story reading

Hearing stories read aloud in a group situation helps build a classroom community. Good stories also help children learn about emotions, support their language development, and help them acquire general knowledge.

Build community

Story reading in the early years provides a context for building positive emotional bonds between adult and child (Bus, van IJzendoorn, & Pellegrini 1995). In one-on-one situations at home or in the preschool, adults often read books to children who sit on their laps or snuggle beside them. But story reading with larger groups can also be a warm and positive experience. After all, stories involve feelings, thoughts, and relationships. Hearing about and discussing these with a thoughtful, warm, and wise teacher supports bonds both among the children and between children and the teacher. For the preschool child, building attachment to this larger world of people is an appropriate social-emotional goal.

Support understanding of other people

Story characters have thoughts, feelings, goals, and motivations, and they act in response to their own current mental state and the perceived mental states of others. For example, characters cry, write letters, notice interesting things on a walk, and build roads, all of which are motivated by something.

Preschoolers learn a great deal about the world, including the minds of others, just from overhearing others talk about different people's mental states (Beals 2001; Gola 2012). Stories present a wonderful context in which this happens very frequently. The text, illustrations, and a teacher's comments (i.e., comprehension asides) provide some of this information, a discussion following a reading provides more, and a teacher's responses to children's questions add still more (Mills et al. 2012).

Build knowledge about emotions and model strategies for regulating them

Teachers often comment about emotions as they read a story, and emotions come up again when teachers and children discuss a story after its reading. This experience helps children develop an understanding of emotions and a language for talking about them (Taumoepeau & Ruffman 2006; 2008). A broad vocabulary learned from stories includes words, such as *sad, astonished, distraught, knowing, remembering, forgetting, wondering, thinking,* and *wishing,* all of which help children understand a story's characters, and also to regulate their behavior in emotionally charged situations (Campos, Frankel, & Camras 2004; Dunn, Bretherton, & Munn 1987).

The ability to regulate emotions affects learning, because it allows children to allocate more mental resources to it (Copple 2012; Raver 2002). In other words, because cognition and emotion are intertwined, children learn better when they are less occupied with intense emotions (Bell & Wolfe 2004; Blair 2002; Cole, Martin, & Dennis 2004; Tamouepeau & Ruffman 2008).

In addition to teaching about emotions, stories also model some effective strategies for coping with them. One strategy, **cognitive reframing**, involves turning a negative situation into a positive one (Morris et al. 2011). The resolution of the central problem in many stories involves this strategy. For example, Ernst, the main character in *The Puddle Pail* by Elisa Kleven, cognitively reframed his strong desire to collect puddle reflections (i.e., they disappeared once placed in his pail), by deciding to paint the reflections he had collected in puddles. This idea allowed Ernst to keep the reflections he had seen, though not in their original puddle form.

Support language development

Story reading fosters all aspects of language development, including vocabulary.

Vocabulary development from stories. Stories expose children to a range of words, both common (i.e., heard in everyday talk) and sophisticated (i.e., rarely heard in daily conversation). Stories provide opportunities for children to hear many sophisticated words. When it comes to sophisticated word knowledge, children need both breadth (i.e., a lot of words known at least minimally) and depth (i.e., some words known deeply) in their vocabulary (Coyne et al. 2009; Ouellete 2006).

Story reading fosters vocabulary breadth by exposing children to many new words. It fosters vocabulary depth by exposing children to subtle variations in word meanings, because they encounter the same word in different contexts. For example, in the story *Possum's Harvest Moon* by Ann Hunter, children are exposed to new meanings of *great* (i.e., large) and *grew* (i.e., to become). In *Mouse Paint* by Ellen Stoll Walsh, the word *cried* means shouted or cried out, not *cry* as in producing tears.

Some depth in vocabulary knowledge helps children comprehend stories during their preschool years, and also later on, when reading challenging texts on their own (Ouellette 2006). A broad vocabulary allows children to understand more during their preschool years, when listening to books or engaging in conversation. Additionally, as discussed in Chapter 1, a broad vocabulary also seems to support a child's phonological awareness (Dickinson, Golinkoff, & Hirsh-Pasek 2010; Metsala 1997).

We also discussed in Chapter 1 how a larger receptive vocabulary acquired in the preschool years contributes to reading and comprehension in later years (Dickinson & Porche 2011; Storch & Whitehurst 2002), no doubt because simply learning words minimally early on provides a starting point for learning more about them, as time goes on. This early vocabulary foundation, upon which deeper meanings are built, benefits reading comprehension as books become more challenging, especially from fourth grade on (Lesaux & Kieffer 2010; Ouellette 2006). Although technical language used in content areas, such as biology, earth science, geography, and history, can be learned best as children study these areas (Nagy & Townsend 2012), preschoolers do learn initial meanings for some technical words in stories. These meanings can be deepened when preschool, kindergarten, and primary teachers read informational texts and provide first-hand experiences (see Chapter 4).

Support for understanding the complexity of language. Reading and discussing books also helps preschoolers understand

▲ *syntax*: word order in sentences

▲ *grammar*: how sentences are constructed, and how various words change depending on their position and the features of other words in the sentence

▲ *pragmatics*: the understanding of the effect of context on language

High-quality stories also help children learn sophisticated language structures because they expose children repeatedly to many varied sentences. For example, consider the complex language in *Possum's Harvest Moon*, a story about a possum who wants to celebrate the waning days of the season with a party but encounters disinterest from animal friends who want to work or sleep (p. 12):

> "How could they work on such a beautiful night?" Possum asked himself. "How can they think of sleep in such moonlight?" He put on his hat and sat alone, looking up at the great harvest moon.

As Possum asks these "how" questions, children hear language that reveals Possum's thoughts about characters' motivations. This information prompts engagement in contrastive thinking (i.e., Possum's rationale for a party and the animals' disinterest). The modifying phrase, "looking up at the great harvest moon," is considerably more nuanced than simply saying, "He put on his hat and looked at

Box 3-2 Peer Effects on Children's Language Learning

Our experiences with multiple language classrooms are varied. Some included nine or 10 children out of 18 who spoke a language other than English, with as many as six or seven different languages represented. English was the language of instruction, and also of play among the children, because children who spoke a language other than English typically had no home language peers. Other classrooms served fairly large numbers of children who spoke primarily one language other than English (e.g., Portuguese, Spanish, Chinese, Vietnamese, Somali), and only a few children who spoke English. English was the language of instruction in these classrooms, although one teacher in each class was usually bilingual (i.e., knew the home language of the children who were also learning English).

But because our own competence in languages other than English was always quite limited, we never collected detailed case data on any of the English-speaking children's use of a second language in play situations with peers. Thus, the example of peer interaction provided here is of a 3-year-old dual language learner, JK, who began preschool as a monolingual speaker of Korean.

According to Wong Fillmore (1976; 1991), children learning a new language use several strategies to engage with peers who already know it: (1) join in and act like they know what's going on; (2) use a small number of well-selected words from the new language; and (3) don't worry about details at first. Tabors (2008) has also written about the importance of peer interaction for children learning a new language and about the negative consequences of social isolation among children who attend English immersion preschools.

In the classroom from which our data were collected, the teachers supported peer interactions and offered a program rich in play opportunities. They also maintained a consistent daily schedule and used established routines to manage transitions. The language of instruction was English, and English was the first language of about two-thirds of the children. The remaining six or seven children spoke a language other than English (e.g., Chinese, Arabic, Farsi, Greek, Hebrew, Hindi, Italian, Korean, Russian, Spanish), and some were trilingual (e.g., Arabic, Farsi, English; Hindi, Russian, English).

September–October

1. At snack time (late September), JK took a Cheerio from a friend's supply, held it up to her eye, peeked at her friend through the hole, and said, "Gi!" (first syllable in friend's name).
2. One week later during center time, JK said "Come here" in Korean to a friend as she motioned with a wave.
3. In mid-October, JK said, "Triangle" when referring to a shape on a peer's geoboard.
4. A week later, JK said, "Sit down, please" to a child who was standing up in the car she had made with blocks.

During this time period, JK engaged with peers in play or conversation by using children's names, Korean sentences, one-word English labels, or formulaic English utterances, usually accompanied by gesture (e.g., hand motions) or other nonverbal behavior (e.g., smiling and shared eye gaze).

November–December

1. JK said, "Meeting time, Gabrielle. Stop!" when a classmate continued playing after the teacher had given the clean-up signal. The peer responded by sitting down on the floor where morning meeting was always held after center time.
2. After a peer knocked over a block structure, JK turned to the child and said, "Shhh! Baby sleeping!" The child she shushed looked at her from the pile of toppled blocks.
3. JK said, "Baby head! Baby head!" as she handed a baby doll to a peer in the house play area. The peer accepted the doll carefully by cradling its head.

During this time period, JK used English with peers more frequently and with increasing skill. JK now used multi-word utterances, similar to a monolingual's telegraphic speech (e.g., "Meeting time" and "Stop" rather than "It is meeting time"). Like other English learners, JK also picked up the language of classroom rules and routines and "tried it out" (Tabors 2008). In example 2, JK used the –ing form of the main verb, *sleep*, but omitted the auxilliary verb, *is*. In example 3, she omitted the possessive morpheme –'s, which is also typical morphological development of monolinguals (Brown 1973). In example 2, JK's directions to a peer indicated a play role that JK had adopted. This prosocial mechanism invites peers into play. In example 3, JK appeared knowledgeable as she offered guidance about holding a baby. This characteristic, which makes play interesting and moves it forward, increased JK's appeal and status as a play partner.

January–March

1. On the snowy playground, JK asked, "What doing?" as a peer cleaned snow off the playhouse roof.
2. At the water table, JK initiated a pretend scenario by saying, "Misha, here's your juice," and offering a cup of colored water.
3. At the end of the song "Everybody Wash" at circle time, JK laughed, turned to peers seated nearby, and said, "That's funny."
4. JK shouted, "Hey! Who eat ice cream?" to a peer walking by the doorway of the playground playhouse.

By now, JK used some full English sentences, including wh-questions and contracted verbs (e.g., "Here's your juice" and "That's funny"). Her strategies supported a variety of social purposes: (1) asking questions about peers' ideas in ongoing play; (2) making bids to others within pretend play roles; (3) telling others her opinion; and (4) inviting peers to play without breaking her role. JK's central desire was always to engage in play with peers.

April–June

1. JK said, "I'm help you" as she began to fasten a bike helmet's snaps for a peer.
2. In the block area, JK said, "Yes, there are four children here" to a child who wanted to know if the limit for this play area (four) had been reached.
3. Directing a peer's attention to the garden on the playground, JK pointed to a plant and said, "Look, that's growing!"
4. When scooping goop at the water table, JK initiated a conversation with a peer by exclaiming, "Hailey, look at my hands!"

By year's end, JK used English fluently throughout her play with peers to offer help, confirm limits in a center, comment about growth (i.e., vegetables in a garden), and initiate conversations about play.

Concluding thoughts

Together, these examples demonstrate how a classroom, rich in opportunities for play, provides varied opportunities for dual language learners to use language with English language peers and other dual language learners. Strong teacher support for play, and a consistent daily schedule and routines, are also important.

Another critical element that is not evident in the specific excerpts is direct teacher support during children's play. By joining in play with dual language learners, teachers serve as magnets that draw other children in. From this position, teachers coach children about play and model strategies when occupying a role. Of course, teachers move in and out, as needed, to leave plenty of room for the children to play and talk with one another, on their own.

Young dual language learners acquire considerable language from interacting with English speaking peers, although more than just these interactions is needed for the development of the academic language that is so necessary for later success in school. A balanced preschool program provides plenty of time for teacher supported and facilitated play, as well as for teacher-led group activities, in which English technical vocabulary and grammatical structure, and other literacy-related learning, are supported directly and explicitly.

the moon." Later, when hearing, "It was a moon that made them dream of dancing, of eating and singing" (p. 15), children learn causal detail from embedded clauses ("that made them dream . . . ") and are exposed to an ellipsis, a literary device to indicate omitted words, assumed to be understood.

Finally, inferential thinking is fostered by the structure of the language in high-quality stories. In "The mice danced until the crickets played every jig twice, and the frogs grew hoarse from singing," children must infer that the party and dancing lasted so long that the crickets ran out of original songs and the frogs sang a lot (p. 24). Putting this all together, a child can conclude that everyone ultimately enjoyed the party.

Storybook reading also develops understanding of language *use* across different social contexts. For example, stories model how children talk to friends versus adults, how feelings and different points of view are expressed, and how language use depends on the speakers and the situation (e.g., in libraries, on the playground, when raising a hand to offer a comment during group time).

Of course, even extensive opportunities to listen to good stories and to participate in discussions about them cannot provide all of the support that preschoolers need to develop language. Adults must also talk with children in a variety of situations throughout the day. Children also need opportunities to play and talk with peers.

Children with less language skill benefit from classmates with more (Justice et al. 2011; Mashburn et al. 2009). The effect of the more skilled peers' language on children with less initial skill probably occurs indirectly through the influence on teachers (i.e., they might talk more and use a wider range of language with children who have more language skill, and other children listen in), as well as directly from interactions with their more highly skilled peers.

Children learning English as a second language also benefit from many opportunities to play and talk with English-speaking peers. These opportunities occur most frequently in classrooms that have a variety of languages represented, because classrooms comprised mostly of children who speak the same language other than English interact mostly with one another. Of course, the few children who speak only English in such classrooms benefit greatly from exposure to the language used by the other children, because, in today's world, knowing two or three languages is an advantage. (See Box 3-2 "Peer Effects on Children's Language Learning" for excerpts from a year-long case study of a 3-year-old English language learner's use of English with peers.)

Build general knowledge

Even though informational books, not stories, are designed specifically to convey information, narratives also provide some information about a wide range of topics. For example, *Dreams* by Ezra Jack Keats and *The Puddle Pail* provide information about shadows and reflections, respectively. Similarly, children learn about bats, mammals, and fish versus amphibians from *Stellaluna* by Janell Cannon, *Amos & Boris* by William Steig, and *Fish Is Fish* by Leo Lionni, respectively. Of course, the primary purpose of these stories is to inform about friendship, separation, adapting to circumstances, solving problems, and accepting one's limitations. Yet, some content knowledge is also conveyed.

Whole-group story reading

Preschool teachers read to children in multiple contexts that allow varied grouping. For example, during center time, teachers can read to children individually or in small groups of two or three. It is also common for preschool teachers to read daily to the whole group. Here, we consider a few issues that teachers typically consider when reading in this context.

Seating for whole-group story reading

All children must be able to see the teacher and the book's illustrations. When reading to the whole group, a teacher holds the book up, facing outward, and makes sure that children can see exactly where he is pointing at an illustration.

Several rows of children, a few feet in front of the teacher, work better than one big circle that places some children too far back from in front of the teacher, and others too close to the teacher's immediate right or left. When organized into two to three rows in front of the teacher, taller children are placed in the back and shorter ones in the front, with seating positions in rows staggered to prevent children from blocking views of others. Quite soon, children take a place in the row where assigned, out of consideration for others in the group.

Teachers also consider carefully where to sit. Because sitting on the floor rarely makes a book's pages visible to all children in a large group, teachers often sit on a chair. Additionally, when teachers sit on the floor in this context, the physical conditions can unintentionally "invite" children sitting closer to approach the book, thus blocking other children's views or encouraging them to get up too. Sitting on a chair, instead, sends a clearer message that children should remain seated rather than approach the book to look at or touch it. Sometimes, story time turns into a negative experience, rather than one of joy and delight, as teachers devote considerable time to managing children's behavior. It is better to sit in a location (i.e., on a chair) that helps children show respect to others in the group, rather than send mixed messages.

Appropriate book size for a whole group

Illustrations in a storybook work with the book's text (i.e., words) to convey story meaning (Sipe 2000). Illustrations also help support vocabulary learning, because many items referred to by name in a story's text appear in its illustrations (e.g., *overalls* and *escalator* in *Corduroy* by Don Freeman; *slug, swallowtail butterfly, skink,* and *sparrow* in *Some Smug Slug*).

Because "big books" make pictures more visible, many teachers use them rather than standard format books. Large-size books, however, can draw too much of a child's attention to pictures and divert it from listening as the teacher reads the text (Beck & McKeown 2001; Schickedanz & Collins 2012). When teachers select standard size books carefully (i.e., illustrations are reasonably easy to see from a distance), they can support a better balance in the allocation of a child's attention between listening to the text and looking at illustrations. Children can look more closely at illustrations in storybooks in the book area, where storybooks should be placed after they have been read aloud.

Of course, a big book format should be used if a book's standard format has small and detailed illustrations that are hard to see from a distance. Teachers also consider the children in the group. For example, children with visual or hearing disabilities or delayed language often need more picture support, although teachers also sometimes provide an individual standard format book for some children to hold, while other children in the group focus on the standard format book the teacher holds and reads. If available, a teaching assistant can also assist an individual child by pointing to pictures that relate to text read by the lead teacher.

Some teachers also use big books to teach print concepts (e.g., underline print from left to right, ask children to find specific letters or words). While research shows that children *can* learn about print from storybooks when adults focus on it while reading (Justice & Ezell 2002), this does not mean we *should* focus on print at this time. With stories, we think it is wiser to focus children primarily on meaning, rather than on print, because many other contexts can be used to support print-related learning, while only the story reading context can support meaning directly. Moreover, many predictable text books are more appropriate than complex stories for teaching print concepts (see Chapter 5).

Thinking of the group, not just individuals

Each child brings unique experience with stories and different content knowledge to the group. In this context, a teacher cannot always respond at length to an individual child's questions or linger on pages for an extended discussion of one child's ideas. Teachers learn to respond to individual children, even while taking more than an individual child's needs and interests into account.

Comprehension: Supporting meaning

The most important goal when children listen to a story is to comprehend it. This requires understanding characters' feelings, motivations, and goals, and how these are connected to characters' actions. Story comprehension also sometimes requires understandings about the physical, biological, and social worlds, for example, what happens to hair or clothing in a rainstorm, why animals run away if approached, or why people should not go outside in a bad storm. Finally, because a story's author never tells everything, story comprehension requires reasoning to fill a multitude of gaps. (See Table 1-1 in Chapter 1 for an illustration of the gaps in the story *One Dark Night* by Hazel Hutchins.)

To provide the help that preschoolers need to comprehend good stories fully, adults can use several strategies: (1) introduce each story; (2) use voice, gesture, pacing, gaze, and expression when reading; (3) point to illustrations; (4) provide comprehension asides; (5) respond to children's comments and questions; and

	Table 3-1	**Introducing a Story for a First Reading**

Inch by Inch by Leo Lionni

Reading the Title and the Names of Author and Illustrator	"I have a new book to read today. Its title is *Inch by Inch*. The author of this story is Leo Lionni. Mr. Lionni also made the illustrations for this story."
Introducing the Main Characters	"Here on the cover, we see the main character—a little inchworm (point to). He's a little caterpillar who got the name, *inchworm*, because he's about one inch long. Several birds are also characters in this story, but they aren't pictured on the cover. We'll meet them as we read the story."
Stating the Story's Problem	"In this story, the little inchworm was busy, one day, eating leaves and grass, when a hungry robin spotted him. The robin thought 'Oh, what a nice lunch you would make.' Birds like to eat worms and insects (eyebrows raised, eyes wide open). But, of course, the little inchworm did not want the robin to eat him."
Transition Language	"Let's read the story and find out what that little inchworm did."

Swimmy by Leo Lionni

Reading the Title and the Names of Author and Illustrator	"Our new book today is *Swimmy*. Leo Lionni is also the author of this book. Remember, we just read another book that was written by Mr. Lionni—*Inch by Inch*. Mr. Lionni wrote the words for this story, and also made the illustrations, just like he did for the story *Inch by Inch*."
Introducing the Main Characters	"We see the main character of this story, a little fish, right here on the cover (point to). His name is Swimmy."
Stating the Story's Problem	"Swimmy is a brave and smart little fish, and it's a good thing, because, one day, in the big ocean where Swimmy and his brothers and sisters lived, something very bad happened. After this bad thing happened, Swimmy had to figure out what to do about it."
Transition Language	"You'll see what I mean when we read the story. Let's begin."

Some Smug Slug by Pamela Duncan Edwards

Reading the Title and the Names of Author and Illustrator	"Our new book today is *Some Smug Slug*. The author is Pamela Duncan Edwards, and the illustrator is Henry Cole."
Introducing the Main Characters	"Mr. Cole, the illustrator, made a very big picture of the main character in this story—a slug—right here (point to). A slug is an animal that is very similar to a snail, except that slugs do not have a shell. There are other animals in this story, but they are not shown on the book's cover. We'll meet them as we read the story."
Stating the Story's Problem	"In this story, the slug goes for a walk and climbs up a slope—a hill—and is in for a very big surprise—something happened that he did not expect."
Transition Language	"Let's read the story and find out what happened."

(6) engage children in thoughtful discussions after the story reading. Teachers can also read a story multiple times, over a week or more, to give children the time they need to absorb it (Martinez & Roser 1985; Morrow 1985; Yaden 1988).

Story introductions

Because the problem in a story is not always explicitly stated (Paris & Paris 2003), young children often miss it. If they do not understand the problem, children can't judge well the significance of story events or characters' actions and motivations (Benson 1997). Preschoolers might also have trouble identifying characters or settings, especially early in a story. A good introduction helps to prevent these problems (McGee & Schickedanz 2007).

When introducing a story for its first reading, the teacher can start by reading the title and the names of the author and illustrator, and then introduce the main characters. Next, a teacher might situate the story in its setting, and then state the story's problem. An introduction can end with a comment that beckons curiosity and leads right into the reading (e.g., "Let's find out what the slug does one day when out for a walk"). (See Table 3-1 "Introducing a Story for a First Reading" for examples.)

A teacher shows the book's front cover during the introduction and when reading the title and author and illustrator names, and underlines the print, using good speech-to-print matching. The cover is also in view as characters are introduced, if they are pictured. The back cover, end pages, and title page are also sometimes used to support the story problem, characters, or setting (McGee & Schickedanz 2007).

Introductions should not be used to query children about the book (i.e., to make predictions) or to conduct a picture walk. These approaches distract children from focusing on relevant information for constructing meaning. For a good discussion of the negative consequences of using these approaches to introductions, see "When Bad Things Happen to Good Books" (Serafini 2011).

Voice, gesture, gaze, and pacing

The volume, pitch, and pace of the reader's voice, along with gestures, gaze, and facial expression, all convey meaning beyond just reading the words. For example, when reading *Possum and the Peeper* by Ann Hunter, speaking the words that the bear utters very slowly, and closing eyes and yawning, help to convey the bear's sleepy state and the meaning of *blearily*. Rolling eyes quickly suggests that something is nonsensical. Squinting can convey characters' states of minds or the meaning of their actions. Likewise, the gesture of raising one's eyebrows can imply "Well, I'm not so sure about that" or can model surprise and curiosity (e.g., "Oh, no!" or "Why did that happen?").

Meaning is also conveyed by reading dialogue with appropriate intonation. For example, throughout the story *Farmer Duck* by Martin Waddell, the farmer asks his hard-working duck, "How goes the work?" The duck utters a consistent response, "Quack!" with waning enthusiasm and energy, indicating increasing fatigue. To remedy the duck's plight, his farm animal friends roust the farmer out of bed and chase him away. When the unknowing duck encounters his friends as they return, he says "Quack?" By reading, "Quack?" with the appropriate rise in intonation, the reader indicates that the duck is now *asking* about the situation. The reader's intonation conveys the different meanings of "Quack!" which is used throughout most of the story, and "Quack?" which is used near the end.

Referring to illustrations

Because text and illustrations work together in picture storybooks to convey meanings, teachers often refer to the illustrations. For example, when reading *Swimmy* by Leo Lionni, a teacher might point to the little black fish among the many red ones to help children understand the text: "A happy school of little fish lived in a corner of the sea somewhere. They were all red. Only one of them was as black as a mussel shell" (p. 2).

Similarly, pointing to the slug near the toad's mouth on page 28 of *Some Smug Slug* prompts children to notice information that is related to what has happened when they see the next page (p. 29), where the toad is licking its lips. On this last page of the story, the teacher can point to the toad's tongue, while commenting, "I don't see the slug anywhere, but I see the toad licking his lips. Oh, my. What do you think happened to the slug?" (This question prompts the story discussion.)

Pointing also helps to fill in actions mentioned in the text, but not illustrated. For example, the text in *Whistle for Willie* by Ezra Jack Keats says that Peter jumps up off his shadow and then lands back on top of it, although the illustration only shows Peter suspended above the shadow, not landing. A teacher's finger can move from Peter in mid-air, down to the shadow on the sidewalk, to demonstrate the action.

Research on visual literacy explores how children interpret illustrations of various kinds to derive meaning (Duke et al. 2010). Visual "literacy," however, is not purely "visual" because it requires background knowledge, attention to text information, and reasoning (Schickedanz & Collins 2012). Thus, adults must take account of not only what and how something is pictured in an illustration, but also how young children might interpret and use illustrations, when helping them understand a story.

Not surprisingly, preschoolers often misinterpret illustrations in storybooks, in part because they do not understand that these are creative art, not realistic representations of the world, and in part because they apply their own personal experiences quickly, without taking critical illustration details into account. As a consequence, preschoolers often misapply their own experience. Understanding the various sources of confusion that contribute to young children's story misunderstandings can guide a teacher's response. (See Box 3-3 "Story Misunderstanding and Adult Response.")

Comprehension asides

A teacher's comments during story reading make a character's emotional state clear, explain an illustration, or indicate what various characters do and do not

Box 3-3 Story Misunderstanding and Adult Response

Although we might think that children understand a story fairly well after hearing it the first time, their comments often indicate otherwise. When misunderstandings arise, adults have opportunities to clarify each specific meaning and also to help children learn to use relevant sources of information.

In the first example, which occurred during a second reading of *Max's Dragon Shirt* by Rosemary Wells, the teacher discovers that some of the children do not understand one of the characters.

Before reading the text, the teacher points to two rabbit characters.

Teacher: Who do we see here?

Children: Max and Ruby.

Hannah: Ruby is Max's mother.

Teacher: Is Ruby Max's mother or his sister?

Children (several): His mother.

Children (others): His sister.

Teacher: I think the book tells us some information about that.

Teacher: (reading p. 1) "Max loved his old blue pants more than anything. 'Those pants are disgusting, Max,' said his *sister*, Ruby."

In this book, Ruby behaves much like Max's mother (i.e., takes him shopping for new pants at a department store and dresses up as an adult might for the trip). The rabbit children's mother never appears in the book's illustrations, and she never enters directly into the text. Thus, a preschooler has no contrasting depiction of the mother. Furthermore, Ruby's identity is provided only a few times, and indirectly at that (e.g., at the end of one sentence the narrator adds, "said his sister, Ruby").

The teacher is appropriately direct in leading children to the critical information. Although the children had heard the text during the story's first reading, they apparently missed some details. This is not too surprising, given the children's likely attention to other picture details and to the salient part of the text here in which Ruby tells Max his pants are "disgusting."

In a second example, which arose during the fourth reading of *A Hat for Minerva Louise* by Janet Morgan Stoeke, the teacher's behavior and the illustration design both probably contributed to children's misunderstandings.

Teacher: "Her friends didn't like them one_____?" (pauses at end of sentence on p. 2)

Children: (several speak at the same time) Two! Three! Four!

Teacher: "bit." (reads the correct word on p. 2)

In response to the teacher's pausing, the children deployed a familiar counting routine, which indicated a lack of understanding of the story, and an inability to link the meaning of text on one page ("Minerva Louise liked snowy mornings") to the meaning on a following page. Furthermore, the multiple pictures are a more prominent feature of this illustration than the details that some hens are sleeping, have heads tucked under wings, or are watching Minerva Louise leave.

In this example, it would have been wise to read the entire phrase in the text, "They didn't like them one bit," and then follow with a brief explanation of "not one bit." A teacher might then have focused on the consequence of the hens' decision, by saying: "Those other hens didn't like snowy days *at all*, not even a little bit." Then, the teacher might have asked, "What did they do all day while Minerva Louise went out to explore the snow?" to help children focus on their whereabouts (i.e., in the henhouse, with heads tucked under their wings).

know. These comprehension asides not only call children's attention to critical information, but also model how to reason using the information. For example, in *Peter's Chair*, Peter's mother does not know that Willie knocked over the block building. Here's how a teacher might help children understand this situation:

> **Teacher:** Peter's mother is in another room (i.e., draws inference using information from the illustration—mother is not shown).
>
> **Teacher:** She thinks Peter knocked the blocks over. I think his feelings are hurt. Look at his face (i.e., makes emotions explicit, and indicates information that is used to draw the inference).
>
> **Teacher:** Peter probably *did* remember the new baby (i.e., infers a character's knowledge) and tried to be quiet (i.e., infers a character's intentions), but his mom didn't know that (i.e., infers a character's knowledge).
>
> **Teacher:** Let's read more and see what happens (i.e., transitions back to the reading).

Story understanding develops as much through apprenticeship as through asking children, "Who knows why _____?" because preschoolers usually don't know the answer. Even babies and toddlers learn by observing what happens in the world and listening to what people say and do (Beals 2001; Gola 2012; Horner 2004). Preschoolers also learn a lot by listening in to what others say (Mills et al. 2012), including a teacher's comments and explanations.

Responding to children's comments and questions during a story

Responding to comments and questions supports children's comprehension, although sometimes, in a whole-group setting, a teacher cannot respond immediately. If a question indicates that a child has missed something critical, a teacher should answer fully, but as briefly as possible, and then continue reading. Turning the child's question into a discussion during the story causes a long break in the story reading, and long breaks in the first reading make it hard for young children to hold onto their understanding so far.

If the answer to a child's question is provided later in the story, a teacher can say, "I think we'll find out about that pretty soon." This response acknowledges the child and also alerts all about important information to come. When an answer is revealed on the very next page, a teacher can use eyes and a head nod to indicate, "I hear you, and we'll find out *very* soon," then finish the current page and move immediately to read the next one. After reaching the relevant portion of the text, and reading it, the teacher can comment in a way that links the information read to the child's previous question.

Guiding discussion

Guiding a good discussion *after* a story reading deepens the basic understanding that children have built *during* a story. Saving actual discussion until after the story reading maintains the story's flow and also gives children considerable information to draw upon (e.g., text information, illustration information, and information from the teacher's asides). The read-aloud experience is also more enjoyable for children when they have deep understanding and information to use in a discussion.

Table 3-2 Avoiding Discussion Pitfalls

Avoid this Pitfall . . .	Because . . .	Instead . . .
1. Asking children to retell the story	This taps only memory for story events and characters, not analytical thinking or reasoning. Retelling does not constitute a discussion.	Use specific events and literal questions as a means to establish facts needed when analyzing and synthesizing story events to answer inferential questions.
2. Forgetting what you had thought you would talk about for a story's discussion	Opportunities to execute a carefully planned discussion are missed.	Jot the question down on a sticky note and attach it to the book's back cover, until you are comfortable with remembering the language for your discussion prompts.
3. Letting a child's tangential comment redirect the discussion (e.g., "I played in the snow one day...and I got snow in my boots")	These personal experiences comments often divert a teacher from pursuing a more beneficial discussion question, such as "What do you think Peter and his friend from across the hall might do in the snow when they go out to play on this day?"	Reframe the response to address the question you are pursuing (e.g., "Oh, that must have felt cold, but we are talking now about what we think Peter and his friend might do in the snow. Do you have an idea about that to share?").
4. Using low-level (i.e., literal) questioning for a lot of the discussion (e.g., "And then what happened?")	Literal questions do not require children to reason about cause and effect, consider characters' motives, or make informed predictions. Unless children learn to think in these ways, they will not comprehend stories very well.	Create a discussion that includes questions and statements that prompt examination, such as "What did Peter learn about the snow, from having played in it?" Use examples from the text to support children as they engage in thinking about the question.
5. Using discussion time as a "Question and Answer" session	It feels drill-like and performance-oriented, and doesn't prompt higher-level thinking. The goal of a discussion is not simply having children perform or demonstrate their knowledge, but also to foster their learning about how to reason and draw inferences.	Conduct the discussion as a conversation. Intersperse key questions with your comments, and add short embedded vignettes that are related to a point. Clarify what children say, and explain why and how a child's comment is or is not related to a point.

Avoid this Pitfall . . .	Because . . .	Instead . . .
6. Asking children to relate the story to a personal experience (e.g., "Tell me about a time when you received a birthday present you really liked")	These questions pull the discussion away from the content available in the story, which usually needs discussion if children are to reach a deeper understanding. These questions also reduce opportunities for the teacher to use and explain some key vocabulary words, as is possible during a more story-based discussion.	Solicit accounts of personal experience *sparingly* after several rounds of discussion have solidified basic comprehension of content, and when children are poised to make thoughtful connections between text and their own lives. Pose a question that requires thinking, not just "Have you ever....?" For example, "What do you think you might add to your snow person, if you made one?"
7. Relying on just generic open-ended questions, such as, "Can you tell me more about that?" or "Why do you think so?"	The aim of story discussion is not simply to get children to produce language. What they talk about matters. To meet goals for a discussion, a teacher often must scaffold children's thinking by suggesting relevant information to consider, or by asking fairly specific questions. If a child says just a little bit in response to a question, and has more to say, or should provide evidence, fairly specific follow-up questions are perfectly okay.	Craft detailed questions to provide the information children need to understand. When responding to children's questions, use specific language to indicate what you understand about their thinking or to ask for more clarification (e.g., "Are you asking about why the Peeper's throat is puffed out like a balloon?").
8. Telling children the correct answers	Children must learn to consider information in the text and illustrations, and to engage in reasoning to sort out confusions. If you simply provide correct information without revealing its sources or how you used it in your reasoning, children will not learn how to use information sources or to reason about information.	Refer children to sources of helpful information, such as illustrations, text, and what you think they already know (i.e., prior knowledge). Model thinking and offer explanations about why children's thinking seemed accurate to them, but was not, because some information was not considered.

Good discussions follow from questions that focus on something important to the story and to the children. A topic for discussion after a first reading might explore the story problem and its resolution.

"Personal affect" questions (e.g., "What did you like about the story?" or "What was your favorite part?") do not deepen children's story understandings very much. Teachers can spend the little time they have for discussion after reading a story on topics that prompt reasoning about the story events and characters. Personal questions (e.g., "What was your favorite part of *Some Smug Slug*?") can be saved for conversations at mealtimes or at the end of the day, when a teacher can spend more time talking with an individual child.

Teachers should also avoid letting a discussion get off track (see Table 3-2 "Avoiding Discussion Pitfalls"). By doing this, story time discussions can focus more centrally on helping children to think analytically about the story's events and the characters' thoughts and feelings.

Discussion questions are of two kinds. *Literal* questions seek factual information from the story's text and illustrations (e.g., "What piece of baby furniture did Peter at first think he would save?") and require only the mental process of recall. The answers to *inferential* questions, in contrast, are not provided explicitly in the text or the illustrations (e.g., "Why did Peter change his mind about his little chair?"). Thus, to answer inferential questions, children must integrate and reason about text and illustration information, and use background knowledge.

Preschoolers are quite good at acquiring literal facts from hearing a story read two or three times. In contrast, without help from adults, children do not obtain understandings that require reasoning (Collins 2004; van Kleeck, Vander Woude, & Hammett 2006). Thus, it is best to spend precious story time on inferential, not literal, questions.

Sometimes, though, children do need help in noticing and recalling specific information that different parts of a story provide (i.e., literal facts) before they can answer an inferential question. Thus, literal questions have a place in story time discussions, as long as the ultimate goal for asking them is to support children in drawing inferences. (See Box 3-4 "Strategic Use of Literal Questions: *Peter's Chair*" for an example.)

As the example in Box 3-4 illustrates, the teacher's explicit guidance helps children identify relevant information and to learn how to use it in reasoning to draw the relevant inferences. The teacher guides the discussion by clarifying and connecting children's responses, because this helps children to understand which information is important, where it fits into the inferential question, and where the group's current thinking about the question is going.

Supporting vocabulary

Children acquire the meanings of a few new words, just from listening to a story, especially multiple times. But children's learning of new word meanings can be increased when teachers identify key vocabulary in each story and use specific

Box 3-4   Strategic Use of Literal Questions: *Peter's Chair*

In this example, a teacher uses literal questions to help children focus on story information needed to answer an inferential question.

Teacher: (after reading the last page) Why did Peter decide that Susie should have his little blue chair? (showing p. 19) What did Peter find out about his little chair when he tried to sit in it?

Child 1: It didn't fit.

Child 2: It was too little.

Child 3: Peter was too big.

Teacher: Yes, Peter found out that he didn't fit in his little chair anymore. I guess he hadn't sat in his chair for quite a while, because he tried to sit in it as if he thought he could. Maybe he's not so interested in keeping the chair for himself, now he knows it's too little. (showing p. 20) What did Peter's mother say to Peter here?

Child 1: You should eat lunch and come back in the house.

Child 2: She said she made a special lunch for him.

Teacher: Yes, and she was talking very nicely to Peter, wasn't she? She called him "dear." People talk like that to someone they love. Maybe Peter noticed that his mother spoke nicely to him. It looks like he's thinking pretty deeply here (points to Peter's face). What do you think he might be thinking about?"

Child 1: He's sad, because he can't sit in it.

Child 2: He doesn't want it anymore, because, because, he doesn't.

Child 3: He's going to give it to his baby.

Teacher: Maybe Peter is sad but maybe not. Maybe he's thinking that he doesn't need his little chair anymore, after all, because he can't sit in it, and he's thinking about giving it to his baby sister.

Teacher: (showing p. 25) Do you remember what kind of chair Peter was sitting in here?

Child 1: A big one!

Teacher: Yes, he sat in a grown-up chair because he is big enough now. Look at his face (pointing) and how he is sitting all the way back in that chair. And look at Peter's father's arm (pointing to arm around Peter). I think Peter might have realized here that his father loves him still. And what else was he probably thinking about?

Child 1: His chair?

Child 2: He wanted to paint it, and he had to ask about that.

Teacher: Yes, he was probably thinking about his chair, and about asking if he could help paint it, because this is when he asked his father about that.

Child 1: He said, "Could we paint it?"

Teacher: Yes, he wanted to help. He said, "Let's paint it for Susie."

Teacher: (summarizing) So, Peter changed his mind about keeping his chair, because he realized he couldn't fit into it anymore, and probably because he felt a little better about what was happening to his baby chair after his parents were so kind to him and gave him some attention.

strategies to support these words during a story's reading (Biemiller & Boote 2006; Bus, van IJzendoorn, & Pellegrini 1995; Scarborough & Dobrich 1994).

Identify key words

The first step is to identify and select sophisticated words in each story, not words used in everyday conversations (Dickinson & Porche 2011; Weizman & Snow 2001). Teachers might use the tiered system suggested by Beck, McKeown, and Kucan (2002) to guide this selection. **Tier 1** includes words that children hear almost every day (e.g., car, walking, red, dog). **Tier 2** words (e.g., industrious, vehicle, reflection), on the other hand, are less common than everyday words and also more important for comprehending texts, both in preschool and later on. Tier 2 words are also used across many topics or fields of study (e.g., science, math, social studies), which makes knowing them especially useful. Beck, McKeown, and Kucan suggest that teachers select mostly Tier 2 words for explicit support during story reading. (See Nagy & Hiebert 2011 for a more detailed discussion of word selection.)

Of course, when a book has an abundance of Tier 2 words, teachers select those that, if not understood, may decrease children's comprehension of the story the most. For example, in *Possum and the Peeper*, which is about hibernating animals who were awakened at spring, the words *clamor, crest, burrows, glorious, overheard, speck, proclaimed, deny, swamp, reeds, pond, din, muskrat,* and *grumbling* are used. From among these, a teacher might select *din, clamor, reeds, overheard, proclaimed, deny,* and *grumbling* to support explicitly.

Finally, a teacher decides whether to include sophisticated words in comprehension asides, when these are not used in the story's text. For example, in *Whistle for Willie*, Peter spun around so fast that lights in a traffic signal seemed to move out of their sockets. Even though the text does not use "dizzy" to label Peter's mental state, a teacher can use this word in a comment that explains what is going on. Similarly, if reading *Henny Penny* by Paul Galdone, a teacher can use *sly, sneaky,* and *gullible* in comprehension asides, even though they are not in the text. For example, the teacher might say, "I'm so surprised that none of these birds is asking Henny Penny why she thinks the sky is falling. I'm thinking these birds are a bit *gullible*— just believe everything they are told. I hope she knows what she's talking about."

Using illustrations, explanations, gesture, and voice

Pointing to illustrations in storybooks helps children learn key word meanings (Collins 2010; Elley 1989), especially nouns (e.g., barnyard, forest, tailor's shop, thunderstorm, lightning bolt). In a process called **fast mapping** (Carey 1978), young children link the meaning of a new word to its referent (i.e., the actual object a word names), after only one or two exposures, if the named item is in the immediate physical environment or is pointed to in a book's illustration.

Even though children still have much to learn about a word (Justice, Meier, & Walpole 2005), fast mapping gives children a quick *start* in learning many words. A teacher follows up with explicit support in subsequent book readings and also in activities outside the book (Wasik & Bond 2001). (See Chapter 4.)

Although a teacher usually points to the illustration almost simultaneously with reading the word in the text, this need not be done when a word is in the middle of a long sentence or if she feels that concentrating on pointing will disrupt her fluid reading. If a teacher feels distracted by pointing as she reads key words in the text, she can finish reading the sentence, and then say, "Oh, here's the *hedge* at the edge of the lawn, right here," while pointing to the hedge in the illustration. Although this approach stops the reading briefly, this is better than reading a sentence very awkwardly, or losing phrasing or good intonation, because attention is on trying to point at just the right moment. If a teacher has planned a comprehension aside to support meaning in this part of the book, she can point then to the relevant illustration and use the key term in her comments.

Gestures that model meaning are helpful, especially for verbs. For example, a teacher can convey the meaning of *inhale* by breathing in deliberately to demonstrate. Limiting gestures to what you can show while seated avoids distracting children from the story reading. For example, a teacher would not get up to demonstrate "dashing," but could use a hand gesture to indicate very fast movement.

Onomatopeoia—the use of sound/pronunciation to convey a word's meaning—is a perfect strategy for some words, such as *peep,* which can be read in a high-pitched, staccato tone. Other words (e.g., *murmur, snarl, mumble, whisper, whine,* and *sputter*) also lend themselves to onomatopoeic renderings.

Synonyms (e.g., "*Chilly* means cool") or brief definitions (e.g., "*Clamor* means a loud noise") also support vocabulary development. Synonyms can be tucked into the reading (e.g., on page 14 of *Rabbits and Raindrops* by Jim Arnosky, "*Baby rabbits can become soaked—very wet—and catch cold*"), but tucking in longer explanations (e.g., "—soaked means that their fur would get very, very wet—") can make it difficult for a young child to grasp the entire sentence, especially if learning English as a second language. It would be better to just read the sentence in the text, with a very brief explanation of *soaked* (e.g., "—very wet—") or wait until after reading the sentence to add, "Soaked means that the baby rabbits' fur would become very, very wet," if a longer explanation is preferred.

Of course, when a word is hard to explain, a teacher should not try. For example, a verbal explanation of *edge* in *Rabbits and Raindrops* would become far too wordy and complicated. It is probably best to support this word simply by pointing to the lawn's edge in the illustration.

In a first reading, skilled teachers use verbal support (i.e., synonyms or brief explanations) that is connected to the text (e.g., "Soaked means that the baby rabbits' fur would become very, very wet"), not decontextualized meanings (e.g., "Soaked means something is very, very wet"). We also agree with literacy experts who suggest that preschool teachers should not ask children what *soaked* means (Beck, McKeown, & Kucan 2002; Elley 1989), even though others advise this practice (e.g., Christ & Wang 2012).

Teachers usually plan one or two strategies to use for a first exposure and then plan other strategies when the word comes up a second time in the first reading, or in the discussion or a subsequent reading. (See Box 3-5 for "Questions about Supporting Key Word Comprehension in Storybooks.")

Box 3-5 **Questions about Supporting Key Word Comprehension in Storybooks**

1. Should I simplify words or substitute an easier word for a sophisticated word?

No. Use the sophisticated word and multiple exposures, both within the book context and in other settings. Simpler words—synonyms for the sophisticated word—can be used to explain the sophisticated word in a story's first reading. Brief explanations (i.e., child-friendly definitions) can be used to give more information about each sophisticated word in later readings.

Sometimes, if a book has very long sentences and many new words, its text can be simplified for a first reading without harming the plot, by deleting whole sentences or some clauses, phrases, or words. The same strategies for word support apply to new words that remain. In a second reading, the teacher puts some text back. The original text can be read by the third or fourth reading. This method eases children into a more complex and word-rich text, over several readings.

2. How should I adapt my reading and word support for English language learners?

Provide the same quality and frequency of exposure to words and discussions as for other children. Standards and expectations for learning are the same; supports for learning can and should vary.

- Multiple exposures to words are especially important for English language learners (ELLs). Use key words from the book in teacher asides too, and in the discussion.

- Explain some Tier 1 vocabulary; don't confine key word selection to just Tier 2 words.

- Read in small groups, in addition to the large one. This offers a comfortable setting for producing the second language.

- Recognize that engagement and rapt attention are marked by nonverbal behavior (e.g., eye gaze, facial expression). Although a silent period is common during the first few months of exposure to a new language (Tabors 2008), receptive language is being cultivated even if young ELLs do not produce the second language (English).

- As you would for all children, pronounce words clearly.

- In story discussions, simplify the language used, but not the question. For example, change, "Why did Henry frown?" to "Henry frowned. Why?" Repeating the question a time or two is important for all children, especially ELLs.

- Accept word production warmly, interpret what is said, and repeat the word with an accurate pronunciation in a genuine response (e.g., "Yes, that is a *porcupine*. See all those quills?").

- During the discussion, expand and rephrase children's responses. If the child says, "Henry not like it. He chocolate," the teacher can say, "Yes, Henry did not want vanilla frosting because he liked chocolate frosting better."

- If books can be translated or are available in the home language or if parents read well in English, send books home for reading and discussing (Roberts 2008). Remember that older children can read to their preschool sibling, and can also benefit from the experience.

- Guard against regarding storybook reading as primarily a language production opportunity, because this can undermine a focus on comprehension. Red flags for this include: (1) a steady diet of predictable texts, which limits exposure to varied language structures and vocabulary, and typically encourages imitation without much understanding; and (2) the use of low-level prompts (e.g., "What's this?") to elicit labeling only, without supporting inferential thinking.

3. Should I present (teach) key words before I start reading the book?

Preteaching takes words out of context and results in a very didactic instructional experience. A good story introduction is more important. Picture walks—going through the book, page by page, before its first reading, showing illustrations and commenting about each one, but not reading any of the text—also take illustrations out of their print-related context and can preempt attention to the necessary order in which important details unfold. Picture walks also can ruin suspense and intrigue, which decreases children's attention. Children can also become impatient for the story while the talk, talk, talk, and quiz, quiz, quiz, drag on. When teachers are strategic, with word support and comprehension asides during reading, story time remains a delightful experience.

4. Should I ask children to provide word meanings?

No. Asking preschoolers for the meanings of words requires a full stop and a long break. It is not terribly effective because preschoolers cannot easily use a teacher-provided correct explanation after hearing two or more incorrect meanings from peers. In cognitive science parlance, preschoolers do not delete or revise their mental files very well to take account of new information. In addition, children are confused when kind and warm teachers acknowledge all meanings offered (e.g., "Okay, thanks for sharing that good idea. Who has another?"), but then offer one that contradicts all of them.

With age, mental flexibility increases, and children develop organized frameworks of knowledge (e.g., they realize that roots, stems, leaves, buds, and flowers are related because all are parts of a plant). With these new cognitive capacities, children begin to filter incoming information (Willingham 2009) and judge the word meanings they hear. But preschoolers are just beginning to acquire organized frameworks of knowledge.

A final difficulty is that asking children for word meanings can dominate the focus of story reading. Although vocabulary provides strong support for comprehension, learning to integrate background knowledge and storybook information and to draw inferences are also important. Furthermore, learning to use these supports for comprehension *must* take place during book-reading, while vocabulary can and should be supported in many other contexts (Nagy & Townsend 2012; Schickedanz & Collins 2012; Schickedanz & McGee 2010).

Other opportunities to expose children to a word

Repeated exposure to the same word aids learning (Elley 1989; Karweit & Wasik 1996; Nagy & Townsend 2012; Sénéchal 1997). Beyond the exposure to a word in the text, in a book's first reading, teachers can use it in comprehension asides (e.g., "The rabbits' fur looks darker here because it is *soaked*") and also during the story discussion (e.g., "Some animals might not mind getting *soaked* in a rainstorm. Let's take a look"). A thoughtful teacher also sometimes reuses one key word when explaining other key words that are encountered later in the story. For example, when reading *Rabbits and Raindrops*, a teacher used the word *lawn*, explained earlier in the text, when supporting the meaning of *hedge* later.

Box 3-6 ## Supporting Key Vocabulary from Stories during Other Parts of the School Day

During center time, vocabulary is supported best when adults talk with children about ongoing activities. Some specific vocabulary materials can also be used to support children in reviewing vocabulary from storybooks or other teacher-guided activities. The meanings of key vocabulary words from storybooks can also be deepened if children are engaged in playing some word games during circle time.

Materials for supporting vocabulary during center time

A teacher can make lotto cards using pictures of key vocabulary from stories. When playing, children have opportunities to use the names of items pictured (Figure 3-1). A teacher can also include items that are not from storybooks, along with those that are.

If teachers prepare pictures for lotto games for each unit of study, they will soon have a fairly large collection to use in a variety of ways. For example, sets of pictures can be organized around categories, such as animals, plants, birds, reptiles, vehicles, furniture, clothing, or cooking utensils. Make a background board with two columns, and label each column with a category name (e.g., Vehicles/ Furniture, Birds/Reptiles). Children

Figure 3-1. Labeled picture lotto board and tiles.

Teachers can also reuse words, both from the story's text and comprehension asides, in the story's discussion. For example, in discussing *Henny Penny*, a teacher can probably find ways to re-use *sly* or *gullible* (e.g., "I know we were worrying about how *gullible* those birds were, as we read the story. And, yes, that *sly* fox knew how to get those birds into trouble, for sure").

Some exposure to key words from storybooks can and should occur outside the book, such as during center time activities and in small groups. For example, in *The Little Red Hen (Makes Pizza)* by Philemon Sturges, Hen uses numerous kitchen utensils and food items. To support children in learning the meanings of *colander* and *whisk*, teachers can offer these items for children to use in cooking projects.

play with six or seven pictures that are examples of items belonging to each category identified by the column headings, by placing each picture into the column where it belongs.

If the background boards are laminated without designated category names, create category labels (also laminated) that can be removed and replaced with new ones, using masking tape or pieces of Velcro.

A category focus helps children think more about individual words than does simple matching of pictures to identical twins (i.e., as in lotto). In addition, children understand more about new items they encounter if they have category labels and know basic features required for membership (Gelman & Coley 1990). For example, if children have never seen a praying mantis, and one appears in a storybook, they would know something about it if the teacher said, "It's a kind of insect." If children do not know category labels, a teacher's use of them won't advance a child's learning. Some examples of developing category level knowledge about insects are provided in Chapter 4.

Knowing some details about human-made items, such as their functions, also helps children learn and retain new words (Booth 2009; Nelson, O'Neil, & Asher 2008).

A word clue game for circle time

In this game, which uses key vocabulary from storybooks, a teacher starts by telling children they are going to hear clues about some words from specific storybooks. On any one occasion of playing, the teacher selects words to support from just one or two storybooks, and shows the books' covers, at the start.

The teacher uses a category clue first, along with a few specific details (e.g., "This is a *toy* that is small and round, and made of glass. Children play games with these small round toys"). If children do not guess the item's name (marbles) from the first two clues, the teacher provides a story-related clue (e.g., "Noisy Nora's sister had some of these little, round, glass toys, and Nora spilled them onto the floor on purpose"). Because story-related clues usually lead children right to the item's name, using these first removes the opportunity to use a category clue. This is why we recommend using the category clue first.

To provide a good first clue for *bat* (a key word in the story *Stellaluna* by Janell Cannon) a teacher might say, "This is the name of an animal that is a mammal. But this mammal flies, and other mammals do not." This clue uses two category names—animal and mammal.

Small-group activities with these items help children comprehend and produce items' names, especially when teachers provide explicit support for the words in this context. Teachers can support the words more, if the items are available for children's use at the water table or for dramatic play in the house area. Teachers can also play a word meaning clue game during circle time, using key words from stories. (See Box 3-6 "Supporting Key Vocabulary from Stories during Other Parts of the School Day.")

Multiple readings: Why once is not enough

From a first reading, children gain a basic understanding of a story and a beginning understanding of important vocabulary (McGee & Schickedanz 2007). Yet, hearing a story only once is not enough to support learning fully or to foster true love of a story. Additionally, because children bring more knowledge to second and third readings than to a first, each reading provides a unique opportunity for them to integrate knowledge, and for a teacher to model inferential thinking and engage children in analytical talk (Dickinson & Smith 1994).

For example, in one classroom, the book *Dreams* was part of a shadows and reflections unit, and the children had opportunities to experiment with shadow creation, including changes in size, after the book's first reading. During the book's second reading, one child commented, "Oh, it's not a monster! It's a shadow of that mouse, and it got bigger and bigger and bigger!" This comment indicated an increase in the child's understanding of the paper mouse shadow compared to the first reading.

Introducing a second or third reading

For a second reading, which typically occurs within a few days of the first, the story's problem is reviewed briefly and a critical event can be mentioned. For example, for the story *Swimmy*, a teacher might say: "We read this book on Tuesday, and you probably remember that it's about a little fish named Swimmy and what Swimmy does after something bad happens. We're going to read the story again today and talk about it some more."

It is wise to avoid asking a lot of questions before beginning a second reading, because children often end up retelling most of the story, which is then followed by the teacher's reading and a discussion. Doing all of this can make story time last for 35 to 45 minutes, which is far too long for children in this age group. One of the benefits of reading a story multiple times across several days is that any one story time need not last for more than 15 or 20 minutes.

The introduction to a story's third reading acknowledges again children's familiarity (e.g., "We've read this story two times already, and I know you know the title. Read it with me . . . "). Then, the teacher can describe the children's role in the day's reading (e.g., "Today, you are going to help tell the story . . . "). The teacher can then turn to the first page and prompt children to begin reconstructing the story (e.g., "Here, when the story starts, where is Swimmy, and what is he doing?").

Strategies for supporting meaning and vocabulary in second and third readings. Although the same story meanings and key vocabulary are supported in all readings, teachers can add more verbal explanations in second and third readings to deepen children's initial understandings (Justice, Meier, & Walpole 2005). Stopping now during the reading to insert synonyms or brief explanations is less likely to distract children from the story because children's knowledge from the first reading anchors their engagement.

The teacher can ask a *few* questions in a second reading to prompt children to connect events and causes or to infer characters' motivations. The teacher also continues to use comprehension asides, but many will differ from those used in a first reading because children know more now and can benefit from somewhat different asides.

Children's familiarity with a story often prompts both more questions and comments during its second and third readings, and also brings new cognitive challenges. For example, children learn things from a first reading that story characters will never know until the end of the story (i.e., characters, unlike children, never get wiser across multiple readings). But children sometimes insist that characters do something, thinking that they have learned what the children learned from a first reading (e.g., the peddler in *Caps for Sale* by Esphyr Slobodkina should just throw down his hat and not go through all the other actions). A teacher might say, "Well, *we* know that because we heard all of the story, but the characters stay just the same in each part of the story, every time we read it."

In a third reading, a few days or a week after the second, children are usually familiar enough with the story to retell its events. Teachers still provide asides that clarify or model reasoning after children retell parts (e.g., "You are right. The slug ignored the squirrel's warnings, too. I think the slug must have thought the bumps on the toad's back were pebbles on a road. He had no idea that he was walking up the bumpy back of a predator!").

In addition to teacher asides that focus on characters' thinking and causal explanations, prompts now can include a few "why" questions ("What was happening here?"). These foster analytic talk, which can be supported by teacher scaffolding of the children's thinking, and by pointing to illustrations that contain relevant details (McGee & Schickedanz 2007).

For example, while showing page 9 of *Max's Dragon Shirt* by Rosemary Wells, a teacher might point to the hem of the yellow dress in the illustration on page 9 (Figure 3-2a) and ask: "Why did Max think this person here was his sister?" Children would likely say, "Because he knew that Ruby was wearing a yellow dress." The

Figure 3-2a
He went to look for her. He saw her yellow dress and followed it out of Girls' Better Dresses . . .

Figure 3-2b   After a while Max woke up.
Ruby was gone.

teacher might then turn to the dressing room scene on page 8 (Figure 3-2b) and say, "Right. Max didn't notice that Ruby's yellow dress was still on a hook in the dressing room, and he was asleep when she left wearing one store dress to go find another to try on."

Discussion in multiple readings. A teacher keeps an open mind and pays attention to children's understanding in readings. Thus, questions for the second reading, and especially for the third, emerge from both teacher planning and children's spontaneous questions and comments. With study of a book, and careful attention to children's comments and questions, teachers can generate a number of questions that are suitable for a story's discussion after each of its readings.

After a second reading of *Peter's Chair*, a discussion might focus on personal things versus things that belong to the family: "Do you think Peter's parents would give some of his old toys to his baby sister, without asking him first, the way they did with his furniture?" Exploring this topic helps children to distinguish between truly personal items from those that are "in the family and shared by all."

After a third or fourth reading of a story, a teacher might consider using an informational book as the basis for the story discussion. (See examples in Chapter 4.)

Use of digital texts

In today's world, teachers and parents have access to stories in digital form, not just traditional print stories. Digital texts have a place in the preschooler's life, as long as the materials are carefully selected and used appropriately. A discussion of digital texts and best practices for their use is provided in Box 3-7 "Sharing Digital Texts."

Concluding thoughts about story reading

We are past the era of "just read" to children. As this chapter explains, teachers must consider many things, including features of both individual books (e.g., story complexity, language richness, and knowledge) and a year's collection (e.g., connections to units, diversity in universal themes), and interactions that can support meaning and language development.

It takes considerable time to prepare story introductions, select strategies for explaining vocabulary, craft comprehension asides, and identify discussion

Box 3-7 Sharing Digital Texts

Jessica L. Hoffman

Digital texts are electronic versions of literature, available in a wide variety of forms, also known as ebooks, online storybooks, and CD-ROM books. Digital texts share key features with traditional print-based picture books, such as the integration of text and image to convey meaning. They are also distinct, because they have live animation and interactive components, and require the user to operate technology. Digital texts can be shared with preschoolers using the strategies outlined throughout this chapter.

Although digital texts function in different ways from printed texts, and therefore offer new and important skills and literacies, caregivers must carefully consider when and how to share digital texts. As was noted in Chapter 2, after age 2, children's total exposure to all forms of digital media (games, television, computers) should be limited to relatively brief periods that **total no more than about an hour per day** (AAP 2011).

When young children engage with digital media, high levels of interaction with an adult should always be a part of the experience (AAP 2001; NAEYC & Fred Rogers Center for Early Learning and Children's Media 2012). The "new co-viewing" (i.e., adults and children using digital media together) is just as important to learning from digital media, as it is to television viewing (Penuel et al. 2009; Stevens & Penuel 2010; Takeuchi & Stevens 2011).

Choosing digital texts

Digital texts are available in two forms, digitally scanned images of printed books and digitally originated literature (i.e., books constructed specifically for the digital form and involving embedded multimedia features) (Unsworth 2006). The advantage of digitally scanned books is that countless titles are readily available online and in downloadable applications, or **apps**, for portable electronic devices, available to anyone, anywhere, anytime, often in multiple languages. These digital texts can be accessed (free and for purchase) from a variety of retailers, from apps for many electronic devices, at local public libraries, or through online sources of free children's books such as The Rosetta Project (www.childrensbooksonline.org and the International Children's Digital Library (http://en.childrenslibrary.org).

Digitally originated literature is more difficult to evaluate and choose. Labbo and Kuhn (2000) suggest looking for *considerate* digital texts—those that "include multimedia effects that are congruent with and integral to the story" (p. 187). Considerate texts include animations that portray story actions, as well as audio components (e.g., characters' speech) that complement the written text. *Inconsiderate* digital texts, on the other hand, "include multimedia effects that are incongruent with or incidental to the story" (p. 187). Informative reviews written by an independent reviewer help adults find high-quality digital children's literature (e.g., Digital Storytime (http://digital-storytime.com). Recommended sources for accessing digital texts with multimedia elements include the sources listed in the previous paragraph and TumbleBooks (www.tumblebooks.com/library/), an online collection of animated, narrated picture books, including English and Spanish titles. TumbleBooks allows users to click to turn pages and turn the narration on or off. Many public libraries subscribe to TumbleBooks and provide online access for cardholders.

(Continued on p. 72)

Engaging preschoolers with digital texts

Even though many digital texts are designed for children to use independently, they can only promote language and cognitive development to the same extent as reading traditional books if adults scaffold digital texts using the same practices: referencing illustrations and animation to label images with words, explaining concepts and events presented in the text and connecting the text to the child's background to make language more comprehensible, and asking questions to prompt the child's participation and language use. Adults also scaffold children's use of the media (scrolling, swiping, clicking), and model and prompt children's use of a digital text's interactive features (Labbo 2009; Smith 2001).

Some studies on the effects of using digital texts found them more effective than print books in promoting children's understanding of stories, especially their implicit features (e.g. character motivations) (Verhallen, Bus, & De Jong 2006), while other studies found that features of some digital texts distract from story content and make them less effective (De Jong & Bus 2002). Still other studies found that preschoolers benefited equally from digital and print texts (De Jong & Bus 2004). A revealing finding from research is that *different* learning comes from different forms of book reading (Smith 2001), all of which can contribute to children's learning of multiple literacies.

Research has also emphasized that distracting features, such as irrelevant music, animation (De Jong & Bus 2002; Labbo & Kuhn 2000), and ongoing narration, discourage adults from reading and discussing the text (Kim & Anderson 2008). If adults are to use interactive reading strategies, digital texts must (1) allow control over the pacing of the book sharing, rather than simply "play" continuously; and (2) provide narration turn off options that allow adults to read the text aloud (Labbo 2009). When the adult can control both the pace and reading of a digital text, patterns of adult and child talk are very similar to those found with print-based texts (Fisch et al. 2002), through which the adult and child construct meanings collaboratively (Labbo 2009).

Although digital texts are useful, not all children have access to this technology (Common Sense Media 2011).

topics and prompts for each storybook's multiple readings. But the time is worth the benefits that careful planning brings to young children.

We offer one caution about story reading in today's world. Now that policy makers, politicians, and educators understand the importance of the early years, and have established high expectations for early learning, there is a danger that meeting these expectations will change preschool practices in ways that reduce children's delight in learning. For children, story reading must be as interesting and full of delight as ever, even as teachers make every effort to maximize the learning that children take from it.

4 Sharing Informational Books with Preschoolers

Mr. Jacoby was sharing the story *Raccoon on His Own* by Jim Arnosky with his preschoolers (Figure 4-1). After reading, "Mother found a crunchy crawfish" (p. 5), he said, "Here's the crawfish (pointing to illustration). The mother raccoon is going to eat it for breakfast."

"Where is it?" asked a child. Mr. Jacoby pointed to the crawfish again and explained that its head was inside the mother raccoon's mouth. He told the children he would bring some books with pictures of crawfish to school the next day so they could see one better, and talk about them.

Figure 4-1

Mother found a crunchy crawfish.
Two of the young raccoons dug
for crawfish near the boat.
The third young raccoon
was not hungry.
He wanted
to climb.

Situations such as this one occur frequently during story reading, because many items appearing in stories are not explained. When children become curious or puzzled about something in a storybook, teachers can do as Mr. Jacoby did— read informational books to help answer their questions. Informational magazines, such as *Ranger Rick* and *Big Backyard*, published by the National Wildlife Association, are also sometimes useful resources.

In this chapter, we describe some features of informational books and discuss why it is important for preschoolers to experience them. We also discuss contexts in which informational books might be used and strategies teachers can use when reading them. Additionally, some non-book forms of information and their uses in preschool classrooms are discussed briefly.

Informational book features and text formats

Several features distinguish informational books, a type of nonfiction, from other kinds of books, such as narratives (Duke 2000). As their name implies, informational books provide facts or explain processes (e.g., the number of legs that insects have, how whales breathe). Many informational books have a table of contents, an index, and a glossary, and are divided into sections marked by headings. By using these features one can find specific information and use a book selectively. In contrast, the parts of a story work together and must be read as a whole. Informational books also contain more technical vocabulary than stories, and have realistic photographs, diagrams, and charts, not creative art. The labels and captions that accompany many illustrations in informational books provide explicit information that support and supplement the text.

Informational books are written in a variety of styles (i.e., text structures): (1) informational; (2) informational-narrative; and (3) informational-poetic/verse (Duke 2000). An example of a book with an informational text structure is *From Wheat to Bread* by Stacy Taus-Bolstad. The book's text is straightforward ("Wheat seeds are called kernels. Trucks take the kernels to a factory" [p. 6]). *Chameleon, Chameleon* by Joy Cowley features informational-narrative text ("The gecko will not hurt the chameleon. The chameleon moves on" [p. 14]), while *Birds* by Kevin Henkes offers facts about birds in a poetic form ("Sometimes they are so black that you can't see their eyes or their feathers, just their shapes" [pp. 6–7]).

Why read informational books?

Teachers of young children typically devote more time to stories than to informational books, and also include more storybooks in classroom book areas (Duke 2000). These practices are based on beliefs, such as thinking that informational books are more difficult and less appealing for young children than stories. Interestingly, in a small study, researchers found that teachers in the United States thought narratives were easier than informational books for preschoolers, and also far more appealing, while Korean teachers held exactly the opposite view. Not surprisingly, the books these preschool teachers read aloud and included in their classroom libraries strongly reflected their attitudes (Lee et al. 2011).

Preschool and kindergarten teachers will probably provide more balance between storybooks and informational books in the years ahead because the Common Core State Standards require more informational book use in the primary grades (National Governors Association Center for Best Practices, Council of Chief State School Officers 2010). This change is important because informational books benefit young children's learning in so many ways.

Informational books are interesting

The content of informational books is interesting to almost all preschoolers, and some young children actually like informational texts far better than stories (Caswell & Duke 1998; Correia 2011; Duke 2004). Having access to books that are preferred can affect a child's interest in books and in reading.

This affective response is related to a child's reading success (Guthrie, Schafer, & Huang 2001), which makes sense because children who are interested in books read more and develop greater reading skill. They also acquire more content knowledge and associated vocabulary. In fact, the majority of new vocabulary acquired during the school years (i.e., third grade and beyond) comes from the books that children read (Nagy, Anderson, & Herman 1987).

In the U.S., about 40 percent of school children read only what they must for school, and not at all just for enjoyment (Gambrell 2011). When preschool teachers read informational books and include them in the classroom book area, all children have a better chance to develop interest in books.

Informational books support vocabulary development

Because informational books contain many sophisticated technical words and explain them explicitly, reading this kind of book helps children learn higher-level vocabulary. In contrast, stories contain fewer technical terms and provide very little explicit information about their meanings. As a consequence, children must infer the meanings of unfamiliar words when listening to stories, or they learn them from information teachers or family members provide, in ways we describe in Chapter 3.

A few examples from *Crayfish* by Lola M. Schaefer illustrate the explicitness of explanations typically found in informational texts. This book's first page says, "Crayfish are sea animals without bones. They are invertebrates" (p. 4). In this case, *invertebrates* is explained in the first sentence (i.e., "without bones").

Preschool teachers can also provide additional support for word meanings, because young children do not always link information from one sentence to information provided in another. A teacher's comments can also foster broader and deeper word learning. For example, children learn more about a technical term's meaning and how it applies to other instances. Children also learn related words, and increase their understanding of a story event that is related to the content of the informational book shared. Unlike the connected ideas and flow found in storybooks, many informational books are written with one fact or explanation per page, which makes it easy to stop and comment after reading each one.

Mr. Jacoby commented after reading the first page of *Crayfish*, in the discussion that followed his second reading of *Raccoon on His Own*. Here's what he said:

> Many other animals have bones inside their body, which make up their skeleton. People have skeletons (holds up a poster of a human skeleton, and skeletons of a bird and a snake), and so do birds, snakes, and many other animals. Feel your wrist, like this (puts fingers of right hand on left wrist). Animals with bones inside their bodies are called *vertebrates*. That's a great word—say it with me. Animals

who do not have bones inside their bodies are called *invertebrates*. The crayfish in the story was fairly easy for the mother raccoon to chew up and eat because it didn't have any hard bones inside. Then a child said, "A raccoon couldn't eat me, because I have lots of hard bones." Mr. Jacoby agreed.

The illustrations in informational books also provide strong support for the meanings of technical vocabulary. For example, the photograph accompanying the text, "Crayfish have *jointed legs*" (p. 5), shows very clearly a crayfish's jointed legs. Similarly, on page 21, which says, "Little crayfish come out of the eggs. They are called *instars*," a photograph shows the instars.

After reading the text on these pages, Mr. Jacoby pointed to the relevant part of each photograph and also commented. For example, on page 5, he said, "This is the joint of one of the crayfish's legs, and this line goes up from the joint to a label that says, 'jointed leg.' The knees in our legs are joints. Joints allow us to bend our legs and our arms, and even our fingers." (Children bent their fingers and their arms and legs.)

"Jointed legs" and all other key vocabulary in *Crayfish* are in bold face print. Bold facing of key vocabulary, which is common in informational books, helps teachers know which words to support, and it also makes the words easy for children to find, if interested, when they look at the books (see examples in Figure 4-2).

As discussed in Chapter 1, background knowledge supports deep understanding of vocabulary, which is critical for good reading comprehension (Ouellette 2006). Because deep understanding of words depends on having related content knowledge (Nagy & Townsend 2012), children learn content and associated vocabulary best when they have access to both concrete experiences and informational books (Leung 2008).

Figure 4-2. Selected book pages from *Daddy Longlegs* and *Caterpillar*.

Informational books help children acquire content knowledge

Informational books help children learn about things that are impossible or impracticable to experience first-hand. Even when first-hand access to information is possible, informational books allow children to see things they might not otherwise notice.

Suppose that children found a bee or fly outside. Teachers might identify the bee or fly by name, tell a little bit about it, and prompt children to observe some of the insect's physical features and behavior. The problem, though, is that children cannot safely approach some insects, and others fly away before children can observe them thoroughly. Informational books benefit learning, in part, because they make things "sit still" for examination in ways they often do not in the natural world.

For example, if children can have access to books about insects, and adults who read the books with them, the legs of various insects can be counted to learn that all have six (see maps for bees and flies in Figure 4-3). Children can also learn that insects are born as larvae, that larvae feed before turning into pupae, and that an adult insect emerges from a pupa after a few days or weeks. Children might also learn from informational books that, unlike insects, spiders have eight legs and babies that look like spiders and simply grow bigger as they mature.

Informational texts expose children to dense and abstract language

Because informational books are packed densely with content words, their syntax differs from the syntax in stories (Nagy & Townsend 2012). Informational books also contain verb forms that are timeless (e.g., "Crayfish are . . ." "Crayfish live . . ." "Rocks do not melt . . ."), rather than mostly past tense verbs that one finds in most stories.

Figure 4-3. Bug Book "maps" from *Bee* and *Fly*.

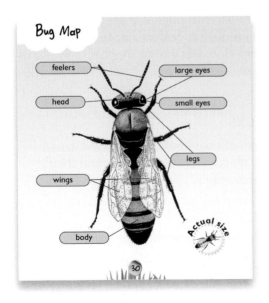

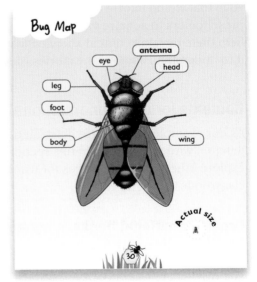

Thus, in addition to giving children access to vocabulary and content information, hearing informational books read aloud acquaints children with language of a specific kind. This familiarity helps all children comprehend content area books they read later in school (i.e., science and social science textbooks), and it seems especially helpful to children who are learning English as a second language (Council of Chief State School Officers 2012; Kelley et al. 2010).

Informational books help children understand narratives

Although children do not need to understand *all* of the facts in every story to enjoy and comprehend most of it, the more a child understands, the better. For example, a young child can enjoy the story *Raccoon on His Own* without knowing much about crawfish because crawfish are not central to the story's problem or plot. Many stories are like this, but others are not.

A good example of such a story is *Farfallina & Marcel* by Holly Keller. Children will realize why Farfallina (a caterpillar, early in the story) does not return to her friend, Marcel, for such a long time only if they understand that the life cycle of a butterfly or moth includes a metamorphosis from caterpillar to the adult butterfly. Similarly, children will only realize that the butterfly appearing later in the story is still Farfallina, not a different creature altogether from the caterpillar they met earlier, if they have knowledge of a butterfly's life cycle.

When content knowledge is central to a story, it is a good idea to provide experiences from which young children can acquire the relevant information and concepts before they hear the story the first time, or at least within the time period of the book's multiple readings (e.g., three readings across a period of about a week). With either of these approaches to scheduling relevant content experiences, children will have opportunities to integrate the content knowledge with information provided in the story's text, and to draw inferences about story events and characters' behavior based on these multiple sources of information.

It takes time, of course, for children to acquire the full range of content knowledge that would inform all of the stories they hear. Although it is not possible for preschoolers to acquire vast stores of information, it is realistic for teachers to help them develop content knowledge in some domains and to support their use of it to understand some of the stories they hear.

Contexts for using informational books

As our examples so far have illustrated, informational books can be used in conjunction with storybooks. In this section, we discuss this use further, and then explore other times and places for using informational books in the preschool classroom.

Use informational books in conjunction with storybooks

In the opening vignette, an informational book was used in the discussion following a story's second reading to help explain something a child had asked about in its first reading. In addition to using informational books to respond to something that arises spontaneously in a story, many educators plan for the coordinated use of stories and informational books within units of study (Pollard-Durodola et al. 2011). We have used this approach with children, and recommend it, because it ensures more than one exposure to vocabulary words (i.e., just in a story) and allows children to build knowledge that supports their comprehension of the stories used in a unit.

Carefully planned hands-on science activities must be central to preschoolers' study of a topic, and these must be integrated well with both storybooks and informational texts. Teachers should avoid relying too much on informational books for teaching content to young children. Even books that are well designed, with diagrams and explicit text, are not sufficient to secure preschoolers' learning of many science concepts (Leung 2008).

It is not necessary to link every individual storybook in a unit of study to an informational book, nor must teachers use all informational books in the same way. It makes sense sometimes to read a variety of storybooks, all of which are related to a major concept, and then use an informational book to address the concept. At other times, it might be useful to read several informational books in conjunction with concrete experiences, and then read several stories after that.

Finally, it is not necessary to use informational books only during story time. It works just as well to read them in other teacher-guided experiences, even when following up on questions that arise during story reading. For example, informational books can be read during small-group science or social studies activities or even in a whole-group session that is devoted to content teaching and learning. They can also be read in the library area, with an individual child or two or three who are especially interested.

Use informational books to introduce a small-group experience

Sometimes, informational books can orient children to a small-group experience. For example, after children have explored magnets during center time, using trays of objects (e.g., paper clips, small wooden beads, bread twist ties, plastic discs), a teacher might organize a small-group experience that focuses on some practical uses of magnets, such as in can openers.

Before demonstrating how a magnet in the can opener keeps the lid from falling into the can once it has been cut off the can, the teacher could use the book *Magnetic and Nonmagnetic* by Angela Royston to show pictures of other uses for magnets (e.g., to hold keys on a rack, to connect toy train cars, to hold pieces in place on a game board). The teacher would use only the pages that discuss practical uses of magnets, and would read only some of the text that explains each picture. The teacher could then demonstrate the use of a can opener to familiarize children with this particular use.

Use informational books to support activities in centers

Informational books placed in centers can support activities in current units of study. For example, books about insects and spiders might be placed in a science center that is focused on the study of insects and other small creatures. Or, for a unit on festivals and celebrations in various cultures, books about piñatas and other objects could be placed in a center along with examples of the real objects.

Similarly, if block building is related to a zoo or farm topic, books about the various animals can be placed in the center, along with model animals. Children and teachers can use the books to learn about the individual animals, and this information might be used to make small props for the play. For example, to support farm animal block play, grains of wheat or corn could be glued onto green construction paper for chickens to eat, and pieces of blue paper could be laminated to make ponds on which ducks and geese could swim.

Books can also be provided in a math or manipulatives center where both math and language and literacy materials are available. For example, after reading and discussing the book *More* by I.C. Springman, which is about quantity words (e.g., more, less, too much), a teacher might place the book in the manipulatives center along with concrete items that children can use to create representations of the words (e.g., more, too many, several, plenty, enough).

A few pictorial examples of informational books in centers are provided in Figure 4-4.

Of course, with the information currently available on the Internet, children can also use computers during small groups or center time to access information. To benefit the most, children need guidance and conversation with a teacher. Teachers can also use interactive whiteboards to display what is on a computer's screen to a large group of children. An example of an interesting use of new technology in the classroom to support children's science learning (in this case, about elephant seals) is provided in Box 4-1 "Preschoolers Using Information Media and Technology."

Figure 4-4. Informational books used in centers.

Figure 4-4a. As part of a unit on plants, a teacher provided books about flowers, with one clipped open to the relevant seed pages. Children used magnifying glasses to inspect seeds that had been glued onto a piece of poster board. Each group of seeds was labeled with the name of the flower that would grow from them, and a picture of the flower was also attached beside the seeds.

Figure 4-4a

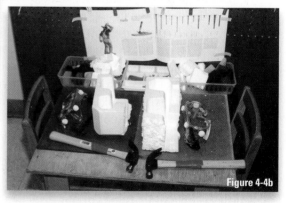

Figure 4-4b

Figure 4-4b. As part of a construction tool unit with 4-year-olds, the teacher provided a book with a page showing many different nails at the small table where the children could hammer nails into pieces of Styrofoam. (Note: Styrofoam can break down into small pieces that may pose a hazard. Use caution and supervision when using this material with young children.)

Figure 4-4c. A teacher gathered books together to help organize a center about musical instruments. This activity, which focused on drums, was one of several about different kinds of musical instruments.

Figure 4-4c

Include informational books in the book area

Informational books should also be available in the classroom's book area. See Box 4-2 "The Classroom Book Area" for information about other kinds of books that should also be included, the number of books to include, and how to display them.

The informational books placed in the book area include those used recently with storybooks or in small-group activities, because children almost always want to inspect their photographs and diagrams further. For example, Mr. Jacoby placed

Box 4-1 Preschoolers Using Information Media and Technology

Three children sit excitedly around the computer. Their teacher, Miss Janirys, says, "I wonder what Miss Liz and Miss Cindy have for us today." Miss Cindy and Miss Liz are at a conference in California. She clicks to a picture of an elephant seal sleeping on the sand. Next to it is an avatar photo of Miss Liz. Miss Janirys clicks on a photo of Miss Liz, and the children listen to what she posted for them earlier in the day. Miss Liz says, "This is an elephant seal. Elephant seals don't have any ears, and an elephant seal is so big it could never fit in your mommy's or daddy's car." Miss Janirys turns to the children. "Who would like to tell Miss Liz something?" They all bounce at the chance.

Miss Janirys helps Juanita write, "What do elephant seals eat?" Tommy asks to speak into the microphone. He says, "An elephant seal won't fit into your grandma's or grandpa's or Aunt Bonnie's or Angelo's car." It's Shea's turn next. She says, "Why does an elephant seal have no ears? How can it hear with no ears? Because I can hear when I have ears."

The children scamper off to the other centers, knowing they can check back for their responses from Miss Liz and Miss Cindy all the way across the country. They are excited to hear what their teachers have to say. Later in the day, they get their answers. Miss Liz answers Juanita's question about what elephant seals eat and reaffirms that elephant seals would not fit in anyone's car. She adds, "Elephant seals would even weigh more than the car." Miss Cindy adds, "The elephant seals do not have ears; you are absolutely right. What they have are little holes on either side of their head, and the little holes are just like ears that allow them to hear."

Source: Adapted from Fantozzi, V.B. 2012. "Exploring Elephant Seals in New Jersey: Preschoolers Use Collaborative Multimedia Albums." *Young Children* 67 (3): 42–49.

the *Crayfish* book he shared with the children in the book area, and also left the skeleton poster in the group area for interested children to examine.

Informational books that are not related to a current or previous unit of study can also be included in the classroom book area, to spark new interests or to allow children who already have a specific interest to pursue it. Teachers also often include informational books that are related to things that simply come up—a new baby in a child's family, grandparents visiting from another country, or a child's broken arm.

Include informational books in a lending library

Children often have many questions about the illustrations in an informational book or about something they heard as the teacher read it. Teachers do not always have time to address questions as fully as children would like. When children can take informational books home, an older sibling or cousin, or a parent or grandparent can read with the child. No matter their literacy level, family members have considerable knowledge about things in the world. Children benefit enormously when an adult helps guide their looking at illustrations and talks with them about a topic of interest.

Many alphabet books are actually informational books that are also good candidates for a lending library. For example *P is for Pakistan* by Shazia Razzak, *A is for Africa* by Ifeoma Onyefulu, and other books in this series contain a wealth of information about different countries. All of Jerry Pallotta's alphabet books are actually content books (*The Frog Alphabet Book*, *The Yucky Reptile Alphabet Book*, *The Boat Alphabet Book*, etc.). And, of course, the classic by Lois Ehlert, *Eating the Alphabet*, is a book about the many fruits and vegetables we eat.

Because these and many other alphabet books contain detailed illustrations and a great deal of information in their text, doing them justice requires one-on-one engagement with an adult. It is difficult for teachers to find time to read and discuss these books with individual children during center time in the classroom book area. Parents and other family members, including older siblings, can come to the rescue if books such as these are included in a classroom's lending library.

Strategies for using informational books

Strategies for reading informational books depend on each book's features and on the specific purposes for which a book is used. The context in which an informational book is used also affects the adult's strategies.

Read only selected parts

Teachers sometimes use selected portions of an informational text that are specifically relevant to the question at hand and are at a suitable level for preschoolers. Often, teachers use mostly the pictures in an informational book, without reading much of the text. For example, when a teacher's goal was to acquaint children with the idea that different birds have different beaks that can do different things, she used all of the pictures in *Unbeatable Beaks* by Stephen R. Swinburne in a class discussion on birds' beaks, but read only the labels that name the birds pictured, not the main text. The teacher then followed up with children who were especially interested by reading some or all of the main text to them in the book area during center time.

Read an informational book in its entirety

Using an entire informational book with a group of children is appropriate sometimes. For example, when an informational book is used in the context of a unit of study, instead of to follow up on a child's spontaneous question about a storybook, children bring knowledge to the book from first-hand experiences the teacher has provided. This knowledge often helps children engage well with the reading of an entire informational book. In turn, the book extends the knowledge the children gained from their first-hand experiences.

Model the use of informational text features

Young children learn how to use informational book features, such as a table of contents, an index, diagrams, and a glossary, as teachers model their purposes. For example, if children spotted some ants while out on the playground, and someone asked, "Where are they coming from? Where do they live?" a teacher might find a relevant book to answer the child's question, and start by consulting its table of contents. The teacher would stop running her finger down the column of topics and reading them when an entry matching the information of interest is found. The teacher would move her finger across to the page number and comment, "This number tells us that information about where ants live is on page 5. Let's turn to page 5 and see what it says."

Children also learn how to use lines and arrows that link labels to their referents in diagrams and photographs, when teachers explain their purpose and demonstrate their use, as Mr. Jacoby did when pointing out the joint in the crawfish's leg. In *Crayfish*, photographs always show the body of a crayfish with a line extending from a key vocabulary word boxed in the margin of the page. The key vocabulary word in the main text is also in bold face type (e.g., "Crayfish look like large bugs. They have two *eyestalks*" [p. 8]). If these words are pointed out and the line from a label to the illustration is traced, children will sometimes use these devices when looking at books on their own.

Many informational books also have glossaries that provide an alphabetic list of key terms used in the book. After reading a book, a teacher can use glossaries to review the book's key vocabulary, and can even flip back to relevant pages of the text, if this approach seems useful.

Some informational books provide supplemental material at the end, after the main text. For example, *Carry Me! Animal Babies on the Move* by Susan Stockdale provides more information about each animal that was discussed in the main text. Similarly, each book in the series about animals, written by Cathryn and John Sills,

Box 4-2 The Classroom Book Area

The book area houses a selected collection of books for the children's use. This area should accommodate four or five children, comfortably, without crowding.

Books to include

A variety of purchased books should be included in the classroom library—informational books, storybooks, concept books, and books of poetry and verse (see Box 3-1 in Chapter 3 for a discussion of four basic kinds of books). Many of the books in the book area are those the teachers have read during story time and circle time, or in content-focused small- or large-group gatherings.

In addition to including a variety of purchased books, teachers can also include books that children have made. These might include photo albums of the children at school, on a field trip, or at home, and albums that document long-term science activities (e.g., plants growing from seed to maturity, caterpillars growing and then changing into butterflies). Teachers can also place illustrated copies of recipes that children have used in cooking projects in a binder to make them easy to browse in the book area.

How many books?

Experts suggest that a classroom library include the equivalent of four to six books per child, to provide adequate choice (Vukelich & Christie 2009). Depending on the total amount of space and the number of display shelves available, this number must sometimes be decreased. Rotating books across time is a good way to provide a wide range of books to children over the course of a year.

Book area shelving

Ideally, some of the shelving in the book area can display book covers (Figure 4-5a), because children more often choose books whose covers they can see than books from shelves that show only their spines (Martinez & Teale 1989, cited in Fractor et al. 1993). Front-facing bins (Figure 4-5b) that show-case several books, perhaps all related to a topic, can allow children to flip through books easily to make selections.

Figure 4-5a

Including items other than books

Sometimes, a book area contains additional items, not just books. These items might include puppets, a flannel board and flannel pieces for a specific story, and bulletin boards that feature a specific author or children's dictated responses about a story they recently heard.

These additional items can crowd a book area or pull children away from looking at books. For these reasons, we prefer to place a flannel board and book-related flannel pieces in another area of the class-

Figure 4-5b

room, and to set up a small puppet theater someplace else, as well. (We would have one or the other of these options available at one time, not both.) Some flannel piece sets can relate to informational books, such as the life cycle of a butterfly (e.g., *See How They Grow: Butterfly* by Mary Ling) or the sequence of events from planting a seed to its growth into a mature plant (e.g., *One Bean* by Anne Rockwell).

With preschoolers, we also prefer concrete approaches to author study, such as placing several books by the same author that the teacher has read to the children all together in a small basket in the book area. Such sets of books need not be confined to stories, but can include sets of informational books by the same author. For example, a teacher might provide several books by Gail Gibbons, such as *Chicks and Chickens*, *Owls*, and *Snakes*, especially after children have used these in units of study. Similarly, *About Hummingbirds*, *About Penguins*, and other titles in the Cathryn and John Sill series might be placed together in a basket.

For the same reason, we would gather together children's dictated responses to a specific story and make a class book for the book area, instead of arranging these on a bulletin board mounted on the wall. If in book form, the children can have hands-on access and are more likely to share the experience with a friend.

If teachers want wall decorations in the book area, they can obtain book-related posters. Or, if able, they could draw large pictures of characters from stories children had heard recently, and place these on the book area walls. In a classroom we observed, the children loved seeing the story characters, and sometimes even talked to them! Teachers might also attractively display pictures of plants and animals related to a current unit of study on a piece of poster board, and put the display on the wall.

has small pictures of each animal in an Afterword that correspond to their appearance in the main text, paired with more detailed information about each one. The more basic main text is suitable for reading to a whole group of children, while the additional information can be shared with children who are interested, when they are in the book area or a small group.

Exposing children to printed information in non-book form

Although the primary focus of this chapter is informational texts, a great deal of printed information is available in non-book form. Children enjoy seeing and using many of these printed artifacts in their pretend play, and some are useful in specific classroom activities.

Providing informational print artifacts for children's dramatic play

Many print artifacts (i.e., props) support children in playing out scripts that go with their roles in dramatic play. These artifacts include restaurant menus, grocery ads from newspapers, appointment books, telephone books, and address books. They also include tickets required to travel by bus, train, or plane, and even by car, when one must pass through a toll booth or enter a parking garage.

Teachers can provide some real props for children to use in their play (e.g., grocery ads) and make others (e.g., menus for a play restaurant, an appointment book for a play doctor's office). Children can use models of some information print artifacts as guides for making their own (e.g., bus tickets, speeding ticket forms, order forms for wait staff in a restaurant).

Providing informational magazines

Informational magazines, such as *Ranger Rick* and *Big Backyard*, can be included in both the classroom and a lending library and can also be used as props in dramatic play. For example, the reading material in the waiting room for a pretend doctor or veterinarian's office can be stocked with such magazines, as well as with brochures or booklets about eating healthy foods and brushing teeth, or taking good care of pets.

Providing informational charts for the classroom

Sometimes, charts that teach can be placed on classroom walls (Roskos & Neuman 2011) or used during small-group activities. For example, a large illustrated recipe chart used in teacher-led cooking projects allows the children and teacher to work together to select ingredients or to find information about how to prepare them. An illustrated chart of steps to follow in planting seeds or bulbs can also be helpful for an individual child or a small group of children engaged in a small-group activity.

An example of an informative chart that a teacher placed on a wall for children's use during center time, in the context of a unit on color, included paper crayon wrappings mounted on poster board to expose their printed names (e.g., asparagus, espárrago, asperge). The English version of each color name was also provided in larger print beneath each crayon wrapping, and a picture of the item that inspired each color name was placed below the name. Two examples are shown in Figure 4-6, one for the crayon named *asparagus*, the other for the crayon named *dandelion*.

Figure 4-6. Parts of a chart about the source of crayons' color names.

Other charts used in a classroom might include one that shows steps for good hand washing. These can be obtained from a local public health department, and could be posted near sinks in the bathroom and in the classroom. Other informative charts include pictures of healthier foods versus less healthy foods.

Modeling authentic use of a calendar

While we agree with Beneke, Ostrosky, and Katz (2008) that calendar time (i.e., days, weeks, months) is beyond the capacity of preschoolers to understand, and that daily exercises in reciting the days of the week or the current month and year are a waste of time, we think that a calendar can be used with children for its intended purpose, which is to mark and keep track of important events. Children often become somewhat familiar with calendars that family members and teachers use to note appointments and special occasions. Teachers can use calendars for similar purposes, and to support some units of study.

We provide a description of one teacher's use of a calendar in booklet form, in conjunction with the monthly poster in her classroom, to help children anticipate and record events during a unit of study on the development of butterflies (see Box 4-3 "Using a Calendar in a Butterfly Unit").

Box 4-3 Using a Calendar to Keep Track of a Butterfly's Development

The teacher started by attaching a small picture of a caterpillar on the monthly chart mounted on a classroom wall during circle time to mark the arrival date of some caterpillars that were ordered a few weeks earlier. The children had expected their arrival, because the teacher had talked with them about the upcoming unit of study and showed them the form used to order caterpillars for the classroom. At that time, she also used an informational book (*See How They Grow: Butterfly* by Mary Ling) to review the life cycle of a butterfly.

Of course, once the caterpillars arrived, the children fed them and watched them grow. When they began to form their chrysalises, the teacher marked this date on the monthly chart, using a picture tile of a caterpillar partially enclosed in a chrysalis. On this day at circle time, the teacher also told the children that it would take quite a long time for the caterpillars to change into butterflies, and that the current month posted on the classroom wall would be all used up before the butterflies emerged.

She showed the children a calendar that was in booklet form and located the current month (May). Then, she turned to the next month (June) in the calendar booklet, read its name, and marked a date on this page with a butterfly sticker. She told the children that the butterflies would emerge from the chrysalises during this month, on about this date. She explained to the children that once the monthly poster chart on the wall was changed to the new month, she would put a sticker picture of a butterfly on it too so that the children would have some idea of how much longer they must to wait for the butterflies to emerge.

In the meantime, the teacher placed the calendar booklet in the classroom book area. She had written children's names on their birth dates on the various month pages in the calendar booklet. The children were accustomed to seeing a new month's name posted on the wall chart, and looking at dates marked on it to indicate children's birthdays, school holidays, and any expected classroom visitors. Now they could search the entire calendar booklet to find their own birth date and the birth date of friends. And, of course, children with summer birthdays, who usually did not get to see their birth dates marked on the classroom monthly chart, could find theirs, too!

After the butterflies emerged from their chrysalises, the children observed them in a net cage for a few days, and then took the cage outside to set them free. This day was marked on the monthly poster too, and also in the calendar booklet, which remained in the classroom's book area.

Children probably become somewhat aware of calendars as family members use them to note appointments and special occasions, such as birthdays, weddings, and festivals. Children learn a bit more about calendars from classroom experiences of the kind just described. Children often enjoy having a calendar booklet in the playhouse area for noting appointments for themselves or their babies, and they also like smaller calendars, such as those with months for the entire year printed on a small card, for the wallets and purses they use when pretending they are grown-ups in the house play area.

Concluding thoughts about sharing informational books

Informational books are of interest to young children and can be used to answer questions that arise during story reading or in a variety of other contexts. They help to extend children's knowledge beyond what is learned from hands-on experiences. Early experience with informational books supports children later in comprehending content area textbooks, not only by augmenting children's vocabularies, but also by familiarizing them with the specific language structures typically found in these books.

Printed information that is not in book form is also of great interest to preschoolers. They can use some print artifacts and magazines in their pretend play, and can use charts in some small-group activities and during center time. Preschoolers can also learn about calendars in authentic ways.

Experience with informational books helps to prevent a cascading barrage of barriers to good comprehension—lack of interest in books, lack of academic content vocabulary, lack of content knowledge (concepts), and lack of experience with some written language structures.

One early literacy expert has even suggested that a content knowledge gap is responsible for much of the achievement gap (e.g., see Neuman 2010; Neuman & Celano 2013). Preschool teachers are uniquely positioned to help close the achievement gap by using informational books in the ways this chapter suggests.

5 Young Children and Literacy Skills Development

Twenty-six-month-old Chara pushed a play stroller to give her doll a ride. She stopped in the kitchen to remove C from the set of letters on the refrigerator. She held and admired it for a moment, then placed it gently in her doll's lap and continued on.

A few days later, Chara said, "Chara," "Mommy," and "music" when the babysitter removed chalk from her pocket at the playground. She listened and watched as the babysitter named letters and wrote each word on the sidewalk. When it was her turn, Chara made 10 short lines while reciting the names of letters in her name.

At 28 months, when Chara scribbled on paper, she sometimes asked her mom to join in. Often, her mom wrote Chara's name and "Mommy," and then Chara scribbled over and around these words. Sometimes, Chara's mom wrote names of familiar foods, such as "cheese" and "chocolate" (Figure 5-1).

Figure 5-1

Chara's mom's words and Chara's scribbles with Cs.

At 33 months, while snipping pieces from thin strips of paper, Chara noticed a strip on the table lying across the end of another. "T, for Tricia," she announced, with authority and delight.

At 33 months, Chara could identify many uppercase letters and was aware that letters are used to make words. She also routinely included C-like marks in her scribble drawings (Figure 5-2a) and started writing grocery lists, using wavy lines, arranged horizontally (Figure 5-2b).

Chara's scribble drawings with Cs and a grocery list.

Figure 5-2a

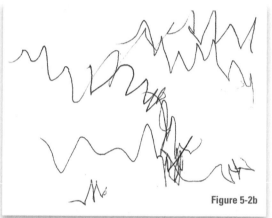

Figure 5-2b

Although most young children experience literacy at home during their early years, the onset, frequency, and focus of these experiences differ across families. Some children's families cover a wide range of activities, including many that focus specifically on print and how it works, while other children's experiences are both more limited in range and more general (Purcell-Gates 1996; Taylor & Dorsey-Gaines 1988; Teale 1986).

As discussed in Chapter 1, print-focused experiences support the acquisition of literacy skills, while book reading and conversation support the development of oral language and content knowledge (Crain-Thoreson & Dale 1992; Hood, Conlon, & Andrews 2008; Sénéchal & LeFevre 2002). If anything, book reading, outings (e.g., farms, vegetable stands, playgrounds) and conversation dominated Chara's experiences. Her alphabet and word experiences are highlighted here to illustrate that some children begin to learn print-related skills at home before they are 3 years old (Baghban 1984; Schickedanz 1990), and find delight in it.

This chapter focuses on three areas of understanding and skill: (1) alphabet knowledge, (2) phonological awareness, and (3) print conventions and functions. Because complete alphabet knowledge includes the understanding that letters in printed words represent sounds in spoken words, we discuss alphabet knowledge and phonological awareness in the same section, before discussing print concepts and functions separately.

Alphabet letter name knowledge

Although there was a time when no one expected preschoolers to learn the names of alphabet letters, researchers and early educators know now that preschoolers have an amazing capacity to learn all kinds of things, including letter names. While there is concern that adding literacy learning to preschool programs will displace other important experiences (see Copeland et al. 2012; Milteer, Ginsburg, & Mulligan 2012), it is both possible and necessary to support literacy skills learning while maintaining other experiences.

By the end of a year of a literacy-rich preschool program, a typical older 4-year-old can often name at least 18 or 19 uppercase letters (U.S. Department of Education 2008) and 16 or 17 lowercase letters (Piasta, Petscher & Justice 2012). Some older preschoolers actually learn all 26 uppercase and 26 lowercase letters (Piasta, Petscher & Justice 2012).

While it might seem like a lot for preschoolers to learn some lowercase, as well as uppercase, letters, many lowercase letters are relatively easy to learn because they closely resemble their uppercase matches (e.g., Ff, Tt, Ss, Mm, Yy, Oo, Zz, Pp). Because the words in books that children will read later contain mostly lowercase letters, it is important to get a good start in learning both uppercase and lowercase letters in preschool.

Using children's names

Research has not determined any best order for teaching alphabet letters, nor has it found any advantage to exposing preschoolers to just one or two letters at a time. The one fairly definitive finding is an "own name advantage," which means that a child usually learns the first letter in his own name (Justice et al. 2006; Treiman & Broderick 1998; Treiman et al. 2007) and in the names of family members before learning other letters (Bloodgood 1999). For example, Chara linked C to Chara, M to Mommy, and T to her Aunt Tricia.

Because children's motivation for learning must always be a major priority (Berhenke et al. 2011; Guthrie & Wigfield 2000), it makes sense to start supporting letter name learning using the first letters of children's names. If there are 18 to 20 preschoolers in a group, there are fewer unique uppercase letters available (about 13 to 14), because some children's names begin with the same letter—Justin, Jose, and Juanita; David, Danielle.

Teachers need not worry about exposing the children to many letters all at once. First, children see many letters in their everyday environment. Second, the accurate naming of letters rests on good letter discrimination, which requires active comparison of them (Gibson 1975). If children's exposure is restricted to one letter a week, or even to two or three, opportunities to compare and contrast letters are reduced. (See Box 5-1 "Three-Year-Old Sara Learns about A and H" for an illustration of how exposure to multiple letters aids learning to distinguish among them.)

Of course, simply putting children's names around the classroom is not enough. Although children will notice their names, and might even begin to recognize them in stable locations on cubbies or an attendance chart, they will not learn

Box 5-1   Three-Year-Old Sara Learns about A and H

At the end of a morning of preschool, 3-year-old Sara occupied herself by writing on a full sheet of white paper with a thin, black marker. First, she created two lines of letters in the upper left quadrant of her paper (Figure 5-3). The class's student teacher watched, commenting, "You have written some As and Hs." Sara glanced at the student teacher, but did not smile.

Sara began writing again, this time in the upper right quadrant of her paper. After pausing, the student teacher again commented about the As and Hs that Sara had written. When Sara glanced up this time, it was clearer that she was not happy.

Figure 5-3. Sara's As.

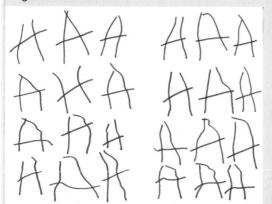

The student teacher was puzzled about Sara's negative responses. As she and her supervisor discussed the situation, the supervisor wondered, "Might Sara have considered all of her marks As?"

The next day, when Sara played with an uppercase alphabet puzzle, one of her teachers discovered that she knew letters S, R, and A, but not others—including H! This explained Sara's negative reaction to the student teacher's comments—it stemmed from having been misunderstood.

The teacher named H and other letters, and commented that H is a lot like the letter A in Sara's name, except that its top is always closed, while both the top and bottom of an H are open. From that day on, Sara always closed the tops of her As, even if an additional short line was required.

Because many alphabet letters vary from one another by just a tiny bit, knowing fully the configuration of one letter often depends on knowing another similar letter. When a child does not know the other letter that contains an important contrast, the child might unknowingly vary the known letter in a way that moves it into the "territory" of the unknown letter. Sara seemed very glad to know about H and wanted to make sure that *her* A was never again confused with it!

Preschoolers are fully capable of detecting small differences that distinguish one letter from others. In fact, babies just 3 or 4 months old can detect very small differences in the configuration and orientation of lines (Cohen & Younger 1984; Fantz 1963). Preschool children are naive, at first, about the small differences that distinguish one letter from others, because these differences are much smaller than the differences that distinguish between the exemplars in most categories.

For example, despite the wide variations found among forks, we call all pronged eating utensils *fork*, whether they have two, three, or five prongs. We indicate different kinds of forks by adding a modifier (e.g., pickle fork, salad fork, pitchfork). In contrast, if just one more line is added to F it becomes the letter E.

Babies begin to develop visually-based categories late in their first year of life (Quinn, Eimas, & Rosenkrantz 1993). Thus, when they encounter alphabet letters as older toddlers or young preschoolers, they respond with expectations that apply to most categories in the world. In other words, they group together letters that are quite similar in features, thinking they are different variations of the same letter (e.g., E/F, O/Q, M/W). With exposure to many letters, children realize that each letter is its own category, which can vary somewhat across fonts, but not in other ways.

letter names or how print works, unless letter names are used intentionally and named explicitly in routines and other contexts (Masonheimer, Drum, & Ehri 1984; Reutzel et al. 2003).

For example, when reviewing assignments on the classroom helpers chart (Figure 5-4), a teacher can name the first letter in a child's first name and also underline the name, rather than just read it while pointing quickly at its middle.

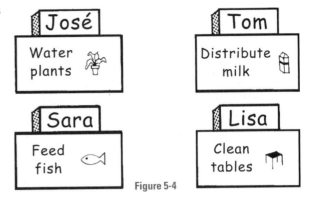

Figure 5-4

Teachers can also design attendance charts in ways that increase children's focus on the print.

Similarly, teachers can point out and name the first letter of each child's name on a name card when holding these up to dismiss children to wash their hands for lunch or to go to their cubbies to put on their jackets for playing outside (i.e., in transitions). Or, when helping children find their places at breakfast (i.e., find their nametag on the table), a teacher can locate a child's name, point to and name its first letter, and then underline and read it.

After a month of reviewing names on a helpers chart during a morning meeting, a teacher can place the name cards on the chart before children arrive for the day, and then ask children to check whether they have a job. By now, children are familiar with the first letters in their names, and also know to look at the big letter (i.e., uppercase letter) at each name's left end, especially if it is in color.

Of course, children whose names share the same first letter (e.g., José, Jason, and Jamilla) will probably need help figuring out whether a J they see in a name posted is theirs or a classmate's. As a matter of fact, preschoolers often treat the first letter in someone's name as if it belongs to that person (Ferreiro 1986; McGee & Richgels 1989). They sometimes say, "K is Kevin's," "D is Danielle's," and so on. These responses reveal that a child does not yet know that each letter is used to write many words, not just one. Asking children to check a helper chart for their names not only provides additional opportunities for a teacher to help children learn letter names but also to increase their understanding that the letters in their names are used in a multitude of words.

For example, if Jamilla calls out, "Hey, is this me?" her teacher can read the name to her and explain: "Both your name and Jason's start with the letter J (points to it). Then, both of your names have a little 'a' (points to it). But, then, after 'a,' Jason's name has 's,' and yours has 'm.' That's how we know that Jason waters the plants today. Maybe you will have a job tomorrow." (See Box 5-2 "Maximizing Learning from Helper and Attendance Charts" for information about designing and using helpers and attendance charts.)

After about two months of preschool, a teacher might also begin to play a name game at circle time. One uppercase letter tile is held up at a time, as the teacher explains, "If your name starts with the letter __ (e.g., M or L), raise your

Box 5-2 Maximizing Learning from Helper and Attendance Charts

The design of both helpers and attendance charts affects the opportunities they provide for letter learning. The teacher's use of these charts also affects children's learning. For example, in addition to the teacher's specific attention to first letters when reviewing helpers for the day, as we

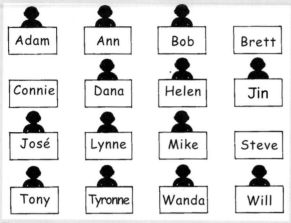

Figure 5-5

have already discussed, assigning jobs on a daily, rather than on a weekly, basis, gives children more opportunities to interact with the names posted. This greater frequency aids children's learning of letter names, and also assists them in learning to recognize classmates' names.

Many preschool teachers also use an attendance chart. When constructing one, teachers typically organize names on an attendance chart alphabetically. Of course, a child soon learns the physical location of his name pocket and stops looking at his name printed on it. When providing children's names for the pockets in a large box lid or basket, however, children must inspect the print of peers' names to find their own, if no routine organization of the names is used. Providing names in this varied way daily supports quite a lot of letter learning.

Attendance chart nametags should have only a child's name, because children will not inspect the print if a picture is there too (Figure 5-5). Some teachers start the year using nametags with a picture of each child and then change to nametags with names only after the first month of school because, by this time, children can usually find their nametags based on print features, such as their name's first letter.

Some teachers post jobs on children's attendance chart pockets, instead of using a separate helpers chart (Figure 5-6). In this approach, small squares of Velcro are placed on each child's attendance chart pocket and on the back of each job tile.

hand." When confirming each child's raised hand, the teacher might say, "Yes, Kanye, your name does begin with the letter K." If a child whose name starts with the letter does not raise her hand, the teacher pulls that child's name card from her set, and points to and names its first letter (e.g., "Manuel, your name also starts with the letter M. You may raise your hand").

At about this time of the year, one preschool teacher also used children's names in a small-group activity (making a bookmark) that was related to a paperback book each child received to take home and keep. Children were asked to arrange letter tiles for their name on the table. A teacher checked each child's letter series, naming and pointing to each letter, and then either confirmed the order or assisted in rearranging letters to spell the child's name correctly, using the child's nametag as a reference. (For children with longer names, this happened quite frequently.)

Figure 5-6. Attendance chart pockets designed for posting classroom jobs.

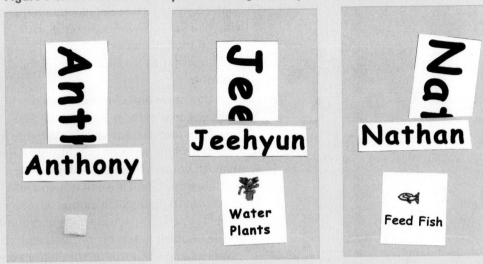

Combining attendance and helper charts reduces the wall space needed for classroom charts, but there is a disadvantage for literacy skill learning—children can see immediately whether they have a job, without inspecting the print. If children's names are used daily in circle time literacy activities and also in transitions, a teacher might judge that a combination chart would work fine, because multiple opportunities each day to inspect names on both a helper and an attendance chart are not needed, that finding their nametags for the attendance chart is sufficient.

Engagement with nametags on attendance and helpers charts provides opportunities for children to continue to learn about alphabet letters and written words, if a teacher can join them to comment. For example, as a child identifies her nametag, the teacher might say, "Yes, that nametag is yours. It says Victoria—V-i-c-t-o-r-i-a" (points to each letter as it is named). Or a teacher might say, "Yes, that is your name, Oliver. I was noticing the other day that your name has a 'v' in the middle and that Victoria's name has a 'v' at the beginning. You are the only two children in our class who have the letter 'v' in your names."

Then, each child used a glue stick to attach the letters to one side of a simple, narrow, rectangle of colored poster board. Children also received a printed conventional form of their name (first letter capitalized; others in lowercase) to glue to the bookmark's other side. Lastly, children glued a nameplate inside their book's front cover ("This book belongs to _____") and wrote their names in its blank. Any form of the name the child produced was accepted, and a teacher assisted any child who said, "I can't. I need help."

Additional letter name materials

Even though a teacher uses primarily first letters from children's names at the start of a year, other letter materials are introduced after a while. For example, in small-group sessions, a teacher might use letter Bingo, letter Memory, and letter-matching materials that include highly confusable letters. (See the example in Figure 5-7.)

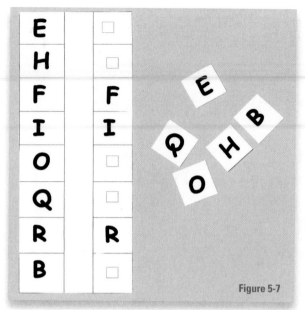

Figure 5-7

Teachers can also use letter-matching materials that show letters in different fonts. Several letters are placed on the left side of a background board (e.g., E, G, H, K), and then the letter tiles provide three or four matches for each letter, in different fonts.

After their introduction in small groups, some of these letter game and matching materials are made available for children's independent use during center time. Of course, teachers also provide alphabet puzzles. Those that help children best to distinguish among letters have a separate space in the background frame for each letter. In contrast, alphabet puzzles in jig-saw form picture letters on irregularly shaped pieces. To assemble these puzzles, children must attend to the shape of the puzzle pieces, not to letter shapes.

Alphabet puzzles used should expose children to both uppercase and lowercase letters, but not all in the same puzzle. Younger preschoolers, especially, become quite overwhelmed when trying to assemble a puzzle that has all 52 letters! Using puzzles that have either uppercase or lowercase letters, not both, provides a more manageable experience.

A teacher might also start using a "Letter Clue Game" at circle time (see a description in Box 5-3 "The Letter Clue Game and Its Benefits to Young Children"). And, of course, from the very beginning of the school year, letter names come up in writing contexts. We discuss ways to support letter name knowledge and other literacy skills in Chapters 7 and 8. We turn our attention now to phonological awareness, which children must acquire to understand how letters function in printed words.

Phonological awareness

Phonological awareness refers to skill in detecting and manipulating sounds in spoken words, while setting aside word meanings, a kind of play with the sound structure of words. In this section, we discuss (1) speech units, (2) manipulations of speech units in phonological awareness tasks, (3) expectations for phonological awareness during the preschool years, and (4) instructional strategies that help preschoolers develop phonological awareness.

Speech units in words

Syllables are the largest sound units in words (e.g., ba-by, ba-na-na). Syllables, in turn, can be divided into two parts—an onset unit and a rime unit. All of the sounds before the vowel comprise a syllable's **onset**. A syllable's **rime** includes the

Box 5-3 The Letter Clue Game and Its Benefits to Young Children

This game helps children realize that two very similar letters can differ physically in only one small way. When children first begin to learn about alphabet letters, they apply to some letters (e.g., E/F; T/L; N/Z) what they have learned about items in categories, such as dogs or forks—"ignore small differences and focus on shared features." In other words, children at first think E and F are two different versions of the *same* letter, not two different letters, because they have *learned* to ignore differences far greater than these when learning about forks, dogs, cats, automobiles, chairs, and so on. Exposure to alphabet letters, especially in this game, helps children begin to realize they must focus on small differences and *ignore* shared features.

How to play

- Tell children that you are thinking of a letter. Write just one part of it at a time, as clues. For example, if P is the target letter, draw a long vertical line on a piece of chart paper, and then pause to give children a chance to guess which letter it might be.

- Children might guess T, L, or M. For each letter guessed, say, "I see what you are thinking," and then form that letter. When responding to T, you might say, "We do start with a long vertical line when writing T (write it), and then we use a short horizontal line across its top (write it). T was a good guess, because it does have a long vertical line, but T is not the letter in my mind."

- You can respond to guesses of M and L the same way. Then, provide a second clue: "This line starts at the top of the long vertical line, then moves to the right, and then moves back to the vertical line's middle, like this. At this point, several children might say, "P." Confirm that this is the letter.

Next steps

- If the letter formed is similar to yet another, you can keep going! For instance, P could lead to either R or B. You could say, "Now, I'm thinking of another letter that is very similar to P. I'll write another P (write it), and then add a line to it. I'm going to add a little diagonal line down here (add the line)." A child or two usually calls out "R." Confirm that the new letter is R, and comment that the only difference between P and R is one small diagonal line (point to it).

- Consider following up this game with others that reinforce the concept. Matching games using tiles of letters in several different fonts (see the section "Additional letter name materials") also help children to understand that each letter may vary somewhat (e.g., E, E, ϵ, **E,**), as long as a variation does not turn the letter into a different one.

vowel and any sounds that follow it. For example, in *bed*, /b/ is the onset and /ed/ is the rime; in *string*, /str/ is the onset and /ing/ is the rime; in *tea*, /t/ is the onset and /ea/ is the rime. A word can also be divided into even smaller sound units called **phonemes**. The word *bed* has three phonemes (i.e., /b/ /e/ /d/). *Plate* has four (i.e., /p/ /l/ /a/ /t/).

Our speech changes at the boundaries between syllables, and between the onset and rime units, in ways that are detectable, even though we don't notice these boundaries when communicating with others. Phonemes, on the other hand, are not distinct, but instead run right into one another in spoken words. Not surprisingly, syllable and onset-rime units are relatively easy for children to learn to detect, while phonemes are hard. **Phonemic awareness** is the most difficult level of phonological awareness for children to achieve. It is also the level most closely related to reading and writing, because alphabet letters represent speech at the phoneme level.

There are other writing systems used throughout the world that represent syllables or whole words/concepts (e.g., water, fire, road) instead of phonemes. Children who are dual language learners might learn writing systems that differ in the unit of sound they represent, such as when the two languages are Chinese and English, or Japanese and English. Children who are becoming bilingual in Russian

Box 5-4 How Different Writing Systems Work

If creating a written language for a society without one, the first step is to decide at what level the new writing system would represent the oral language. We could create a logography (i.e., represent each word with just one symbol), a syllabary (i.e., each symbol represents a syllable in words), or an alphabetic system (i.e., each symbol represents a phoneme in words).

Characteristics of different writing systems

Learning the symbols in a logography, such as Chinese, requires linking a particular design (character) to the object, action, or idea it represents. A logography is a direct writing system, not an abstract one with a code intervening between symbols and their meanings. In a syllabary, on the other hand, syllables are combined in various ways to create all of the words in the language, such as Japanese. Syllabaries are code-based systems. English, Russian, and Spanish writing systems are alphabetic systems—letters represent the individual sounds in spoken words. Letters are combined in a multitude of ways to spell all of the words in a language.

A logography is easy to understand, but a child learning one (e.g., Chinese) must learn several thousand characters (Taylor 1981). A writing system that is sound-based requires a child to learn fewer basic symbols, but because all sound-based writing systems are abstract (i.e., children must learn a code), they are harder to fathom at first. Because syllables are easier to detect in spoken words than phonemes, syllable-based writing systems are easier to learn than alphabetic systems. But even though difficult for children to detect in spoken words, phoneme-based writing systems have the advantage of requiring knowledge of relatively few symbols (i.e., alphabet letters).

Phonological awareness in dual language learners

Children learning English, if their first language is a logography, would find it strange at first that each alphabet letter represents an individual sound in a spoken word, not a whole word. Children whose first language uses a syllabic writing system would also find an alphabetic writing system a bit puzzling.

and English, Hebrew and English, or in Spanish and English are learning languages that do not differ in the level of sound represented in their writing systems. All use alphabet letters to represent phonemes. (See Box 5-4 "How Different Writing Systems Work" for more discussion about different writing systems.)

When children use language for communication, *conscious* phonemic analysis is not required (i.e., children have no difficulty distinguishing between the words *bat* and *bag*, or *silly* and *Willy*). But when learning to read and write, conscious awareness of sound units is needed. Teachers engage children in a variety of tasks to develop their awareness of different sound units in words, including phonemes. (See Chapter 8 for information about helping children develop phonological awareness in writing contexts.)

A teacher can ask children to manipulate any size speech unit in a variety of ways. For example, children might create a word by **blending** sounds the teacher provides (e.g., "I'm going to say some sounds. Hold up your hand if you know what

Luckily, for preschoolers who are learning English, these differences in writing systems are not terribly confusing, because they have not yet learned to read or write in their first language. They often learn to read and write in both languages, at the same time, at preschool or at home, or in both contexts. As with most other things, they simply think, "Well, this is how reading and writing work in Chinese (or in Korean or Japanese), and this is how they work in English." One advantage to bilingualism is that children become more flexible and creative in their language use than if they learn just one language (Hakuta & Diaz 1985).

Children whose home language is based on an alphabet can transfer phonological awareness skills from English to their home language, and from their home language to English (Dickinson et al. 2004). They do not need phonological awareness instruction only in English, because these skills transfer very well from one language to the other. The critical feature of effective phonological awareness instruction is explicitness and adequacy of exposure, which until fairly recently was not offered to children until they entered kindergarten (Hammer, Scarpino, & Davison 2011).

There is an advantage to providing phonological awareness tasks in a child's home language, rather than just in English, because children who are very new to English easily forget the less familiar English words a teacher provides as targets in phonological awareness tasks, and also have trouble generating matches to a target (e.g., other words that begin with the same sound, or rhyme with the target word), because they have relatively few English vocabulary words from which to draw (see Yesil-Dagli 2011).

It makes little sense to spend an inordinate amount of time on phonological awareness tasks in English, thinking that English language learners are performing poorly because they lack specific phonological awareness skills, when the issue is likely the child's small English vocabulary. In addition to providing some phonological awareness tasks in the child's first language, if possible, teachers can use children's first names in tasks, and also use English words that are becoming familiar, such as the names of items used frequently in the classroom (e.g., blocks, sink, paint, puzzle, house, jacket, juice, milk) or key words from storybooks. Teachers can also use pictures of target words so that children are better able to keep the target words in mind. And, of course, all the while, teachers are supporting children in learning English vocabulary using a wide variety of contexts in the preschool.

word they make when we put the sounds together. /s/, /n/, /a/, /k/"). Or, children might **segment** the sounds in a word (i.e., break it apart) the teacher provides into its syllables or phonemes (e.g., "Say *baby* in two parts"). Or, children might be asked to **delete** or **substitute** a sound unit in a word (e.g., "Say *fin* without /f/"), or **generate** words that rhyme or begin with the same sound (e.g., "Let's think of some words that begin with the same sound as *boat. /b/...oat*").

The course of phonological awareness acquisition

Children can detect syllable segments first, then onset and rime segments, and, finally, phonemes. But assessment of a child's level of phonological awareness also includes consideration of the manipulations that she is asked to conduct with a sound unit.

Blending is easier than segmenting, and segmenting is easier than deleting or substituting. Tasks requiring the deletion or substitution of speech sounds are quite difficult, because they involve more than one manipulation. For example, if asked to say *sand* without its /s/," a child must first segment and isolate /s/ from *sand*, then delete it, and say "*and*." Or, if asked to substitute /d/ at the beginning of their own names, children must first segment and delete a sound (e.g., /s/ in *Sue*), and then put /d/ in its place (e.g., *due*).

Generating words with the same first sound or rime unit also requires several steps: (1) Holding a target word and a sound unit in mind (e.g., "Can you think of other words that begin with /b/ like *boat*?"), (2) searching the vocabulary store for possible matches (e.g., ball, bib, baby), and (3) comparing each selected word to the target word. Generating words for phonological tasks is especially difficult for younger children who do not yet have substantial vocabulary stores from which to draw words to analyze and for children who are just learning English (see Box 5-4).

Where to start with phonological awareness

If exposed to texts written in verse, children will enjoy their rhythmical quality and their emphasis on rhyming and alliteration (i.e., words beginning with the same sound). As explained in Chapter 3 (see Box 3-1), books written in verse are often described as "predictable texts," because their repeated features, such as refrains, cumulative text, and stable sentence frames (e.g., "On Monday, he ate through one apple . . . On Tuesday, he ate through two pears . . ." in *The Very Hungry Caterpillar* by Eric Carle [pp. 7–8]) help children to remember them.

Although experience with verse, by itself, will not develop conscious phonological awareness, nothing is better, as a basic experience, for exposing children to language in a form that is enjoyable, because sounds in words are highlighted and sentences flow musically. Additionally, children love to "read" these books by themselves in the library area, and doing so can enhance alphabet knowledge, letter and sound association knowledge, and print knowledge in several ways (see Box 5-5 "Finger Point Reading of Predictable Text Books"). Experiences with verse can be provided daily in a preschool program's circle time, throughout the year.

Teachers can also use books that play with language to draw children's attention to interesting sounding words. For example, clusters of words on the pages of *Roadwork* by Sally Sutton provide information about the sounds that construction vehicles make. These include "Screech! BOOM! WHOOSH!" (p. 3) and "Squelch! SPLUCK! SPLAT!" (p. 14). *One Duck Stuck* by Phyllis Root includes the words "clomp, clomp" (p. 5), "slink, slink" (p. 17), and others. These words are just fun for children to say and play with. Yopp and Yopp (2009) provide a list of both English and Spanish books that play with language.

With respect to specific phonological awareness tasks, teachers usually start with those requiring the blending and segmenting of syllables, and then move to tasks in which these same manipulations are used with smaller units of sound. Teachers usually save deletion, substitution, and generation tasks for later.

Research indicates, however, that children need not master lower levels of awareness (i.e., syllable tasks) before they can benefit from experiences with higher levels (i.e., onset-rime and phoneme tasks). In other words, the acquisition of phonological awareness does *not* occur in distinct stages, one after the other (Anthony et al. 2003; Lonigan 2006), but is, instead, quasi-developmental (i.e., skills develop in an overlapping fashion).

Researchers have also discovered that experience with syllable level tasks are not necessary as a foundation for skill in detecting and manipulating onsets

Box 5-5 Finger Point Reading of Predictable Text Books

Finger point reading entails matching a book's printed words to a verbal recitation of its text, which children have memorized after hearing the book read aloud multiple times. Children who can finger point read memorized books have higher levels of alphabet knowledge and phonological awareness than children who cannot. Children without these specific literacy skills engage more globally with print in the books they have memorized, rather than finger point read them (Ehri & Sweet 1991).

Finger point reading may help a child increase his literacy skills. For example, scanning from left to right and top to bottom becomes more automatic, sight recognition of some repeatedly encountered common words increases, and children consolidate information about how various letters or letter pairs represent sounds in spoken words. Some children actually move into conventional reading through repeated use of finger point reading, possibly because it requires the integration of literacy skills to locate specific printed words, and reading unfamiliar text also requires similar integration.

The increase in explicit literacy skill teaching in today's preschool classrooms may allow more children to finger point read familiar predictable text books. Although predictable text books do not contribute as much to vocabulary development as narratives and informational texts, and do not involve reasoning of the kind required by narratives, they are useful in their own right. They expose children to beautiful language and to literary ways of saying things, and also contribute to children's interest in books and reading. Moreover, as suggested here, they can even contribute to literacy skill development, if children take letter knowledge and skill in phonological awareness to these books as they enjoy "reading" them.

and rimes, and phonemes (Ukrainetz et al. 2011), as many early educators had assumed, based on earlier research that allowed multiple interpretations (Lundberg, Frost, & Petersen 1988). Syllable units are certainly the easiest and most accessible speech unit for children to blend and segment, but it makes no sense to linger for several months on a speech unit that children can detect and learn to manipulate so easily, when research suggests that this might interfere with children's progress in detecting and manipulating smaller speech units (Ukrainetz et al. 2011).

We still think that early childhood teachers should start with tasks involving syllables (e.g., blending and segmenting) because children have used language for communication—have focused on meaning—which causes difficulty at first in focusing only on sound. For example, when first asked to think of other words that begin with the same sound as *cake*, a young child might say, "birthday" or "chocolate." These are meaningful responses, not responses focusing only on sound.

In the face of such puzzlement, phonological awareness tasks using larger sound segments (i.e., syllables) introduce children to the general idea that they can play with sounds in words. But because this is perhaps the only advantage of starting with syllables, it is probably wise for teachers to use this sound unit for only a few weeks before moving on to smaller speech units (i.e., onsets and rimes, and phonemes).

Syllable blending and segmenting tasks. If children's names are used in syllable tasks, the sound units are more accessible to children, and the tasks are more enjoyable. For example, as a game during circle time or for a transition, a teacher can ask children to listen carefully as he says each of their names in parts (i.e., syllables). The teacher explains, "If you think the parts I say are for your name, raise your hand and say your name 'the right way.'"

The teacher models the process first, using names of characters from a familiar story, teachers' names, or the names of children who are absent. When presenting names, the teacher repeats the series of their syllable segments two or three times, pausing very briefly in between each presentation. The repetitions give children a chance to hear and process the syllables presented.

Turns for children whose names have just one syllable (e.g., Ben, Sue, Josh) can be provided by displaying three pictures of familiar objects at a time (e.g., cray-on, eas-el, ba-na-na, um-brell-a), and then presenting the syllable segments for the name of just one, after designating whose turn it is. After the first child's turn, the focus picture card is removed from the chart stand and the syllable segments for the names of objects pictured in the next set are presented to the next child. (Display no more than three pictures at once, to limit cognitive load for each child's turn.)

After using this blending syllable task on a few occasions, a teacher might say each child's name naturally, and ask children to join her in saying each name in parts (a segmenting task). After using this teacher-supported task on several occasions during circle time, children can take turns saying a classmate's name in a funny way for the teacher to guess and say "the right way."

Children need not clap the syllables in names or report their number in these face-to-face experiences with a teacher. They can simply listen to and say the sound segments, marking the "beats" of their names verbally (i.e., with stress) and with synchronized head nods. There is no point in making the task more complicated for children when a teacher can listen and watch to obtain information about children's understanding. With some digital-based phonological awareness tasks, asking children to count phonemes is appropriate where phoneme segmentation is part of a game (i.e., the child's game piece moves when the child has correctly counted phonemes in words presented). (See Box 5-7 "Using Educational Technology to Support Literacy Skills Acquisition" later in the chapter.)

Box 5-6 Interesting Learning from First Letter vs. First Sound Name Games

By using children's names in phonological awareness tasks, teachers expose children to some interesting information about English spelling. For example, based on their experience with the "First Letter in Your Name" game, children might think they should raise their hand for the "First Sound in Your Name" game, with children whose names start with the same letter, as they have in the past. Some children discover, however, that they raise their hand with a different child or two in the "First Sound" name task. For example, Gordon and Gustav raise their hands together for the "First Letter" game, and Giovanna joins them. But in the "First Sound" game, Giovanna learns to raise her hand when Jamilla raises hers, not when Gordon and Gustav raise theirs.

When a teacher explains to Giovanna that she should raise her hand for the /j/ sound, just like Jamilla raises hers, Gordon and Gustav might say, "Hey. She's like us, not like Jamilla!" What a wonderful opening for a teacher to say, "You are right that you and Giovanna have names that start with the same *letter*—with G—but your names start with different *sounds*. Giovanna's name starts with /j/ . . . /j/iovanna; yours start with /g/... /g/ordon, /g/ustav. So, in the sound game, you and Giovanna raise your hands at different times."

Preschool children accept these irregularities and often become quite interested in them. For example, once, after a preschool teacher had introduced "Miss Judy" (lead author) to her class, 4-year-old Giovanna, asked, "Are you J or G?" Her teacher smiled broadly, and said, "She wants to know whether your name starts with J or G, because she knows that her name and Jason's have the same first sound, but different first letters."

Many children are interested in these and other irregularities of English spelling. For example, if teachers include diagraphs (i.e., 'ch,' 'sh,' 'th,' 'wh') among their set of letter tiles for use in "The First Letter in Your Name" game, rather than only single letters, children learn that Chauntise's name begins with Ch, not C, that Shawn's name begins with Sh, not S, and that Theodore's name begins with Th not T.

Knowing these simple truths about English writing is likely to pay off when children are learning to read. Children from classrooms where names starting with diagraphs were accepted and used will probably be less likely to focus on 't' alone, when approaching words, such as *the*, *this*, *they*, and so on. Instead, they are likely to respond to the 'th' letter pair, which is what they must do to read these words accurately. Why take preschoolers in the wrong direction during the preschool years, when it is possible and even interesting for them to know more about how English spelling actually works?

Next steps in phonological awareness instruction

After using syllable tasks for a few weeks, teachers move next to blending and segmenting onset and rime units, and phonemes. These tasks can be used with the whole group during circle time and also in daily transitions. Again, a teacher starts with children's names, but focuses now on first sounds. Children should be somewhat familiar by now with the first letters in their names from the "First Letter in Your Name" activity ("If your names starts with ___ raise your hand") and will enjoy a new game, at times, with a first sound focus.

A teacher explains before starting that the game today uses sounds in their names, not letters (e.g., "Instead of looking at letters I hold up, today you will listen for me to say the first *sound* in your name"). The teacher provides some examples, perhaps using teachers' names: "When I say, 'If your name starts with /t/, raise your hand,' then Tanya (the assistant teacher) would raise her hand, because her name starts with that sound. Listen, /t/-/t/ Tanya." Use a second example before beginning to present the first sounds in children's first names.

In each instance, the teacher says the target sound two or three times (e.g., "If your name starts with /d/. . . /d/. . . —with the /d/ sound—raise your hand"), and provides detailed feedback when a child raises his hand (e.g., "Yes, Devone, your name starts with /d/. . . *D*evone." Or, "Your name starts with /t/, *T*anika, not /d/. I'll say the /t/ sound pretty soon. Put your hand down for now"). If a child does not raise her hand when the relevant sound is presented, the teacher provides informative feedback: "Devone, your name starts with /d/—*D*evone. So, you can raise your hand too." (See Box 5-6 "Interesting Learning from First Letter vs. First Sound Name Games" for a discussion of some interesting consequences for children from their participation in both the "First Letter in Your Name" and "First Sound in Your Name" games.)

After playing the "First Sound in Your Name" game multiple times across several weeks, other tasks can also be used in circle time (one each day). For example, words beginning with the same sounds as the children's names can be presented (e.g., "If your name begins with the same sound as /b/ /b/ . . . *b*all, raise your hand"). The teacher first presents some examples (e.g., "If I said, 'If your name starts with /m/ /m/ like milk, raise your hand' and someone's name was *M*olly, then Molly would raise her hand. /m/ . . . *M*olly"). The teacher provides detailed feedback when children recognize the sound that is the first in their names (e.g., "Yes, Nathan, your name does begin the /n/ like *napkin*: /n/ /n/ *n*apkin, and /n/ /n/ *N*athan, both begin with the /n/ sound").

Teachers can also use poems, songs, and predictable text books that children help recite during circle time, as a jumping off point for phonological awareness tasks, because these usually contain rhyming words and words that begin with the same sound. (See Table 5-1 "Circle Time Beginning Sound and Rhyming Word Activities" for examples of phonological awareness tasks for use in circle time, some of which are based on words from predictable text sources.)

Using phonological awareness manipulatives during center time. Materials that provide children with opportunities to practice phonological awareness skills can be provided for their use during center time. Decks of picture cards are the basic materials used in these manipulatives. The example in Figure 5-8 focuses on the beginning sounds in words. A target picture appears on a background board; tiles to match have pictures of objects beginning with the same sound as the target pictures' names.

Teachers can use many sets of materials like this one, but with different pictures. The specific focus of the phonological awareness task can also vary over time. For example, later in the year, the task might focus on ending sounds in words, rather than on beginning sounds.

The items pictured in these manipulatives should be very familiar to help children label them as intended. Otherwise, the picture tiles provided for matching will not work. Teachers need not place printed labels for the pictures on the background board or tiles. This sometimes shifts the teacher's focus from sound (phonological awareness) to letters, which is not helpful.

Today, many digital applications are available to help children learn about letters and sounds. A few examples are discussed in Box 5-7. Studies indicate that children from lower income families have much less access to computers and to apps designed to support learning than do children from higher income families (Common Sense Media 2011). Experience in preschool can help to reduce this new "app gap," while also keeping screen time within the recommended range (AAP 2011).

Using writing to support phonological awareness. Phonological awareness is also supported in writing contexts, and each child's progress can be observed in this context. Although phonological awareness is an oral language skill, which can be developed without reference to print, research indicates that embedding phonological awareness instruction in writing is highly effective (Ball & Blachman 1991; Ukrainetz et al. 2000). We discuss the use of writing to support phonological awareness in preschoolers in Chapter 8.

Figure 5-8. First sounds in words matching manipulative.

Box 5-7   Using Educational Technology to Support Literacy Skills Acquisition

Kathleen A. Paciga

Technology motivates and engages children, and mobile devices like tablets are intuitive and portable enough to add easily to the early literacy environment. There are many options from which to choose, some related to TV or movie characters and some not. Apps that support letter knowledge, phonemic awareness, and phonics skills include

- Letter knowledge apps that provide children with practice identifying, writing, and connecting sounds [phonemes] to letters. Elmo Loves ABCs, Starfall ABCs, and Dora ABCs Vol. 1: Letters & Letter Sounds focus on letter knowledge. Children play letter identification games, listen to ABC songs, and view videos or color pictures of things whose names begin with the same sound each letter represents. For example, in Elmo Loves ABCs (Figure 5-9, courtesy of Sesame Workshop), the child clicks Z, traces it with a finger, and watches Elmo sing "/z/ /z/ /z/ /z/ /z/ zebra is a word that starts with Z." They can also play a hidden picture game (i.e., move balloons around the screen with their fingers to uncover the zipper, zucchini, and zebra). Other letters show Sesame Street videos of animals and objects (e.g., Murray and a child pretending to be a rocket as a video about R). This app can extend traditional letter exploration, while also extending preschoolers' vocabulary and content knowledge.

Figure 5-9

- Phonemic awareness software for older preschoolers and kindergartners focus on segmenting and counting phonemes (e.g., LeapFrog's Toy Story 3), and on rhyming words (e.g., Dora ABCs Vol. 2: Rhyming Words). Toy Story 3 replicates a board game experience in which children count phonemes in orally presented words accompanied by pictures onscreen. Children indicate the number of phonemes in each word by touching the correct number of dots. Correct responses move the child's character that number of spaces (e.g., *fish* would move three spaces on the digital board game).

- Other apps (e.g., Bob Books Reading Magic Lite, Dora ABCs Vol. 3: Ready to Read!, or Phonics Awareness, 1st Grade) include phonemic awareness, as well as phonics, by asking children to touch letters to hear the sounds they typically represent and to move letters or objects on screen to spell or identify words. In Dora's ABCs Vol. 3, children help Dora and Boots cross the lily pads by placing the correct letter at the beginning or end of a word or by identifying the correct picture for a word after hearing a sequence of sounds and blending these into a word. For example, after Dora says, "What picture goes with this word?" the child blends the sounds and moves *rug*. Then, Dora says, "Change *rug* into *hug*," and tells the child, "Touch the letters on top to hear their sounds." Phonics Awareness (Figure 5-10) focuses on connecting letters to sounds that are segmented or blended. For example, for blending, the narrator says, "You can listen to all the sounds in a word and find the word. Listen, /s/ /i/ /t/." A child then moves a bug character onto the word *sit*.

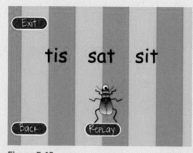

Figure 5-10

Although these apps are useful to support literacy skills, not all children have access to this technology (Common Sense Media 2011).

Table 5-1   Circle Time Beginning Sound and Rhyming Word Activities

Activity	Feedback	Presentation
Tasks that Use Songs, Poems, and Predictable Text Books		
Singing Songs, Reciting Poems and Rhymes, and Reading Predictable Text Books	• Sing songs, recite poems, and read books, using good expression to capture the natural rhythm. • Repeat the same songs, poems, and predictable text books over weeks and months. • Encourage children to join in, as they learn the verses.	• Vary pace to allow children to recite, sing, or read along. • Use eye contact and facial expressions to connect with children.
Teacher Identifies Rhyming Words or Words that Begin with the Same Sound in Familiar Nursery Rhymes, Poems, Songs, or Predictable Text Books	• After using a rhyme, poem, song, or predictable text book several times across two to three weeks, comment, after a new occasion, that some of its words sound alike. For example, for the poem "Little Bird," say, "I noticed that both 'hop' and 'stop' have 'op' as their second part—h-**op** and st-**op**. Those two words rhyme." • After identifying the second pair of rhyming words ("do" and "flew") in the poem, present each word's onset and rime parts (i.e., d-**o** and fl-**ew**). • Proceed similarly over the first three or four months with a variety of poems, songs, and predictable text books, as they become familiar.	• Comment that it is interesting to find rhyming words (or words that begin with the same sound) in poems and songs. Then move on to the next circle time activity. • If children repeat the words after you say them, comment: "Yes, *hop* and *stop* rhyme."
Children Identify Rhyming Words or Words that Begin with the Same Sound in Familiar Nursery Rhymes, Poems, Songs, and Predictable Text Books	• After three or four months, recite a poem or sing a song, as usual, then ask children to listen for rhyming words or words that begin with the same sound, as you recite some verses again. • Ask children to raise their hand if they hear words that rhyme (or start with the same sound, if this task is the day's focus). • Ask a child called on to say the words that rhyme (or begin with the same sound, if this is the focus). Provide detailed feedback.	• Use detailed responses, such as, "Yes, the words, *rocks* and *box*, do rhyme. Their last parts sound alike—r-**ocks** and b-**ox**." • Avoid saying, "Yes, Jonas. Those two words rhyme. Good job!" (See "Constructive teacher feedback" on p. 111.) *(Continued on p. 110)*

Circle Time Beginning Sound and Rhyming Word Activities (cont'd)

Activity	Feedback	Presentation
Blending and Segmenting Tasks		
Teacher Presents Phonemes for Children to Blend into Familiar Words	• Explain that to play a new game with sounds, you will say the name of something in a funny way—in little pieces—and then a child can say it "the right way" when called on. • Use a few picture cards, one at a time, to provide some examples (e.g., "If I said /d/-/o/-/g/, then one of you could say to me, 'You were saying dog'"). • After two to three examples, display three pictures at a time, name the items pictured (e.g., *dog, cat, hat;* or *sock, cup, spoon;* or *gate, coat, tree*), and then present sounds for the name of just one of them (e.g., /k/ -/a/- /t/; /k/- /a/-/t/). Call on a child to respond. Provide feedback. • Set up and name three more pictures. Present the individual phonemes for one item, as before, and let children guess. Provide detailed feedback. • Continue through three to four sets of pictures to present the sounds for three to four different words.	• After children respond, say the word again as presented ("Yes, /k/-/a/-/t/ are the sounds for the word, 'cat'"). • If a child says the name of another object pictured, such as "hat" instead of "cat," say, "Let me say the sounds again: '/k/-/a/-/t/; /k/-/a/-/t/.' What do you think?"
Teacher Presents Words in Pairs or in Triplets and Asks Children to Judge Words that Rhyme or Begin with the Same Sounds	• Tell children that you will say some words and they should tell you whether they do or do not start with the same sound (or do or do not rhyme, if that is the day's focus). • Provide a few examples (e.g., *boat* and *girl*, with feedback; then *doll* and *dig*, with feedback). • Continue with pairs of words for children to judge, and provide feedback. • After a month or two, present three words and ask children which two rhyme (or begin with the same sound, if that is the day's focus). Say the three words twice. Provide detailed feedback.	• "Right. **B**oat and **g**irl don't start with the same sound. **B**oat starts with /b/—**b**oat— and **g**irl starts with /g/-**g**irl. Yes, **d**oll and **d**ig both begin with /d/— **d**oll and /d/- **d**ig." • For incorrect responses (e.g., says that *top* and *boat* rhyme), say, "Mmm... t-**op**, b-**oat**. Their last parts—'op' and 'oat'—do not sound the same. They do not rhyme."
Teacher Asks Children to Help Think of Words that Begin with the Same Sound or that Rhyme	• Provide a target word and ask children to think of words that begin with the same sound (or rhyme with it, if that is the day's focus). • Provide examples to start: "**B**oat, **b**at, and **b**ug begin with the same sound—/b/—/**b**/oat, /**b**/ at, /**b**/ug." • Provide a target word and ask children to think of other words that begin with the same sound: "*Sink* starts with /s/, /**s**/ink. Can you think of other words that start with /s/ like /**s**/ink?"	• Provide examples, if children do not respond. For example, say, "Mmm. Do you think /**s**/oap starts with /s/ like /**s**/ink?" • Provide detailed feedback: "Yes, *sun* begins with /s/ like **s**ink, /s/ **s**un."

Constructive teacher feedback

Often, just a few children in a group can identify words that rhyme or have the same beginning sound. Children who do not respond usually *are* listening, but do not yet understand what they are to do in a specific task or cannot yet detect the sound unit on which the teacher has focused. Sometimes teachers respond to correct answers with only a general comment, such as, "Yes, you are right. *Rocks* and *box* rhyme." Informative feedback, in contrast, makes the features of a correct response obvious to *all* children in the group.

For example, a teacher might say, "Yes, *sand* and *sun* do begin with the same sound, /s/. Okay, I'll read some more lines of this poem, and you can raise your hand when I stop if you think you've heard any words that begin with the same sound." When children respond correctly, a teacher avoids empty talk, such as "Good job!" or "You are such a good listener" because it is completely uninformative. Instructional language, on the other hand, provides specific information that helps *all* children learn.

Phonological awareness tasks are opportunities for instruction, not "quizzes" or "tests." Asking, "*Who can tell* me which words rhyme (or begin with the same sound)?" or "*Who knows* which words rhyme," can suggest that children *should* already know. To suggest that these are opportunities *to learn*, a teacher can instead address task information to the whole group (e.g., "I'm going to recite this poem which all of you know, a few lines at a time. I'll stop and ask if anyone heard words that begin with the same sound. You can raise your hand if you think you heard any").

Print conventions and functions

As discussed in Chapter 1, ***print conventions*** are rules for organizing and using print. These rules specify that print appears and is read from a page in a specific direction and that spaces separate printed words in a sentence. Print conventions also include rules for the use of uppercase letters and lowercase letters, and a variety of punctuation symbols.

Children observe and learn about the convention for reading print from left to right, as teachers underline the titles of poems, songs, and books; when they read signs or lists to children; and when they write with children. The titles of some books, and the information on some charts, also provide opportunities to model sweeping back to the left to read multiple lines of print.

Teachers need not underline on poem and song charts, or in predictable text books, as they recite, sing, or read. Children should hear the beauty of the language in these forms, and underlining often distorts its natural rhythm and flow. If teachers underline all titles of items used daily, and underline directions on charts they use in small groups (e.g., planting a seed, making a food item), children will have adequate exposure to print conventions. Strategies for underlining titles, signs, and lists to help children learn both the direction in which print is accessed and about print and speech mapping are discussed in Table 5-2 "Strategies for Underlining Titles."

Table 5-2   Strategies for Underlining Titles

Because books and poems or song charts are used daily, their titles can be used in circle time or story time for teaching some print conventions. It is important to use effective strategies when underlining titles, and to change these over the course of a year as children's literacy skills increase. This table outlines some underlining techniques and their varying effectiveness in helping children acquire specific literacy skills.

Underlining Technique	Effectiveness
A general, "sweeping" gesture, aimed at a title. Uses no underlining.	Ineffective—only conveys the general idea that the teacher is reading the print.
Points to the middle of each word. Uses no underlining.	Ineffective—only conveys the general idea that the teacher is reading the print.
Underlines each word from left to right, as it is read. Reading is quite fast, as an adult might read when not in an instructional setting. Reading sometimes ends before the title has been completely underlined, or vice versa.	Reasonably effective—models the tracking of print from left to right, which helps children learn in which direction print is accessed. Useful for preschoolers who have little alphabet knowledge or phonological awareness (perhaps at the start of the school year).
Underlines each word from left to right, and at a slower pace than an adult normally reads when not in an instructional situation. Underlining coordinates print and the teacher's speech fairly well, although some mismatches exist.	More effective—allows children to observe a line of print more closely, and may lead them to notice space between clusters of letters (i.e., words) the teacher reads. Suitable for the middle months of a preschool year.
The teacher's finger lingers under the first letter of each word, as it is translated into sound, then underlines the remaining letters as the rest of the word is read. Underlining coordinates print almost perfectly with the teacher's speech. The title is read more fluently a second time, with underlining of each word without lingering on its first letter.	Most effective—specific, and can be used during the last three or four months of a preschool year when children know many letter names and have some phonological awareness. Some children will read along as a teacher uses this approach. Rereading the title a second time, after the more deliberate first reading, gives children another chance to read the title along with the teacher, and allows children to focus on its meaning.

Print functions refer to the many uses of print. In addition to learning about uses, children also learn that print is arranged differently in different contexts of use. For example, the headings on a menu do not resemble headings found in informational books, street signs differ from lists, and concert and theater programs differ from the paint chip booklets found at the hardware store. A telephone book differs from a cookbook, a greeting card differs from a poster, and airplane tickets differ from the number ticket we take to establish our place in a deli counter queue.

Preschoolers become familiar with many print functions as they observe print used for a variety of purposes, at home, in their neighborhoods, and in their classroom (e.g., observe classroom signs and charts, make cards for a family member or friend, add items to a teacher's list, make and use print props in dramatic play). (See Table 5-3 "Print Uses in a Preschool Classroom.")

Concluding thoughts about preschoolers and literacy skills

This chapter has provided an overview of literacy skills that are important for children's later success in learning to read and write, along with many suggestions for activities and instructional strategies to help children acquire literacy skills.

It is important to achieve balance in preschool programs and to do everything possible to develop children's interest in literacy activities. Without opportunities to use literacy skills as they are acquired, children's skill learning will be diminished, or worse, their interest in literacy skills might decline. Chapters 7 and 8 provide many examples of children's use of their developing literacy skills in play and other contexts.

Although literacy skills are important for children's later success in learning to read and write, we must always remember that children's long-term success depends on both literacy skills and on language and content learning. (See Chapters 3 and 4.) It is vital that preschool programs provide a good balance.

Table 5-3 Print Uses in a Preschool Classroom

Preschool teachers can use print for a variety of purposes to expose children to its many functions and forms.

Lists

Turns Lists in Centers	• Children write their names as best they can on turns lists available on clipboards in each center. • When a child asks, "When is it my turn?" the teacher might say, "Helen is using the easel now, and then Tyronne's name is next on the turns list. Your name follows his." • Children cross off their names, after taking their turn, and can notify the child whose name is next.
Shopping Lists	• As children and teachers notice that snack or other supplies are running low, they add items to the shopping list. • Children can attempt to write an item's name, using words on a printed list of typical supplies the teacher provides, or the teacher helps them spell the words.
Field Trip Item List	• The teacher can review the list of items he takes along—class list with the day's attendees checked, first-aid kit, bottle of water, and cups. • Though the teacher's responsibility, reading the list to children and pointing out each item teaches children about the required items and that lists are used for such purposes.
List-Related Props for Dramatic Play	• Emergency numbers (e.g., police, doctor, fire personnel) can be posted on the play refrigerator. • Include common items needed from the grocery store. Children can use these when preparing to go shopping. • Include examination items (blood pressure, temperature, heart and lung checking, ear and eye checking, and height and weight measuring) for doctor's office play. • Add food carton lists for children to take home when items are needed for grocery store play.

Labels

	• Place children's names on cubbies. Use uppercase for the first letter; lowercase for the rest. • Place names of items on both their containers and the shelves to help children know where items can be found and put away. • Write children's names on strips of paper to accompany artwork posted on bulletin boards.

Signs

- Use signs to indicate limits in areas, to ask children to "whisper please" in the book area, and to "walk please" down a hall.
- Create signs with the children to greet, welcome, and inform visitors (e.g., "Hello, Mr. Juarez. Rainbow classroom is this way").
- Help children create signs for the departments in a play grocery store (Figure 5-11), for "daily specials" in a play restaurant, and a sign saying "receptionist" for a play doctor's office.

Figure 5-11: A sign for a play grocery store.

Print Use in Play and on Play Materials

- Miniature commercial road signs for streets and highways made with blocks
- Child-created road and street signs (e.g., DETOUR, CHILDREN PLAYING, and CAUTION)
- Commercial wooden "toppers" for block buildings (Hospital, Post Office, Gas Station)
- Child-created block signs for neighborhood spots (Milo's Subs, Johnny's Neighborhood Market, Anna's Burritos)
- Commercial community figures (e.g., mail carrier's bag is labeled U.S. Mail) for block play
- Commercial vehicles with labels (Taxi, Police, Fire Truck, Ice Cream Truck, Ambulance)
- Road sign puzzles
- Storybook and nursery rhyme puzzles with titles the puzzle pieces depict
- Food cartons and grocery store ads from newspapers in house play area
- Children's books and magazines, and pamphlets for children (brushing teeth, eating good food, wearing seat belts) in doctor's office play area
- Cookbooks for chefs (teacher-created, laminated pages) and menus in restaurant play area
- Maps or an atlas, travel brochures, and a poster with arrival and departure times for train station or airport play area

Building a
Foundation
for Writing

PART II

6 What's Involved in Writing?

The understandings and skills that provide a foundation for reading also comprise a large part of what young children need for learning to write. Some additional knowledge and abilities also come into play, especially in the early years, when the physical act of writing can challenge a young child's fine motor skills.

This chapter provides a brief overview of the two main processes involved in writing—generating and organizing ideas (composing) and representing these meanings. Each process involves a number of understandings and skills. We also describe some milestones of writing development up through adolescence, and discuss major issues related to writing in preschool, kindergarten, and the early primary grades. These include the balance between code-related skills and meaning, the question of where drawing and talking fit into writing, and the amount of attention handwriting should receive.

Creating messages

Writers think about the message they want to communicate, sometimes putting it into oral form (talking it through) before they write it. This meaning-creation part of the writing process is called ***composing***.

Composing draws on the writer's content knowledge (i.e., knowledge of the physical, biological, and social world), understanding of different genres (e.g., fiction, nonfiction, lab report, friendly letter, note, sign), and language and cognitive skills. Planning is part of the composing process, and older writers often prepare an outline before they start.

The degree of challenge involved in composing depends, in part, on the message and its purpose. For example, a short note written to a friend about an upcoming meeting is far easier to compose than a short story or a persuasive essay. When the message is fairly complex (i.e., a story, an essay, a newspaper column), writers usually rework their message several times before it expresses well what they had intended. The reworking of drafts is called *revising*.

When revising, writers scrutinize a draft for accuracy, adequacy (e.g., "Is there enough detail and information?"), clarity (e.g., "Will a reader understand what I mean?"), and appeal (e.g., "Will my intended audience like this?"). Revising by mature writers is a complex process because they look for various problems (e.g., in meaning, sentence structure, and spelling). Once found, the problems must be repaired. Especially important for expert adult writers is skill in evaluating the meaning in their drafts. This requires some of the same skills that readers use to comprehend text (Hayes 2000).

Representing messages

Of course, as writers compose a message, they represent it in some way. For some older preschoolers, school-age children, and adults, representation takes the form of written words, which requires knowing how to create and arrange symbols (i.e., alphabet letters/graphemes) to spell specific words. Language skills (i.e., syntactic and grammatical knowledge) then guide the writer in arranging her words into sentences. By the primary grades, children are also expected to place words on a writing surface, such as paper or a white board, according to established conventions (e.g., from left to right and from top to bottom, leaving space in between them, using uppercase and lowercase letters appropriately), and to use punctuation.

Younger, emergent writers (i.e., preschoolers, kindergartners) usually do not check to make sure their spelling is correct (Adams 1990). For one thing, because they are not yet reading, they have not inspected words carefully, which is how children become aware of the conventional spellings of most words. But even though unconventional, some young writers' spellings show that they know something about their language's basic spelling rules.

For example, when a child wrote a note to a friend near the end of kindergarten (Figure 6-1), he placed two vowels in the middle of *Dear*, an acceptable representation for tense vowel phonemes in some word contexts, but the wrong pair (*Deer*) for this word's standard spelling. Similarly, the child placed a vowel before 'ng' in the grammatical morpheme in *feeling*, but used a more literal spelling (*feeleang*) than the standard 'i.' Specifically, he chose two letters that are an acceptable representation for the tense vowel in this spot in some words (e.g., peat), even though it is not the standard spelling needed for the same sound in this particular word context.

Likewise, he spelled *better* with just one 't,' not two. He did include the 'e' between the 't' and 'r,' which indicates an understanding of the requirement that each syllable have a vowel. Or, if he did not know this specific English spelling rule, he knew that he had never seen the consonants 'tr' in this sequence at the end of a word, but instead had always seen another kind of letter (vowel) in between them. He might have guessed which one to use. The words *I*, *you*, *are*, and *love* were all spelled correctly, which illustrates that young children learn many standard spellings from having seen them frequently, especially as they are learning to read.

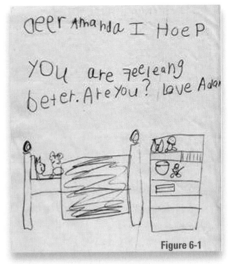

Figure 6-1

Phases of writing development

We can think of writing development in terms of three major phases: (1) emergent, (2) beginning conventional, and (3) more mature conventional. Developing skill in writing takes years. The timeframes for these phases are rough approximations, not sharply delineated stages. There is also considerable development *within* each phase.

Emergent writing

The emergent phase starts around 1 year of age and continues through kindergarten and into first grade (Figure 6-2). There is a world of difference, of course, between an emergent writer who is a toddler and one who is a preschooler, and also between a preschooler and a kindergartner, and a kindergartner and a first-grader. For example, in the early part of the emergent phase, infants and toddlers make marks, but just to explore mark making and the tools used, for their own sake, not to represent messages. The preschool and kindergarten child, in contrast, draw and label pictures that represent objects and events, write their names, and also use scribble writing and mock words (i.e., letter strings that look like words, but are not actual words) to create grocery lists, notes to friends, and signs for block buildings. An older first-grader also spells more words correctly than a kindergartner, invents others that closely resemble their conventional spelling (Figures 6-2c and 6-2d), and separates words by a space (Figure 6-2d).

There are also major differences in the complexity of messages created by younger emergent writers, compared to older ones. Although older toddlers sometimes name scribble drawings after having created them, they have relatively little to say beyond the label. By 4 years of age, children typically set out to draw with intention (i.e., to represent something), and they use details that help convey their meanings. They might also add some scribble or mock word writing to "tell" their message, although they use oral language to relate much of their meaning, and an adult sometimes writes down what they say.

Seventeen-month-old's scribble.

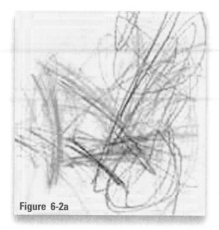

Figure 6-2a

Four-year-old's name used to sign his picture.

Figure 6-2b

Picture with writing ("This kind of dinosaur feeds on trees"). Convention of using space in between words is not used.

Figure 6-2c

Older first-grader's thank-you note to his father, with spaces separating words.

Figure 6-2d

The emergent period of writing can be divided into three sub-phases:

1. **Pre-Representational:** Marks are not intended to convey a message (see Chapter 7).

2. **Intentional Representation with Multiple Symbol Systems:** Marks convey meaning. Scribble or mock words are added to "help" represent meaning, but children convey much of their meaning orally, because neither their drawing nor their writing conveys as much as they wish to express (see Chapter 8).

3. **Intentional Representation with More Balanced Symbol Systems:** Children's drawings convey more of their meaning. Marks intended as writing are more letter-like in form, and creatively spelled words are often readable. Talking about drawings and writing to explain what they "say," is still extremely important for older preschoolers and kindergartners, and also for first-graders, because their full meaning is sometimes hard to convey with

only drawing and writing. By late in the preschool years, many children can represent some simpler meanings with writing marks, alone (e.g., "I love you," grocery list in scribble writing or mock words) (see Chapter 8).

Beginning conventional

From kindergarten through third grade, writing and drawing are almost always intentional (i.e., convey intended meanings). Kindergarten and primary grade children also create more complex messages than preschoolers, and begin to use features that distinguish one genre from another (e.g., stories versus informational text) (Duke & Kays 1998). First-graders, compared to preschool and kindergarten children, also begin thinking more about the content of their writing, and often use sentence forms and content from familiar books (Dahl & Freppon 1995).

Yet, first grade writers are still quite spontaneous—they do not engage in extensive planning before beginning (Graves 1981). They talk a bit about what they are going to write and also talk *as* they write and draw (Cioffi 1984). Moreover, if a message includes several ideas, first-graders formulate each in the moment (i.e., each is an "add-on"). They do not revise the whole as they think of new ideas.

The first grade child forms alphabet letters fairly well. Handwriting skill increases over the primary years and becomes more automatic (i.e., children form letters without thinking much about it). First- and second-graders develop considerable skill in spelling, and acquire more knowledge about punctuation and the appropriate uses of uppercase and lowercase letters. Much of this learning comes from reading.

As children gain skill in these writing mechanics, they can devote more time and energy to thinking about what they will write. But although first and second grade children have considerable skill in creating written words, they still use drawings to represent some of their meanings. Kindergartners and first-graders, in particular, still need to use oral language to communicate much of their meaning.

More mature writing

As language skill, knowledge, and spelling and other technical skills increase, a writer's messages increase in length and depth, and the words used to convey messages increase in specificity. In fact, a good vocabulary is as important for writing as for reading, if not more so (Johnson 2000). Good instructional support for writing also includes vocabulary development (Kelley et al. 2010). For example, when reviewing a draft of an autobiography with a second-grader, the teacher might discuss word use, such as when several words are used where one higher-level word would capture the meaning. For example, a teacher might say, "Right here, you've said, 'I like soccer better than baseball, basketball, or hockey. I like soccer more than any other sport.' For the second sentence, you could say, 'Soccer is my *favorite* sport.' Just that one word would express 'more than any other sport' all by itself."

As children progress through school, they craft sentences to express increasingly complex relationships, and they write more clearly and with more coherence. They also think more specifically about the intended audience and gradually develop skill in writing for a wider range of purposes. Children's writing progress is enhanced if they receive helpful feedback from teachers and peers.

Effective early childhood practices

Unfortunately, research shows that the majority of high school students in the U.S. are not proficient writers (Achieve, Inc. 2005; Persky, Daane, & Jin 2003; Salahu-Din, Persky, & Miller 2008). One misstep in U.S. education followed from the publication of the "Report of the National Reading Panel" (National Reading Panel 2000). This happened because research on writing did not clearly show effects on reading skill development, and the panel's report did not recommend writing practices as a strategy for supporting reading development. As schools tried to make language arts instruction "scientifically based," writing was often neglected. Now that the Common Core State Standards for the English Language Arts (National Governors Association Center for Best Practices, Council of Chief State School Officers 2010), which include writing, have been adopted by all but a handful of states, we will likely see improvement in children's writing.

There are many things that early childhood teachers can do to help children get off to a good start. We highlight some of the ways to help, along with some pitfalls to avoid. Chapters 7 and 8 will discuss specific writing-related information and strategies more fully.

Read to young children

Reading to children, starting in infancy, helps children develop language and become familiar with different forms of written discourse. Children also learn a lot about people and the natural world from books, especially when adults engage children in conversation about them.

Expose children to a range of purposes for writing

Young children benefit from seeing writing used for a wide variety of purposes (e.g., menus, lists, signs, greetings, stories, poetry, labels). They can use scribble writing and mock letters and words for many of these purposes, in house pretend play (e.g., making a grocery list, leaving a note for a babysitter), in play in the block area (e.g., signs for buildings and streets), and when making a card for an absent friend or creating a drawing and note for the teacher at the writing center. (See Figure 8-5 in Chapter 8.)

Using writing for these purposes is highly motivating to young children no matter their level of skill (e.g., scribble, mock letters, mock words). If we confine preschoolers' writing to set tasks, such as alphabet letter and name writing, we stifle their motivation to write and severely limit their opportunities to learn.

Provide mark-making experiences early

Early mark-making experiences gradually lead to the creation of pictures and scribble writing, to which children attribute meaning. Because the physical form of a young child's representations does not give others access to its meaning, very young children relate meanings orally. Early marking provides a wonderful opportunity for adults to talk with children about their meanings.

Talk with children about their writing and drawing

As adults talk with young children about their drawings and writing, they learn not only about oral language, but also about message creation (e.g., how much detail to include, how to organize messages). When adults prompt children to tell more, it helps to develop their narrative skills (Peterson & McCabe 1994).

Keep the focus on meaning

Of course, preschoolers begin to learn how to form alphabet letters, link letters to sounds, and use various print conventions. But if code-based and handwriting skills are the primary focus in the early years, while meaning is given little attention, children are not served well for the long run. It is important for early childhood teachers to keep a primary focus of writing on meaning, and on communicating it, rather than focusing mostly on code-related and handwriting skills. Experiences in the early years must be balanced.

Understanding the young child's approach to representing meaning

Dyson (2000) and Genishi and Dyson (2009) point out that young children, including first- and second-graders, have several well-established ways of conveying meaning, before they can use writing well for this purpose. For example, they engage in pretend play, draw, use gestures, and talk. Of course, young children are more comfortable using these forms, instead of writing, to convey their meanings. Although it takes years for children to develop skill in handwriting and spelling, they try to express complex meanings from very early in life. It's important to keep meaning afloat in these early years, and not focus narrowly on requiring children to represent ideas only in writing, or to include writing with all of their pictures. For example, when a 3-year-old boy drew a fairly detailed picture of a lady in a green hat, he told a lot about it, but did not add writing to the picture. His teacher accepted his oral commentary and did not ask him to add any writing (Figure 6-3).

Figure 6-3. "This is a lady with a green hat and polka dot eyes and nose, and a mouth."

The challenge for early childhood teachers is to help children acquire skill in using written forms of communication, while also maintaining and nurturing their skill in communicating mean-

ings through pretend play, drawing, and talking. Doing this requires giving children freedom to use multiple means to represent and convey meaning (e.g., drawing, writing, talking), and accepting writing as a somewhat minor player in the communication of meaning, for a while.

As a start, early childhood teachers can do more than ask children to label their drawings (e.g., "What is it?") and then move quickly to saying, "Let me write that down" (e.g., "This is a bird's nest"). Learning that "we can write down what we say" is easy for children, and fairly trivial in the grand scheme of things, especially when the teacher elicits only a few labels. If we ask a child first to "tell me about your picture" and he says, "It's a bird's nest," we can ask, "Did you see a bird's nest somewhere?" to prompt him to provide more information. A teacher can then ask a second follow-up question after the child responds, to keep the conversation going, if the child seems interested.

Far better for the child in the long run to talk more about what she means, and worry less about writing it down. Far better too, if the teacher writes down messages for young children, rather than expect them to write complex meanings by themselves. While there is a time and a place for expecting independence in action, pushing independence too soon in some realms stifles what children are willing to think and say, because representing it by themselves is overwhelming.

Concluding thoughts about writing

Early childhood teachers can open up various means of symbolizing and communicating for young children if they provide ample opportunities for pretend play, block building, and drawing, painting, and writing. Notably, the Common Core State Standards for the English Language Arts, K-6 (National Governors Association Center for Best Practices, Council of Chief State School Officers 2010) recognize the importance of drawing and dictating messages in the kindergarten-level writing standards. Preschool teachers can certainly follow suit.

Good preschool programs nurture a balance, tipped at first toward the development of meaning and the use of multiple symbolic strategies (i.e., drawing, talking, and writing) to represent them. To nurture their writing, teachers and parents must provide children with many opportunities and sufficient time, and must interact and assist in numerous ways, all along the way. Chapters 7 and 8 provide many examples of how early childhood teachers and parents might do this.

7 Babies and Toddlers Leave Their Mark

When he was 12 months old, Adam's mother touched the tip of a washable, nontoxic black marker to a piece of paper that was taped to his high chair tray a couple of times before handing it to him. For about five minutes, he made and inspected marks. He seemed fascinated by the marker. He touched it once to the tip of his index finger, and looked astonished when he saw dots of ink. Twice, he turned the marker around to try its other end. After finding no trace of its path on his paper, he returned to using the tip. Adam also made a few marks with a brown crayon. His mom watched closely, thinking he might take a bite of it, but he did not, probably because the visual effects he created held his attention (Figure 7-1a.)

Prior to marking on paper, Adam had marked with his fingers in pureed peas and carrots, on his high chair tray. Washable orange finger paint provided a similar experience for 10-month-old Alex (Figure 7-1b).

A rationale for early marking experience

Although many adults share books with very young children, and considerable research has focused on it (see Chapter 2), marking experiences are provided less frequently to very young children and have been studied very little (see Rowe 2008).

Adam's marks on paper.

Figure 7-1a

Alex's marks in finger paint.

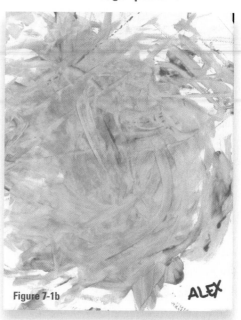

Figure 7-1b

ALEX

A classic book about young children's artwork (Kellogg & O'Dell 1967) starts with samples from 2- and 3-year-olds, a whole year older than the children whose samples we share in this chapter. A more recent book by language researchers, Hirsh-Pasek and Golinkoff, includes paintings and drawings created by children as young as 10 months of age (*Celebrate the Scribble*, 2007).

Books advising about play materials have traditionally rarely suggested paintbrushes, markers, or crayons for children under 3 years of age, because their fine motor skills are still developing and they do not use these materials for representation (e.g., Hughes 1999). But we talk to babies who cannot yet understand what we say, knowing that language understanding and skill emerge only out of this experience. The same principle applies to mark-making. Moreover, a toddler's fine motor skills are plenty good enough to make marks with tools and to learn from the process. A whole world of learning about movement and its effects on tools is possible long before babies and toddlers ever use marks to represent anything.

Consider also that most babies begin exploring a spoon at mealtimes a few months before their first birthday (Gesell & Ilg 1937). Although *skilled* spoon use comes many months later, infants start taking account of the effects of their actions on a spoon, and constantly adapt to make it work better (Connolly & Dalgleish 1989). Mark-making provides a unique opportunity for learning because, unlike other object exploration, it creates permanent visual effects.

This chapter focuses on mark-making in children from 10 or 12 months of age to about 30 months. It chronicles physical mark-making (i.e., what shows up on the paper) and the emergence of the child's insight that lines and designs can represent ideas (i.e., can convey meaning). In addition to this primary focus, this chapter includes information about the vast amount of learning that takes place during infancy and toddlerhood. This learning comprises the cognitive, social, emotional, and language foundations that affect the content of young children's drawing and writing, for years to come.

Babies' actions on objects and the use of marking tools

Early mark-making is a motor, visual, and tactile delight, and infants also take account of the effects of their movements. Indeed, physical actions and thinking are closely intertwined in the young child (Bartlett 1958).

But before we describe the very young child's marking behavior, we summarize some research about babies' learning from physical object manipulation to illustrate how observant babies are about objects and their properties, and how they vary their actions in response. This information provides some background about the knowledge and skill that very young children bring to mark-making, and also indicates the potential contributions of mark-making to early learning.

What the baby and toddler bring to this experience

Throughout much of the first year, infants handle objects and adapt their behavior in response to feedback the objects provide. Here are some examples:

- ▲ **4 months:** Move objects held toward the mouth, more and more, if objects are mouthable (i.e., will fit); move objects to mouth less, if they are not (Rochat 1989).

- ▲ **6 months:** Feel bumpy objects more and mouth them less, and do the opposite with smooth objects (Ruff 1984). Mouth objects more if they don't make sound, and less, if they do (Morgante & Keen 2008; Palmer 1989).

- ▲ **6 months:** Begin to adapt actions on objects to features of surfaces. Bang objects more on a bare table than on a padded or liquid surface (Bourgeois et al. 2005; Palmer 1989), and bang them more on bare floors than on floors covered with carpet (Morgante & Keen 2008).

- ▲ **8 or 9 months:** Bang rigid objects more and squeeze them less, and squeeze pliable objects more and bang them less (Bushnell & Boudreau 1993).

- ▲ **6 to 12 months:** Decrease the mouthing of objects they hold, and look at and manipulate them more (Rochat 1989).

Mark-making provides a new context for learning

Babies and toddlers can also learn a lot about mark-making tools and substances, for example, that crayons must be applied with relatively more pressure than pencils, markers, or pens, and that markers leave wet marks with only a touch of their tip. In contrast, chalk is dry, smears on paper, and leaves dust on fingers. Babies and toddlers also learn that a paintbrush must be dipped into paint, and that paint drips from it, but that the writing substances are already part of other marking tools.

Of course, toddlers could injure themselves with a pencil or pen, if permitted to walk around with one. And toddlers certainly will decorate walls and furniture, if given the chance. For these reasons, adults provide safe contexts and supervise babies and toddlers as they explore with marking tools. With that said, they are ready to begin.

Chara sits at the kitchen table using her mother's pen and notebook, which she had requested after noticing her mother use them.

Early mark-making phases

Early mark-making phases are not sharply delineated stages, but rather, time periods indicating roughly when babies and toddlers acquire new behavior. The first two phases involve exploration without any representation. Babies and toddlers become fascinated with and delighted by what *they* can "make happen." The third phase includes some representational behavior, although children do not yet approach paper intending to create anything specific. Still, they sometimes now attribute meaning to their marks, after making them.

Phase 1: Whatever happens, happens

Between about 10 to 12 and 18 to 20 months of age, children's facial expressions suggest astonishment at what they see, as if surprised by and in awe of the traces *their* fingers leave. They often make many marks in these explorations, and look closely at them.

Several examples of early markings by Livi (12 months), Adam (14 months), and Chara (14 months) are shown in Figure 7-2. Livi marked on a piece of lined paper she requested from her mother's pad (Figure 7-2a). Adam used ballpoint pen, pencil, and red crayon (Figure 7-2b); and Chara used several markers of different colors while sitting in her high chair (Figure 7-2c).

Children love mark-making, and often request the paper, pens, and pencils they spot in others' hands. Adults find it difficult to write within sight of an infant—she wants the materials!

Markings by Livi, Adam, and Chara.

Figure 7-2a

Figure 7-2b

Figure 7-2c

Phase 2: Controlling and contrasting marks

Within a few months of starting to explore marking, children begin to repeat a specific kind of mark, sometimes in ways that contrast it with another kind in the same drawing. This behavior is seen as early as 16 or 17 months of age, and usually no later than 20 to 24 months, in children who have marked frequently from about 1 year of age.

At 16 months, Chara created a patch of dots (Figure 7-3a), which she separated from the other scribble on her paper. Much later, at 28 months, she often scribbled with abandon on one part of her paper, and created controlled C-like marks in parts separated from the scribbles. Sometimes, in response to Chara's request for words, her mother wrote Chara's name and other words that begin with C (Figure 7-3b), and named the letters. This behavior might have sparked Chara's interest in making Cs when she scribbled (Figure 7-3c).

Chara's marks at 16 and 28 months.

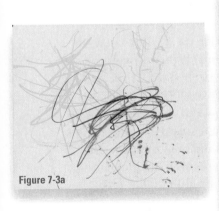

Figure 7-3a

Figure 7-3b

Figure 7-3c

Grayden began controlling marks on a whiteboard/chalkboard easel when about 22 months of age. Sometimes, he even approached the surface with specific forms in mind. He labeled the marks in one session (Figure 7-4a) "spirals," and those in another "round and round" (lower left) and "dot, dot, dot, dot" (Figure 7-4b).

Interestingly, Grayden's father, an artist, sometimes drew for and with Grayden, showing him specific forms and naming them. Chara's mother, an early childhood teacher, wrote words and named letters for Chara. The children picked up specific forms from their parents. Thus, Grayden created and named line forms, while Chara created and named Cs.

Grayden's spirals and other marks.

Figure 7-4a

Figure 7-4b

Several of Adam's line contrast markings appear in Figure 7-5. In the first and second examples (Figures 7-5a and 7-5b), Adam clearly separated contrasting lines, circular and straighter back and forth lines, and vertical and horizontal lines, respectively. The exploration shown in Figure 7-5b even suggests that he conducted a little study to compare two kinds of mark.

But at this time, Adam mostly just *used* contrasting lines for effect. For example, he made circular scribbles with a pencil one day, and then added more circular marks on top of those, using a red crayon. Finally, he made several bold, red, vertical lines, on top of the whole mass of scribbles (Figure 7-5c).

At 20 months, Adam deliberately repeated a specific kind of mark, after creating it first, accidently, amid several small circular marks (Figure 7-6). He knew the shape and name of G from having asked for names of letters on the refrigerator and the rim of his baby dish. When he spotted the G-like designs, he said, "a G!" as if surprised. Then, he made two more, announcing, "'Nother G; 'nother one."

While drawing at 24 months, Sydney started with large, red, free-flowing circular scribbles, to which she added smaller shapes with a blue marker (some closed and reversed curves). Then, she made an S, in the left middle of her paper—her first one ever (Figure 7-7a). Three months later, Sydney separated distinct circular marks from patches of scribbles (Figure 7-7b). She said the tight circular forms were Os, the first letter in *Owen*, her cousin's name.

Adam's contrasting lines at 16 months.

Figure 7-5a

Adam's contrasting lines at 22 months.

Figure 7-5b

Adam's bold, vertical lines at 21 months.

Figure 7-5c

Children's control over their marks increases as they continue exploring with marking tools. But we see already the beginnings of both control and intention, when children repeat a form they accidentally made (Adam's Gs), or deliberately make several specific marks (Grayden's spirals; Sydney's Os). In these instances, the child adapts his movement to create a specific form. Without a doubt, babies and toddlers are remarkable learners!

Phase 3: Attributing meaning to marks

Beginning between 20 and 24 months of age, toddlers sometimes attribute meaning to their marks, when initially random marks coalesce, by chance, into forms that resemble familiar objects. This behavior occurs infrequently for a few months, and then increases.

Adam's Gs at 20 months.

Figure 7-6

While drawing at 22 months, Adam announced, "A man... mouth and eyes!" (Figure 7-8a). His surprise indicated that he had not intended to draw something in particular. In fact, he had just completed another drawing (Figure 7-8b) to which he did not attribute meaning, even though it contained marks and shapes similar to those in the "man, mouth, and eyes" piece. Apparently, the marks in the previous drawing (Figure 7-8b) did not remind Adam of anything, while the arrangement of the marks in the second one (Figure 7-8a) did.

Adam also sometimes attributed meaning to paintings (Figure 7-9), but not until several months after having done this with drawings. Perhaps paint invites children to make large spots of color and fewer defined shapes and designs, especially

Sydney's S at 24 months.

Figure 7-7a

Sydney's Os at 27 months.

Figure 7-7b

Adam's drawings with and without attribution of meaning.

Figure 7-8a

Figure 7-8b

when the brush used is fairly wide. We found no research about this, but wonder whether drawing with markers, crayons, pens, and pencils elicits more attributions of meaning than does painting, and whether adults more often request a child to "Tell me about this" when she draws, compared to when she paints.

Sometimes older toddlers add a bit of detail to a drawing that has reminded them of something, perhaps to increase the similarity between their scribbles and the object the scribbles suddenly brought to mind. For example, 31-month-old Livi added rocks to the right side and the base of her mountain, after having seen in her scribbles the likeness of a volcano (Figure 7-10).

At 27 months, after creating some straight and curved lines, seemingly without any deliberate intention, Sydney looked at her paper and said, "This is an X and

Adam's snakes.

Livi's volcano with rocks added.

Figure 7-9

Figure 7-10

this is a rainbow" (Figure 7-11a). Then, on a second piece of paper, she deliberately recreated the same kinds of lines. When finished, she told her mom, "This is an X and this is a rainbow again" (Figure 7-11b). It seems that after having seen some meaningful objects in one of her scribble drawings, Sydney realized that she didn't need to wait for forms to coalesce, by chance, on each occasion of scribbling, but instead could make things happen.

Interestingly, a book about colors that Sydney's parents had recently read to her included a picture of a rainbow. Her parents had also named X and other letters as Sydney played with letters on the refrigerator and in other contexts.

At about this age, children start using one object to represent another in pretend play, even when the object selected bears little resemblance to the one represented. Prior to 2 years of age, children do not make such substitutions, but use small replicas of the actual object instead, or other objects with similar features (see Box 7-1 "Milestones in Children's Pretend Play Behavior" for information about pretend play development, and its connection to writing).

The onset of this mental flexibility—and perhaps also a new insight that drawings, unlike photos, need not be realistic—allows the child to see more now in the organization of marks than was possible just a few months earlier. There are probably social influences, as well, as adults show interest in children's drawings and paintings, and comment and question (e.g., "Tell me about your drawing" or "Oh, what did you make?").

Some approaches to inquiring are less demanding (e.g., "Tell me about it") than others (e.g., "What did you make?"). A third approach is to share an interpretation,

Sydney notices an X and a rainbow and makes them again.

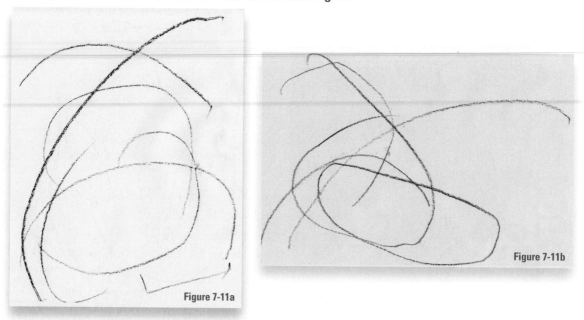

Figure 7-11a

Figure 7-11b

Box 7-1 Milestones in Children's Pretend Play Behavior

Children begin to pretend at about 12 months of age, but their pretending is at first very simple. Over the next two to three years, pretending changes dramatically. Pretend play requires *object substitution*—the attribution of meaning to one object used to stand for another (e.g., use of a stick as a fishing pole, or a cube as a cup). **This is a symbolic (i.e., representational) activity, akin to a child giving meaning to marks on paper.**

When pretending becomes sociodramatic (i.e., pretending that you are someone and coordinating your role with other players' roles), it requires thinking about others' thinking (e.g., what they know, how they feel, what their goals are). **These are the same kinds of considerations required when comprehending a story or when creating one.**

The milestones for pretending provided here indicate the major shifts in pretend play over the course of the infant, toddler, and preschool years.

- **Prior to 10 months:** No pretending (Fenson et al. 1976). Explores objects separately, not functionally (e.g., bangs pot lid on floor, mouths its edge, and hits it with a hand, but does not put it on top of the cooking pot).

- **10–12 months:** Uses objects meaningfully (e.g., puts lids on pots, cups on saucers, and spoons in bowl), but does not pretend (e.g., does not pretend to take a bite of food from the spoon, or stir in the bowl as if mixing food) (Bretherton 1984; Fenson et al. 1976).

- **12–13 months:** Simple pretending. Mimics own ordinary actions (e.g., pretends to sleep when they are not; pretends to take a drink from an empty cup). Does not include others in pretend; materials must be real or replicas (McCune-Nicolich 1981).

So Much More than the ABCs

such as "Oh, this big splash of blue here in the middle of your painting makes me think of the pond where we visit the ducks." In this case, the adult indicates that marks *can* convey meaning and that people are likely to interpret a child's drawings, while not suggesting that the adult's interpretation is what the child intended or that the child should portray something specific all the time.

It is always appropriate and helpful to children for adults to talk with them as they draw and paint. Consider the rich information adults can provide, as illustrated by these examples:

▲ "Oh, the paint isn't food. We don't eat paint. (Child had licked a painted finger.) Does the paint remind you of mushy food you have on your high chair tray sometimes?"

▲ "Oh, I think you made a new color, right there (points to). You mixed the red and blue paint together. That spot looks purple to me."

▲ "Maybe you can slap the paint softly like this (demonstrates). The paint splatters in our faces when you slap it hard like that. We don't want paint in our eyes."

▲ "When you put your hand down like this (demonstrates with own hand on a blank space on the paper), it makes a print of your hand."

Notice that these are not demanding comments—a child would not feel compelled to respond. Thus, they would not disrupt the child's own activity. Moreover,

- **13–15 months:** Begins to direct play actions toward others (e.g., pretends to feed parent or doll; pretends that doll is asleep) (Fein 1984; Fenson & Ramsay 1980).

- **20–24 months:** Combines several distinct behaviors into a connected series (e.g., feeds the doll, pushes doll in stroller, puts doll to bed). Uses objects that are not replicas, if they have similar features. Begins to use actions not yet performed in real life, but observes others perform (e.g., pretends to cook in a pot or reads to a doll). Begins to animate dolls (e.g., makes them talk, puts spoon in their hand) (Fenson 1984; Fenson & Ramsay 1980).

- **26–30 months:** Begins to use objects that do not closely resemble the object pretended (e.g., a cube as a cup, although lacking an essential feature—a cavity) (Fein 1975).

- **30 months:** Pretends to be someone else. Indicates they are "in role" by tone of voice, or states role verbally (e.g., "I am Elmo's Mommy") (Dunn 1998).

- **30 months:** Manages the play of two characters—self and a doll (e.g., the toddler is the Daddy, the doll is a baby; the child puts both "in role") (Goncu 1998). Uses more and more language of roles played (e.g., to a doll baby, "It's good. Eat" and "Go to sleep now"), and tells others what they are playing (e.g., "I am the Mommy" and "I'm going shopping") (Fenson 1984).

- **30–48 months:** Learns to coordinate own role play with roles of other players (Bretherton 1984; Goncu 1998).

- **48 months:** Resists using objects with specific known functions as substitutes for other objects, but increases flexibility in using non-specific objects to represent objects in play (Ungerer et al. 1981).

the comments about the use of the materials provide reasons for changing behavior, rather than simply telling a child "No! Stop that!"

Making mark-making experiences accessible to babies and toddlers

Children can create markings at home or in a group setting, when the environment is organized for these experiences. Here, we describe a variety of effective strategies to foster babies' and toddlers' early marking by using particular materials or set-ups.

High chair opportunities

A baby's first opportunities to mark with fingers will likely occur on the high chair tray, as he enjoys a meal or a snack. As Hirsh-Pasek and Golinkoff note in *Celebrate the Scribble*, "The high chair becomes a canvas and baby foods the paints…. It's all about the feel—truly high touch instead of high tech" (2007, 8). These language researchers advise, "Don't rush to clean up that mess; there's potential in those mashed potatoes."

We agree, although we also understand that caregivers cannot always replicate the leisurely pace of a child's eating and playing in a high chair at home in a setting where care and attention must be given to more than one baby at a time. Potential benefits of the baby's exploration of soft foods might still be realized in group settings by having one caregiver attend to a table with seating suitable for a few babies who are this age.

Babies between 12 and 14 months often enjoy finger paint or markers. A bit of finger paint can be placed directly on the table, in front of each child's place, and a print of it can be made, if desired, by using easel paper. Parents might enjoy seeing these, although babies just enjoy the process of squishing the finger paint and smearing it all around, and sometimes making marks with their fingers.

Always offer markers without their caps on, because caps present a choking hazard. Use masking tape to secure paper to the table.

Easel opportunities

By 2 years of age, children can easily stand at a toddler-size easel to paint. Place a small amount of paint in two or three open cups. Put a brush in each cup, or provide just one, knowing that toddlers usually use the first brush they pick up to dip into other paint cups, even when each has its own brush. Toddlers don't care that the colors become mixed.

Caregivers should expect that toddlers will touch both the bristles of the brush and the wet paint they apply to the paper, to feel the paint. This is all part of their exploration. Special chubby brushes are not necessary. Toddlers can grasp a thinner one just fine, if not better. It is a good idea, however, to choose brushes with shorter rather than longer handles, because these are easier for a toddler to manipulate.

Children can also finger paint at an easel. Provide finger paint paper, not easel paper, or run some large sheets of white paper through the laminating machine, and hang these panels on an easel to create a finger painting surface. Place the finger paint in shallow cups in the easel tray. Children just dip their fingers into the paint, and away they go!

When a child is finished exploring with the finger paint on a lamination film panel, a caregiver can make a print of his markings using a sheet of easel paper, and then wipe the film's surface a bit before the next child's turn. The child who has finished can wash his hands at a sink before a caregiver helps him remove his painting smock.

Water table and other places to finger paint

Toddlers can also explore finger paint in clear plastic tubs designed for water play. The gel type of paint works best here, because it dissolves more easily when the tub is washed. Place just a small amount of two or three colors in the water tub for children to smear around its bottom and sides.

Stands are available for the sand and water table tubs, thereby creating a good place for children to finger paint. Place a color of finger paint in the tray that contrasts with the tray's color, so that it will show up on the tray's surface.

Activity table opportunities

It's best to not place pencils, markers, and crayons out on shelves in a writing/drawing center in a toddler classroom, because it is unsafe for toddlers to walk around with these items in their hands. Instead, place the materials at a table each time the activity is offered to toddlers and make sure an adult is there continuously to supervise.

It is also far better for toddlers to place a few marking tools in a small flat tray, at each place on the table, rather than in sets, in cans or plastic containers, as is customary in preschool classrooms, because toddlers have trouble pulling one marker or crayon out of a cup or can, without tipping the whole thing over. Or they just dump them all out on the table rather than try to select one. Toddlers need only two or three markers, crayons, or colored pencils, not a full set.

Box 7-2 Technology & Mark-Making

Kathleen A. Paciga

In today's world, children need to develop digital literacy. Children can begin to learn about digital tools (e.g., tablets, computers, navigation systems) at an early age when the physical environment allows exploration (Labbo et al. 1996; Roskos et al. 2011) and adults supervise and scaffold the interactions (Labbo 2009; Turbill 2001).

As noted in Chapter 2, both the American Academy of Pediatrics (AAP) and NAEYC discourage all screen media for children under 2 years of age and recommend only one to two hours per day for children older than 2 years (AAP 2011; NAEYC & Fred Rogers Center for Early Learning and Children's Media 2012). This concern relates to children's *independent* use of screen-based technology. Several examples of developmentally appropriate screen-based technologies for children 12 to 24 months of age are provided here. In all cases, these experiences are shared with an adult caregiver in ways similar to traditional marking experiences, and thus can be rich in descriptive language (NAEYC 2009; Takeuchi 2011; Takeuchi & Stevens 2011).

In the sections that follow, both digital marking devices and some on-screen communication and coviewing experiences are discussed.

Digital mark-making: Devices and software

The many applications available for Apple and Android mobile devices are appropriate for use in family and early childhood settings when paints and other marking substances are not available or their use is not practical (Shuler 2009; 2012). Some technological devices and applications for very young children replicate traditional mark-making experiences. That is, the child can draw as she might with finger paint, but on a screen rather than on paper or a tabletop.

The advantages of technological devices include (1) a writing tool (i.e., fingers) that does not break, like crayons or chalk; (2) the absence of choking hazards, as might occur with marker caps or broken pieces of a crayon; (3) no requirement for cleaning up, as when using paint; and (4) the saving and sharing of young children's marks with a global community. But of course, because the child does not learn about various substances (e.g., paint, chalk, wet ink) from screen-based marking experiences, these experiences on technological devices should be provided only as an occasional supplement to traditional marking experiences.

Some of the digital mark-making experiences of my daughter, Annie, on an iPad when she was between 12 and 24 months of age, illustrate a variety of electronic drawing space experiences that mimic pens, pencils, markers, and paint.

Figure 7-12

- Doodle Buddy, a free application, allows children to finger paint, stamp (with sound effects), and type onto a blank canvas or on a variety of other backgrounds (for purchase). Many colors and marking tools are available (e.g., chalk, brush, glitter, smudge, and eraser), and the diameter of the tool's head can also be changed. At 18 months (Figure 7-12), Annie and I explored stamps and lines. She enjoyed the sound effect accompanying the water stamp, and the crying that accompanied the crying face, as she stamped the canvas. I drew yellow swirls (in marker format) with my finger and then encouraged Annie to pick a marker color. She chose purple and said, "Annie." I replied, "Oh! You want to write Annie? Okay. A-N-N-I-E. Annie." As I said the letters, she used her finger to write her name (purple lines). We also explored typing with the letters in the purple text box.

- Magic Marker HD is similar to the Doodle Buddy app (e.g., stamps, tool-size choices), but it also uses stamp heads as cut-out tools and allows the adult to insert a background photo behind a white or black drawing canvas. Thus, when a toddler drags the stamping tool across the canvas, a piece of it is cut out to reveal the background image. When Annie used this app at 23 months of age (Figure 7-13), she explored the orientation and size of the cutouts, especially with the frog. For example, she used the slider on the bottom of the screen to change the cutout size from small to large, and used the slider on the right of the cutout selector to change the orientation (head up, down, or sideways). She chose a background that was her puppy.

Figure 7-13

- Crayola's Color Studio HD (free version) has marking tools and colors, and utilizes tool bar icons similar to those in traditional computer programs. Its "new document," "undo," "redo," and "settings" buttons, which are used in programs and applications like Microsoft Word and Google Chrome and other Internet browsers, give young children early experience in identifying the meaning of these symbols and how they help a person accomplish a task. At 19 months, Annie brought the iPad to me and said, "Draw circles." I entered my passcode to access apps. After swiping the screen to find this app, Annie opened it, and then selected a marker and the color red (Figure 7-14). After she drew circles, I helped her compose an email message to accompany the picture, which we sent to Grandma. (See the next section.)

Figure 7-14

On-screen and coviewing experiences related to mark-making

Mobile devices and computers allow us to share and discuss both digital and print marks with a wide audience. Sharing is appropriate in both home and early childhood contexts. All of the marking software described above allows a screen shot of the marks and the sharing of the picture by email. The language-rich message creation experiences in which Annie and I engaged supported her message creation. All of these activities were language-rich, modeled description, and provided her an opportunity to describe what she saw on-screen.

- Emailing a screen shot of Annie's digital marks to daddy at work or to Grandma. I typed a comment about what she drew, as I talked with her about the message. The recipients always commented on Annie's marks when they saw her. These conversations sounded quite similar to conversations that occur around traditional marking creations as described in this chapter. When creating the email message for Annie's "circles" at 19 months (Figure 7-14), we typed, "Dear Grandma, Hope you like the 4 circles I drew for you. Love, Annie." Grandma replied, "Annie, what BEAUTIFUL purple and red circles! Thank you for sharing. Love, Grandma."

- Annie sometimes looked at herself and others on the screens of a computer, digital camera, and mobile phone (still and video images). We scrolled through digital photos and videos on the mobile phone while in doctors' waiting rooms, identifying people and talking about what they were doing, an experience similar to reviewing a paper photo album. In an early childhood setting, a teacher might review some digital photos of happenings during centers or free play. These photos could also be shared with parents, families, and so on, providing material for discussion at home that connects with the child's child care experience.

- Annie often saw a loved one on the other end of an online conversation (e.g., Skype for iPad or Apple's FaceTime). In one conversation, Annie shared marks she had made on paper by holding the paper up to the web camera.

- Sometimes, she looked at a blank computer screen and said, "Nana! Nana! Call." This behavior indicated her understanding that verbal communication with others is one use of a computer.

- We recorded Annie's voice, which she then heard coming from a mobile device. Many ebook apps (see Chapter 2) also have a voice recording function. For example, we used a *Pat the Bunny* ebook, which utilizes the iPad camera to put the child's image into the mirror. I then narrated the pages of the book, replicating an emergent reading experience, and used prompts, such as "Read this page" or "What happened here?" to encourage Annie's active participation. Similarly, *Don't Let the Pigeon Run This App!* allows children to create their own story about the pigeon. The bus driver prompts the child to select story features from a multiple-choice menu (e.g., snack, a stinky thing, what you don't want the pigeon to run, a number, a game) or to speak the story feature by tapping a giant record button. After the child selects and/or records the features of the story, an adult or older sibling can read aloud the story for the child using his or her selections/recordings.

Although these apps are useful to support mark-making, not all children have access to this technology (Common Sense Media 2011).

So Much More than the ABCs

Pencils, both plain and in colors, should be fairly short and have dull tips. Use hand-held sharpeners to create a short tip, then dull it by running it back and forth across a piece of paper. Thick diameter crayons or the chubby kind do not break as easily as thin crayons under the pressure applied by toddlers. Both thick and thin markers should be placed out without their caps, because toddlers usually cannot remove or replace them, and, most importantly, because, once off, they pose a choking hazard. If there is access to the technology, developmentally appropriate screen-based technologies provide excellent exposure to marking experiences with no choking hazards. (See Box 7-2 "Technology & Mark-Making.")

Paper will stay put as a young toddler draws on it, if it is anchored at its top and bottom with masking tape. Older toddlers learn how to use one hand to stabilize the paper, while drawing with the other. When a toddler is finished marking, a caregiver can write the toddler's name, while naming each letter made, as the toddler watches.

Message content in the making: A look inside the baby and toddler mind

Babies and toddlers are busy learning a lot about the physical, natural, biological, and social worlds. For example, they acquire knowledge about how objects in the physical world behave, about feelings and intentions, and about the differences between animate versus inanimate objects. They also learn to communicate with others and to pretend. Soon after this early period of mark-making, which we have just described, children begin to pull more and more from this foundation as they draw and write, and they use language more and more to tell others "all about it."

Although we can't do justice in a discussion here to all that children learn during the first two or three years of life, we try to give the reader some sense of how busy babies and toddlers are, not only in acting on the world physically, but also in observing and thinking about much that goes on around them. We don't see evidence of all the knowledge that very young children are building in their early markings or verbal expressions. Later, however, we see it in the content of pictures that preschool and older children draw and paint, and in what they tell and write about in stories or informational pieces. We discuss this knowledge acquisition here to fill out the picture of the learning during the infant and toddler years that contributes to aspects of writing other than mark-making.

Knowledge about the behavior of physical objects

During the first year of life, babies learn some rules that govern the behavior of objects in the physical world. For example, by 7 months, babies expect a box to fall off a table, if pushed far off the table's edge. In laboratory experiments, where researchers can prevent boxes in this position from falling by using a hidden prop, babies look a long time at such impossible events, because they know objects do not ordinarily behave in this way (Baillargeon, Needham, & DeVos 1992). Babies this age also show surprise (i.e., look longer) when a ball rolls up rather than down an inclined board (Kim & Spelke 1992) or when an object moving through the air stops and remains suspended, without anything appearing to holding it there (Spelke, Phillips, & Woodward 1995).

Within the first year, babies also learn about physical world cause and effect. For example, they learn how objects behave when other objects knock into them. Because babies are not yet talking, researchers must infer what they know and think from how long they look (i.e., longer when surprised/puzzled). Here's what babies figure out:

▲ **6 months:** Act surprised (i.e., look longer) when any object does not move when another object collides with it.

▲ **8 months:** Know that objects move longer and farther when the colliding object is larger rather than smaller (Baillargeon 1995; Kotovsky & Baillargeon 1994; 1998; 2000).

▲ **9 months:** No longer show surprise when tall, narrow objects don't move when hit. Babies learn from exploring while crawling that some tall narrow objects, such as table and chair legs, and poles between a railing and stairs, are attached and don't budge when pushed, pulled, or bumped into (Wang, Kaufman, & Baillargeon 2003).

▲ **10 months:** No longer show surprise when an unattached object doesn't move when hit. When crawling about, infants pull books off shelves, try to push heavy baskets of magazines, and manipulate various pots and pans. From this kind of experience, they learn that some items are hard to move—are heavy—while others are easy to move—are lighter (Wang, Kaufman, & Baillargeon 2003).

It is no wonder that toddlers painting at an easel return brushes to a cup or the easel tray, rather than release them into the air, and show no surprise when a hole appears in their paper after they have rubbed a paint-filled brush over and over it, but not in the easel frame behind it. It is also no wonder that, when preschoolers represent object relations and their actions, they know enough to make comments, such as, "The ball knocked into that wall (points to in his painting) and then landed over here (points to where it was deflected). It didn't hit a window, like my brother's ball did one time."

Categories of things

By 11 months, infants also know some specific behaviors and functions associated with many categories of things. For example, they are more likely to give a toy person a ride in a vehicle of any kind, than a ride on an animal. Conversely, they are more likely to put any kind of animal to bed, after seeing the researcher model this behavior, than to put vehicles to bed (Mandler & McDonough 1998; McDonough & Mandler 1998).

Between 7 and 9 months of age, when infants see actors on film perform actions, such as walking, jumping, or bending, they distinguish among the actions. Apparently they notice each action's unique features even in people who perform the actions somewhat differently (Pulverman et al. 2006). Later on, when drawing and painting, preschoolers and older children depict people in ways that portray these different actions, using this early understanding, and use the correct term (walk, bend, jump) for each action, as they tell about it, if adults have linked the specific terms to their respective actions.

Infants also begin very early to distinguish animate versus inanimate objects. For example, by 2 months of age they vocalize and smile more to a live person than to a doll (Legerstee 1992; Legerstee, Corter, & Kienapple 1990). By 6 months, they begin to realize that people behave differently toward animate versus inanimate things (Legerstee 1991), and that these two categories of things also behave differently.

For example, 7-month-olds look longer at a ball or a chair that appears to move spontaneously than at a person who moves, because they know that inanimate objects are *not* supposed to do this (Poulin-Dubois & Shultz 1990; Spelke, Phillips, & Woodward 1995). Similarly, 16-month-olds show no surprise when a dog or a person climbs stairs or jumps over a block in a movie, but are surprised (i.e., look longer) when a movie shows a car or a bus jumping over a wall (Poulin-Dubois & Forbes 2006).

Older infants also attribute intentions to humans (Myowa-Yamakoshi et al. 2011). For example, in one study, 18-month-olds saw either a human model or a mechanical model perform the very same action of placing beads beside a cup. When it was their turn to place the beads, toddlers who watched the human model put the beads *in* the cup, while toddlers who observed the mechanical model put the beads on the table, just as they had observed (Meltzoff 1995). Toddlers assumed that the human models intended to put the beads in a cup, but failed.

Knowing the typical behavior of things allows children later to create something funny in a drawing or a painting by violating typical behavior. This knowledge about animate versus inanimate things also allows preschoolers and older children to appreciate fiction without becoming terribly misinformed about the real world.

Building blocks of communication: Emotional expression and identification, emotional understanding, and empathy

Writing is communication—it's the expression of ideas and information using symbolic representation. Here, we look at how very young children develop basic communicative skills, which are the basis for creating messages they capture with emergent writing during the preschool years, and with conventional writing later on.

Newborns cry when hungry or uncomfortable and gaze at a caregiver's hairline or eyes, because light and dark contrast in these areas attracts their attention. Adults interpret an infant's gaze toward their face as regard for them, and respond (Kaye 1982). Between 1 and 2 months, babies begin to smile socially at people who smile at and talk to them, and they begin to gaze more at people's eyes (Brazelton et al. 1975; Stern et al. 1975). By 3 months, infants use smile and gaze to regulate their interactions with caregivers, and also make more cooing sounds. A list of milestones for social interaction and language from 3 months to 36 months are provided in Table 7-1 "Typical Milestones in Social Interaction and Verbal Communication."

Emotional expression and identification. Babies and toddlers are also learning about emotions and social behavior. Infants express emotions from the minute they are born, and adults can soon tell when a baby is happy or sad, or angry or surprised. Infants smile a lot by 2 or 3 months when people talk and smile at them, but not when viewing a sad face (Termine & Izard 1988). By 4 months, babies laugh (Sroufe & Wunsch 1972). By 6 months, they show anger and sadness to unresponsive mothers (Weinberg & Tronick 1996) and wariness toward strangers (Lewis & Rosenblum 1974). Later in the second year of life, between 18 and 24 months, toddlers add more complicated, self-conscious, emotions, such as guilt, embarrassment, and shame to their repertoires (Lewis et al. 1989). Pride is expressed a bit later, at around 28 months (Lewis, Alessandri, & Sullivan 1992).

In addition to experiencing and expressing emotions, infants gradually learn to distinguish facial expressions that signal different emotions in others. By 7 or 8 months, infants have learned to distinguish expressions for happiness, sadness, fear, anger, and surprise (Barrera & Maurer 1981; Bornstein et al. 2011; LaBarbera et al.1976; Nelson, Morse, & Leavitt 1979; Young-Browne, Rosenfeld, & Horwitz 1977).

Between 18 and 30 months, toddlers build a vocabulary for naming and talking about many emotions and affective behaviors. These words include *happy*, *sad*, *funny*, *mad*, *yucky*, *cry*, *laugh*, *surprised*, *scared*, and many more (Bretherton & Beeghly 1982; Dunn, Bretherton, & Munn 1987).

Emotional understanding. Although 7- or 8-month-olds use visual information to distinguish among different facial expressions, they do not yet understand the meanings of the emotions expressed. But by 10 months of age, infants engage in ***social referencing***—look back and forth between a familiar caregiver and something of concern, such as a stranger or a novel toy (Sorce et al. 1985; Vaish & Sriano 2004). For example, if Dad smiles at a stranger, the infant more likely approaches the stranger than if Dad scowls or looks worried. Although infants this age use emotion information they infer from facial expressions to guide their *own* behavior, they are not able to use facial expressions, alone, to predict the future behavior of others until about 18 months of age (Repacholi & Gopnik 1997).

The development of empathy. In laboratory studies, babies between 1 and 9 months of age cry when they hear the recorded cry of another baby (Geangu et al. 2010). But in natural settings with their mothers and other babies, 6-month-olds rarely cry when a peer baby cries. Instead, they might try to touch the baby. In natural settings, babies become distressed and stop showing concern only when crying continues for a long time (Hay, Nash, & Pederson 1981).

Although babies between 6 and 12 months respond with affect and concern to others' distress, and prefer people who help rather than hinder others' actions (Hamlin, Wynn, & Bloom 2007), they do not yet try to provide comfort to the distressed person (e.g., pat the distressed person or offer words of comfort) or seek help. By 16 months, these prosocial behaviors are quite evident, unless the other's distress continues for a long time or is very intense. In these situations, the toddler becomes distressed quickly, and is unable to act prosocially. There are individual differences, though, with some babies more likely than others to become distressed quickly when observing distress in others (Roth-Hanania, Davidov, & Waxler 2011; Ungerer et al. 1990).

So Much More than the ABCs

Table 7-1 Typical Milestones in Social Interaction and Verbal Communication	
Age	**Milestones**
3 Months	Begin to coordinate their smiles, vocalizations, gazes, and other responses with adults (Bloom 1977; Condon 1979). Begin to imitate and repeat pitch, loudness, and duration of mother's vocalization. Communicate and connect with mother in this way (Gratier & Devouche 2011).
6 Months	Begin to follow others' head and eye movements, but look only in the general direction not at the specific target, and are distracted by intermediary objects (Butterworth & Jarrett 1991).
7 Months	Respond more consistently to the pause slots that mothers leave for them, and more often use vocalizations rather than other behaviors (e.g., yawns, smiles, burps), when taking their turn (Snow 1977). Often verbalize to greet a familiar person who looks at them (Kaye & Fogel 1980).
9–11 Months	Locate the target of another's gaze (Corkum & Moore 1995), if pointing is combined with it, when objects are in visual field.
12 Months	Follow point and gaze more reliably to targets not close to the visual field (Flom et al. 2004). Are skilled in the alternating pattern of interaction typical of conversation in their culture (Broerse & Elias 1994). Understand quite a few words, and begin to speak a few.
18–20 Months	Combine words to form rudimentary sentences. Expressive vocabulary begins to increase fairly rapidly.
24–36 Months	Syntactic and grammatical skill increase steadily. Use gaze fairly skillfully to signal listening to a conversational partner (i.e., look at the speaker in sustained way); look away as they begin taking a turn, before looking back at the listener, to make sure she is listening (Ruttter & Durkin 1987). Respond quite consistently when spoken to, and initiate verbal interactions. Learn to talk about the causes of feelings and other mental states, in relation to themselves and others. Use mental state talk in pretend play (Bretherton & Beeghly 1982; Dunn, Bretherton & Munn 1987).

Studies about emotional understanding also indicate that, by 18 months, toddlers begin to realize that different people can have different feelings about the same thing. Such understanding, which continues to develop for years, positions the young child to understand the characters in stories and the conflicts that might occur among them. These topics also begin to appear in young children's writing and drawing.

Concluding thoughts about early mark-making

As we have seen, babies' first early marks take form on the paper by accident not by design. But before long, toddlers begin to exert some control by repeating marks whose accidental appearance catches their attention. This behavior marks the transition from the first to the second phase of early mark-making. A bit later, something new begins. As Gardner described it, "The child is establishing a vocabulary of lines and forms—the basic building blocks of a graphic language—which, like the sounds of language, eventually combine into meaningful, referential units" (1980, 11). The dawning of the idea that marks can represent meaning is the transition from the second to the third phase of early mark-making we describe.

In group settings, teachers can display photographs of children engaged in drawing or painting along with their markings on a bulletin board where parents and other family members can see them. These might inspire some families to provide similar experiences at home, if they do not already do so. For a variety of reasons, though, some parents will decide that they cannot provide marking experiences at home. They will be especially grateful to teachers who make an effort to provide their children with these experiences.

We have also indicated that babies and toddlers are very busy learners who acquire the understanding that humans have goals and intentions, and that conditions sometimes hinder their ability to achieve desired goals. This knowledge positions older toddlers and young preschoolers to both understand and generate stories in which humans and animals behave differently than inanimate objects. It is also possible for preschoolers to violate these typical ways of behaving in the real world to create some humor and also to create stories that are fiction, not fact.

We have also discussed the infant and toddler's understandings of facial expressions. It is no wonder that toddlers sometimes show great interest in the facial expressions of children and adults they see in books, or that they can label characters' feelings when we read to them. Feelings also sometimes show up in young preschoolers' first representational drawings and paintings. (See an example from Chara in Chapter 8.)

Some of the strong correlations between early book-reading experience and later success in reading might come from the fact that books for toddlers (see Chapter 2) involve some of the knowledge and understandings that they are just beginning to acquire. When adults share books and talk with toddlers about them, children's knowledge is strengthened, as is the language needed to talk about it. Even in this early period, we can see how reading books to children and offering opportunities for them to draw and write, and "tell about it" are likely mutually supportive.

8 Writing during the Preschool Years

Chara, now 34 months, made two short vertical lines in her finger paint. When finished, she looked up and said, "Two legs." After making a horizontal line above the legs, she glanced up again and announced, "A mouth." Next, she made a small curved line that resembled an arch. "It's sad," she explained. Before breaking gaze, she added, "I need a head." Chara turned back to her finger painting and drew a circle around the two mouths.

"Why are you sad?" the adult asked. Chara looked up and replied, "I want it sad." Then, she smeared paint over the lines, making them disappear. Next, she looked up and smiled, and then looked down as she said, "I need more paint." After the finger paint had been replenished, Chara continued to explore by squishing it in her hands, rubbing her paint-filled palms up and down her arms, and spreading paint all over her paper.

At almost 3 years of age, Chara knew the names and relative locations of basic human body parts and also understood the facial expressions that matched many feelings. Additionally, her language was adequate for engaging in a conversation, and she knew how people in her culture use gaze to monitor a conversational partner's listening and the beginning and ending of turns.

Given Chara's hefty store of knowledge about all sorts of things, and her long history of mark-making (almost two years of experience by 34 months), this soon-to-be-preschooler was now poised to draw something that was in her mind, and equally equipped to tell all about it.

In this chapter, the discussion of both mark-making and representational skill continues on from Chapter 7. We consider how preschool children combine picture making (i.e., drawing or painting) and writing marks to capture their meanings. We also consider preschoolers' uses of writing and drawing, the complexity and content of their drawings, and their interest in these activities.

This chapter is organized around four phases that match the following ages: (1) 30 to 36 months, (2) 3 to 4 years, (3) 4 to 5 years, and (4) 5 years to about 5 years and 9 months. Our fourth phase includes children who will turn 5 during the school year.

Although the ages of the children who created the samples used to illustrate each phase fit within the respective age range, these age designations are approximations. As we noted in Chapter 7, providing mark-making experiences for infants and toddlers is not as common as is reading to very young children. Thus, we are likely to see even wider variations with respect to the ages at which various writing and drawing behavior appears than we see for language and vocabulary, for example, among children whose early language experiences, including book reading, vary in quantity and quality.

For each phase of writing and drawing, we provide a general picture of what children do, and we link it to learning on three fronts: physical mark-making (i.e., writing letters and drawing pictures), word creation, and meaning making. We comment throughout about conditions that support both skill acquisition and interest.

Phase 1: Writing begins to look like writing and "says" something

In Chapter 7, Chara and Sydney included letter-like forms in scribble drawings, and Grayden made spiral, round and round, and dot, dot, dot marks. But although Chara and Sydney knew that C and S were in their respective names, neither child said, "Oh, that's me!" or "That says . . . " Likewise, after making spirals, Grayden did not say, "Those are pinwheels." Letters and spirals were simple depictions, identified by name. At best, the letters were associated with someone (e.g., "O is for Owen," "C is for Chara," "T is for Tricia").

This marking behavior resembles an early form of pretend play in which children relate objects functionally, but are not "in role." Role pretending (i.e., Mommy or Daddy cooking, Daddy feeding a baby) appears around 28 to 30 months (see Box 7-1 in Chapter 7). A somewhat similar transformation toward the symbolic use of alphabet forms and other designs appears in drawing and writing behavior around 30 months. Although children still sometimes picture various lines and alphabet letters, as well as people and other items (Figure 8-1), they also now use lines or individual marks *as writing* (i.e., the marks "say" something). Sometimes, they now also *set out* to draw something specific, rather than only attribute meanings to paintings and drawings after exploratory marking brought something specific to mind. Finally, preschoolers separate drawing from their writing fairly consistently and organize writing marks linearly.

Getting into the role of writer

A 32 months, Chara wrote a grocery list using wavy lines (Figure 8-2a). As she wrote, she named food items (e.g., *eggs*, *milk*, *sweet potatoes*, *beets*), mimicking her mother's list-making behavior, including writing words on Chara's paper when she requested. (See Figure 5-1 in Chapter 5.) At almost 35 months, Chara added names of the people to invite to her birthday party to her mother's list of items Chara wanted as gifts. (Her mom had explained that some people had asked what Chara might like.) To make her guest list, Chara lined up individual letter-like marks (Figure 8-2b).

Figure 8-1. Adam's pictures of the letter A and people at age 34 months.

Chara's grocery and birthday party lists.

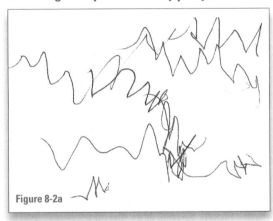

Figure 8-2a

Figure 8-2b

Figure 8-3. Chara's letter practice.

Starting at about 34 months, Chara sometimes wrote just alphabet letters (approximations, not conventional forms), without intending to convey any meaning (i.e., she was not making a list or writing a note to someone), as if practicing. Of course, most letters she wrote did not resemble very closely their conventional forms. In the sample in Figure 8-3, she wrote three Cs first, saying, "C, C, C, C." Then, she said, "H, I, J, K" as she made additional marks.

Adam used wavy lines to write his father's name on a Father's Day card envelope, in response to his mother's request (Figure 8-4a). A few days later, he placed himself in the role of writer to make "a letter to Daddy" (Figure 8-4b).

Adam's Father's Day card envelope and "letter to Daddy."

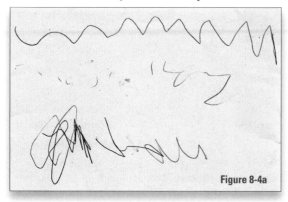

Figure 8-4a

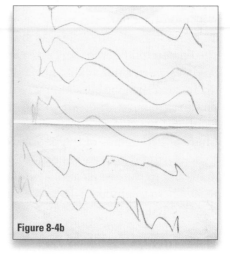

Figure 8-4b

Figure 8-5. Chara's card with name signed at the bottom, 34 months.

Separating writing and drawing, and organizing writing into lines

In the grocery list, birthday party list, card envelope, and letter to Daddy examples, Chara and Adam used only writing—just wavy lines or individual marks organized linearly. But in much of their marking at this time, they used both pictures (or decorations) and writing, which they separated. For example, Chara added letter-like marks (apparently her name) to a card she made for a friend (Figure 8-5), without writing on top of paper decorations she had.

Her mother had written messages recently in some valentines they made together, which modeled separating writing from decorations.

Adam, Monica, and Juliette also separated writing and picture marks. Adam explained that his scribble words (lower right) said: "Dear Mommy, I love you. Dear Daddy, I love you too" (Figure 8-6a). Monica explained: "This is my picture, and my name, and lots of words" (Figure 8-6b). Juliette said, "my name" when pointing to wavy lines at the bottom edge of her paper, and "my picture" when gesturing toward the scribble mass (Figure 8-6c).

Adam, Monica, and Juliette separate writing from pictures.

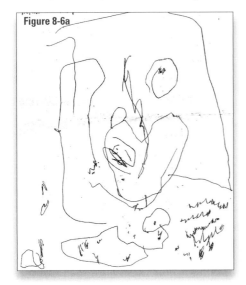

Figure 8-6a

Figure 8-6b

Figure 8-6c

Although many children distinguish between writing and picture marks by about 3 years of age, some children do not. For example, when 3 years and 5 months old, Tyler wrote his name on paper in the block area using a mass of scribble that an adult could easily think was a picture (Figure 8-7). He had limited marking experience prior to preschool, but once enrolled, Tyler spent considerable time in the block area with children who routinely made signs. He also watched his teacher write in some whole-group situations.

With access in preschool to marking tools and models to observe, Tyler figured out that marks intended as writing are organized differently than picture marks. Several months later (at 3 years and 8 months), he began using individual marks, all lined up, for his name. A few months after that, his marks resembled somewhat the letters in his name.

Figure 8-7. Tyler's nonlinear marks for his name.

Attributing meaning to pictures

Although preschoolers continue to paint and draw freely, much of the time, without attributing meaning to their marks, they are more inclined to do so now than when toddlers. Apparently, they realize that people use marks primarily to represent meaning. For example, one day, after painting with watercolors, an adult asked Chara to tell about her paintings. Chara said that one was, "The sun and all the world" (Figure 8-8a), and the other was, "A trail with cool, soft, squelchy mud" (Figure 8-8b).

Chara borrowed the words for Figure 8-8b from a favorite book (*Rain* by Manya Stojic). When the rain stops in the book, the rhino says that he could not feel the rain now, but could " . . . lie in the cool, soft, squelchy mud" (p. 20). Chara liked these words and sometimes repeated them during book readings. Interestingly, her mother had also recently modeled using text from a book in a message that she wrote on a gift tag for some baked goods. Perhaps Chara's idea of using book wording to label her painting marks was inspired by her mother's example.

Meanings Chara attributed to her watercolor paintings.

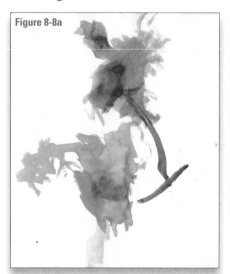

Figure 8-8a

Figure 8-8b

Chara could have attributed any number of meanings to her free-form pictures (Figures 8-8a and 8-8b), because they did not strongly resemble anything. But just as with dramatic play in which children are willing to use one object to stand for another, even when it does not closely resemble it, only a hint of resemblance in a picture (i.e., a few brown spots) is needed for a child to say it is "cool, soft, squelchy mud" or "the sun and all the world." Although this willingness to see something in almost anything declines in the 4-year-old (see Box 7-1 in Chapter 7), younger preschoolers are satisfied with mere hints of a likeness.

Sometimes, children also now set out intentionally to draw a picture rather than attribute meaning only to marks already made, as before. This new behavior indicates increased cognitive growth, including the beginning of the ability to plan.

So Much More than the ABCs

Two examples, each with a single item depicted, are shown in Figures 8-9a and 8-9b.

Adam's person at 35 months.

Figure 8-9a

Livi's house at 35 months.

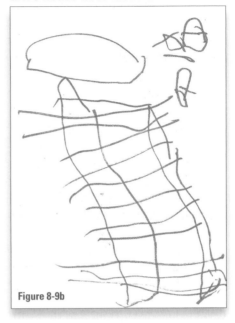

Figure 8-9b

Summing up Phase 1

By about age 3, children get into the role of writer, and often use wavy lines or individual letter-like squiggles, all lined up. Many children this age also begin to separate writing from picture marks, and sometimes try to write their names, although their marks don't always resemble actual letters.

Children are also even more likely now to attribute meaning to pictures that start out as explorations and they begin to draw pictures intentionally. Sometimes, information and scenes from familiar books inspire the meanings children attribute to drawings and paintings.

Writing and drawing skill vary widely among children, even at this age, because their experiences have differed. When assessing a child's understanding, such as the child's knowledge about the organization of picture marks versus writing marks, multiple samples of marking should be drawn from a range of contexts, and the child's intention in each one should also be considered, because these influence the child's behavior. For example, if a preschool teacher were assessing Adam's understanding, it would be appropriate to consider samples shown in Figures 8-1 and 8-6, among others.

A child's history of experience is also considered when drawing conclusions following an assessment. For example, Tyler had virtually no marking experience before entering preschool. Not surprisingly, his writing level differed from Adam's and Chara's. Yet with access, acceptance, and support, this child's writing developed just fine. Readers interested in the assessment of young children's writing might consult Chapter 6 in *Writing in Preschool* (Schickedanz & Casbergue 2009).

Phase 2: Names, mock words, and detailed pictures

During the period between 3 and 4 years of age, children become quite interested in trying to write their names and other words, and they include more details in drawings and paintings. Children also have more to say when adults talk with them about their writing and drawing.

Children write their names

Samples of Adam's name writing, from 32 to 45 months, are shown in Figure 8-10. In the first, one mark resembled A, but the others did not resemble any letters in his name. By 33 months, Adam had added an M of sorts, using a little circle inside "goal posts" to carve out its inside (Figure 8-10b).

By 41 months, As and Ms were very recognizable, and D was a circle whose left side Adam "flattened" by adding lines (Figures 8-10c and 8-10d). Adam knew how the conventional forms of these letters looked, and, through experimentation, had managed to create better and better versions. But, at this point, he could not figure out any other way to make D straight on its left side. By 43 months, Adam had solved this problem (Figures 8-10e and 8-10f), perhaps by taking advantage of demonstrations his mother provided (e.g., "Here's another way to make D with a straight side"). She modeled using two separate strokes, starting with a straight vertical line on the left, and then adding a curved line to its right side.

Because children typically see letters in their finished state, they do not realize that two or more strokes, not just one, are made to compose most letters. They also sometimes envision more strokes than are actually used in a letter (e.g., two short horizontal lines to form the top of T, not one continuous line). The alphabet clue game, described in Chapter 5, helps preschoolers to realize that many letters are composed of multiple line segments, and that others have fewer lines than the child at first imagines.

Figure 8-10. Evolution in Adam's name writing.

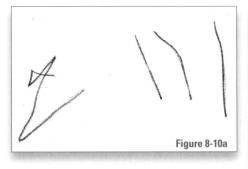

Figure 8-10a

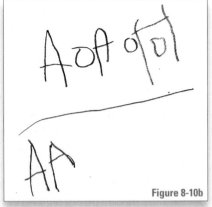

Figure 8-10b

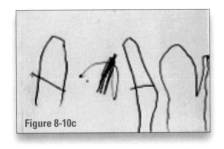

Figure 8-10c

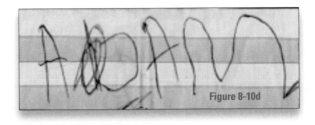

Figure 8-10d

Figure 8-10e

Figure 8-10f

Some children are content for a while to use mostly placeholders for the letters in their names. For example, 3-year-old Audrey wrote six circles when signing a picture at preschool (Figure 8-11), as she said "A-U-D-R-E-Y." R and Y are difficult letters to form, which encourages placeholder use. Additionally, Audrey was familiar with Chinese characters, but not with English letters, when she entered preschool. Within a few months, however, her letters became quite recognizable.

Figure 8-11. Audrey's placeholder letters.

Interest in words

Between 3 and 4 years of age, children often become interested in words other than their names. These include names of siblings, preschool friends, and parents and grandparents (e.g., Mommy, Nana, Papa, Daddy). Children copy these words or write letters that adults dictate. At 39 months, Adam wrote "Daddy" on a birthday card envelope, as his mother dictated each letter (Figure 8-12a). Four months later, he wrote "Mommy" on a valentine card envelope, as his father dictated the letters (Figure 8-12b).

Adam's writing of the words Daddy and Mommy.

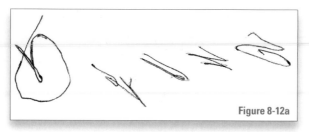

Figure 8-12a

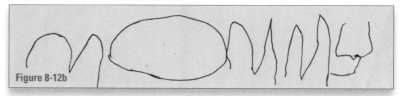

Figure 8-12b

Figure 8-13. Adam's writing of TIGER, at 44 months, which he copied from his mother's paper.

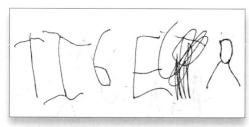

When they are a bit older, children are sometimes interested in spelling the names of familiar things. For example, one day, when at school with his mother (lead author), Adam wanted to see a classroom. He noticed the chalkboard and asked his mother to write words that he dictated. She wrote *cat, tiger, dragon, picture,* and other words, which he copied onto pieces of paper (Figure 8-13). A month later, at home, Adam requested the word game again. Just as before, he dictated the words, and then copied them after his mother had written them.

Figure 8-14. Adam's list of mock words, 43 months.

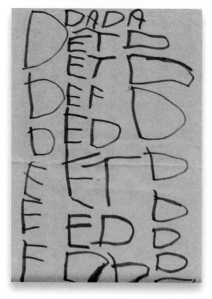

Sometimes, 3-year-olds also create ***mock words***—strings of letters that look like words, but are not. Mock words are based on visual information that children have acquired from observing words in the environment. But visual information, alone, does not provide information about how letters are selected. (See Table 8-1 "Preschoolers' Word Creation Hypotheses" later in the chapter for a discussion of the various strategies preschoolers use to create words.)

At 3 years and 7 months, Adam started with a known word (DADA) and then, using these and a few other letters (E, F, T), created several mock words (Figure 8-14).

Juliana's grocery list (mock words), 47 months.

Figure 8-15a

Jennifer's mock words, 38 months.

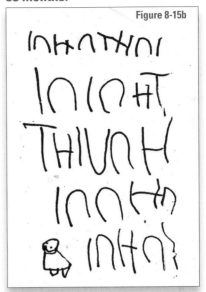

Figure 8-15b

Juliana created a mock word grocery list in her house area play (Figure 8-15a), and Jennifer used mock works to fill the pages of a blank book (Figure 8-15b).

Pictures become more detailed

Children's pictures become more detailed between 3 and 4 years of age, and often "tell" of an event or situation, rather than simply depict a single object. For example, at 37 months, Livi drew several people and said, "This is our family at the circus" (Figure 8-16a). (They had recently gone to the circus.) At 42 months, Adam drew "A cave with frosting decorations and a mommy, daddy, brother, and sister inside" (Figure 8-16b).

Detailed pictures now tell stories.

Figure 8-16a

Figure 8-16b

Figure 8-17. Details in drawings of people.

Sometimes, children still draw single items, but these do not typically include more details than pictures they drew when younger (see Adam's "Man with a Beard" in Figure 8-17).

Every drawing provides an opportunity to talk with a child, if that child is interested. In the process, language development is nurtured, knowledge is expanded, and narrative and expository skills are honed. These conversations have consequences for children's later composing skills (Peterson, Jesso, & McCabe 1999). Talking with children about their drawings is discussed further in Box 8-1 "Talking with Children about Their Drawings."

Box 8-1 Talking with Children about Their Drawings

When reading with young children, we know that talking together about the book is as important as reading it. Although there is no specific research about the effect of talking with young children about their drawings, we can apply what is known from studies of parental talking with young children about their immediate past experiences (Peterson, Jesso, & McCabe 1999) and of the effects of teacher-child talk in a variety of preschool contexts (e.g., Dickinson & Porche 2011). In general, studies point to several features of talk that support children's language development:

- Teachers extend conversations—keep it going—by contributing information and asking questions.

- Teachers use sophisticated vocabulary—higher-level words—rather than more common words.

- Teachers correct inaccuracies of fact in children's statements (e.g., "Oh, that's called a whisk not a broom, because we mix things up with it. We don't sweep with it. Brooms have bristles, and this whisk has wire loops").

A picture, such as Livi's of her family at the circus (Figure 8-16a), which was drawn at home, could be used to help Livi tell personal narratives. Consider the richness of this potential conversation:

Livi's Mom: Oh, yes, we did go to the circus last week. How did we get there?

Livi: We drove a long time.

Mom: Yes, we had to drive all the way into Boston, and that's quite a long distance.

Livi's Dad: After we parked the car, we had to ride the train to the circus, didn't we?

Livi: And the sky went away.

Dad: Yes, we rode underground on the trolley, and we couldn't see the trees or buildings, or the sky for a while.

Mom: What animal at the circus did you like the best?

Livi: I like the elephant, and the people ride on him!

Mom: Oh, yes, the elephants were carrying people in seats on their backs, weren't they? Were there any other animals you liked a lot?

Summing up Phase 2

Between 3 and 4 years of age, children become more aware of letters, especially those in their names, and they write these in ways that resemble more closely their conventional forms. There is variation in skill across children, of course, due to differences in fine motor skill or a lack of familiarity with letter forms.

Children also become interested in writing words at this time, and create letter strings that look like words. Of course, children have little, if any, understanding at this point of how letters are *actually* selected to make words. (See Table 8-1 "Preschoolers' Word Creation Strategies.")

Children's pictures become more detailed and provide wonderful starting points for conversations with adults.

Phase 3: Writing and drawing come into full bloom

During this phase, which spans 4 to 5 years of age, children put writing to even more uses, create letters that are closer and closer to conventional form, and begin to understand why specific letters are selected to spell different words. Drawings also become more complex, because children have more cognitive power and a wider range of experience from which to draw content.

The samples in this section are from a diverse group of children, some monolingual, some bilingual, some trilingual, and some with developmental challenges. We discuss several children by showing multiple samples of their writing and drawing in different contexts, across a few months. For others, we provide only a sample or two.

Using writing for a variety of purposes

When Tracey was 4½ years old and decided to use a watercolor painting as a gift to her mother, she needed a gift tag (Figure 8-18a). She knew how to write her name and the word LOVE. (She had requested it many times.) Like many 4-year-olds, however, Tracey did not plan the use of the limited space on the small piece of paper she had selected. After finishing T, R, A, and C, and realizing that she would likely run out of space, she made a very skinny E. Even with this adaptation, she still lacked enough space for the top of Y. To solve this problem, she placed its top on the line above, after E in LOVE, and then drew its long lower part down to join the letters in her name.

One day, after building a library, Angelina wanted to make a sign. The teacher she asked for help in spelling *library* segmented the sounds in the word and dictated the letters used to represent each one. When Angelina reached the paper's edge after writing R, the teacher advised, "Go over to the other side and put A under L." But Angelina insisted that A belonged under R, explaining, "They have to go together" (i.e., letters that follow in a word should be placed close physically). Angelina had not yet learned to sweep to the left and then move to the right when placing print or reading it (Figure 8-18b).

A gift tag.

Figure 8-18a

Library sign.

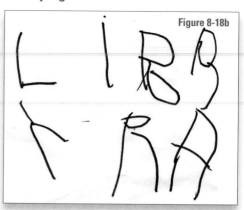

Figure 8-18b

Tracey and Angelina wrote for many other purposes, as well, and so did Sean. For example, he made a grocery list, copying the first two names from food cartons (soup, juice) and making up the others (milk and bread) (Figure 8-19a). He also wrote his name on drawings (Figure 8-19b), made a license plate for a block car (Figure 8-19c), and wrote a pizza order (Figure 8-19d). And, one day, he and a friend collaborated in making a book, drawing pictures first, as they composed, then asking a teacher to listen to their story and help write the words. The teacher wrote some words and asked the children to write others, while helping with spelling. Figure 8-19e shows the cover, and Figures 8-19f and 8-19g show two pages of "The Cat and the Mean Dog."

Samples of Sean's writing and drawing (ages 4 years 6 months to 4 years 9 months).

Grocery list made during house play.

Figure 8-19a

Signature for a drawing.

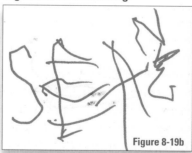

Figure 8-19b

License plate for car built with blocks.

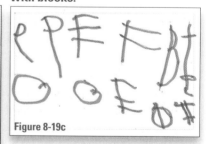

Figure 8-19c

So Much More than the ABCs

Pepperoni pizza order in play restaurant.

Figure 8-19d

Cover for a book cover.

Figure 8-19e

Page of book with drawing of cat's house.

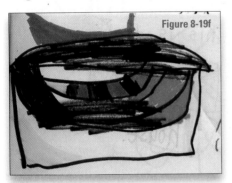

Figure 8-19f

"That is the cat's house," (with page number).

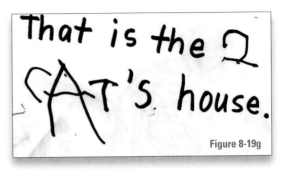

Figure 8-19g

Gabriella also wrote for a variety of purposes. For example, she wrote her nickname, Gabi, in mock cursive (Figure 8-20a) or decorated it and added funny letters and an overabundance of the lowercase i, which she turned into flowers (Figure 8-20b). She also once wrote two names for a new classroom gerbil (Brownie and Pinky). A teacher segmented the sounds in the words, and Gabi selected letters to go with these sounds, and wrote the words. After realizing that she didn't have a letter to represent /n/ in *Brownie*, Gabi squeezed one in, writing M rather than N (Figure 8-20c), which she did again when writing *Pinky*. With this word, she also placed K above the other letters, because she ran out of space on her little piece of paper. (It looks a bit like a short T.) She also used K to represent the last two sounds in *Pinky* (/k/ /e/), which makes perfectly good sense to 4-year-olds, because the name of K contains these two sounds (Figure 8-20d).

Gabi also wrote "Danger, Alligators" (DNG LGAT) signs for block play, and also one saying, "No Pets" ("NO PATS) (Figures 8-20e and 8-20f). In response to her request for spelling help, a teacher segmented the sounds in the words, and Gabi selected letters to represent them.

Gabi's writing at preschool when she was 4.

Fancy cursive writing of Gabi, 4 years 4 months.

Figure 8-20a

Decorated form of Gabi, 4 years 5 months.

Figure 8-20b

Suggested gerbil name—Brownie, 4 years 6 months.

Figure 8-20c

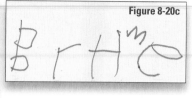

Suggested name for gerbil—Pinky, 4 years 6 months.

Figure 8-20d

Danger, Alligators, block sign, 4 years 8 months.

Figure 8-20e

No Pets block area, 4 years 8 months.

Figure 8-20f

Pages from Mike's book are shown in Figure 8-21. Although he used mock words for pages 1 and 3 (Figures 8-21a and 8-21c), he wrote two real words on page 2 (Figure 8-21b). (He had learned to spell DEAR and OMAMA at home when writing to his grandmother.) He returned to mock word writing to finish the rest of his book (Figure 8-21).

Figure 8-21. Mike's book with letter to grandmother at 4 years 7 months.

Page one of book.

Figure 8-21a

Page two of book.

Figure 8-21b

Page three of book.

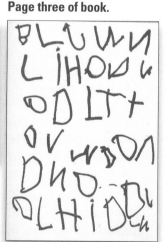

Figure 8-21c

So Much More than the ABCs

One day at preschool, Adam wrote a letter to a favorite student teacher (Figure 8-22a) and a note to his mother (Figure 8-22b). On yet another day, he copied the name of a favorite song, "Head, Shoulders, Knees and Toes," from a list at preschool (Figure 8-22c). At home, during an episode of pretend play, he left a sign on the sofa warning creatures to stay away (Figure 8-22d).

Samples of Adam's writing between ages 4 and 5.

Adam's letter to Sally, 4 years 8 months.

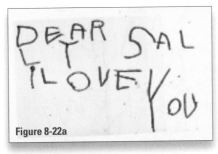

Figure 8-22a

Adam's note to Mom, 4 years 11 months.

Figure 8-22b

Adam's favorite song at preschool. Copied from teacher's posting of song names for the day. 4 years 8 months.

Figure 8-22c

Adam's note left on living room sofa to tell creatures to stay away. Mock words, but used "Roo" name of preschool pet gerbil as a base. 4 years 6 months.

Figure 8-22d

The next set of examples is a group of letters from preschoolers to the lead author. These were written after their teacher shared a book I had sent and suggested that the children write thank-you letters. Some children drew a picture and wrote mock words (Figures 8-23a and 8-23b). One child filled paper with letters and letter-like forms (Figure 8-23c). Another child wrote just words—real ones—with help from the teacher (Figure 8-23d).

The children ranged in age from barely 4 years of age (Figures 8-23e, 8-23f, and 8-23g) to a bit over 5 years. No matter the level of skill, their teacher accepted all of their thank-you letters.

Making words

Young 4-year-olds often use mock words to fill pages of a book (Figure 8-21), to write multi-word messages (e.g., Adam's warning to creatures in Figure 8-22d), or when creating artifacts for pretend play. In all situations, children know they can convey their message when telling interested teachers or peers what their writing says.

Thank-you letters to Judy from 4-year-olds.

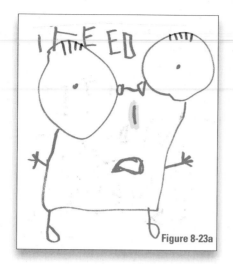

Figure 8-23a

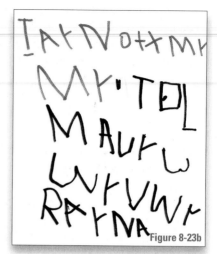

Figure 8-23b

Figure 8-23c

Figure 8-23e

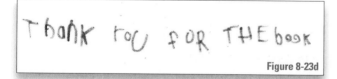

Thank you for THE book

Figure 8-23d

Figure 8-23f

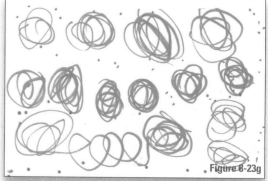

Figure 8-23g

So Much More than the ABCs

In older preschoolers, mock words often coexist with words they make using other strategies. For example, 4-year-old Ella created a turns sign-up list of mock words for a pretend sandbox in the block area (Figure 8-24a), because she said it could accommodate only two children at a time. All but one of the names she created for her list (Coco) were mock words (the pretend children's names). Interestingly, though, Ella's competence at the time far exceeded the mock word approach. For example, just a few months after making this list, she made a maze game with blocks, and a poster to advertise it. She generated spellings for the ad by segmenting sounds in words and matching these to letter names ("Please come to the . . .") (Figure 8-24b). After making the poster, she also wrote a note to a teacher, asking her to come ("Please come") (Figure 8-24c).

At about the same time, Ella made a long book (stapled half-size pieces of paper together) about fairies (Figure 8-24d). She invented spellings on the first page ("One day the fairies went out and they saw a toad"), and used some on the second. For page 3, she resorted to mock words. Beginning on page 4 and continuing through page 24, she used scribble writing. Generating spellings for words, and even writing specific letters for mock words, was too much work for the long book she had in mind.

Four-year-old Ella's word creations.

Turns list for sandbox in block area, 4 years 5 months.

Figure 8-24a

Poster, 4 years 10 months.

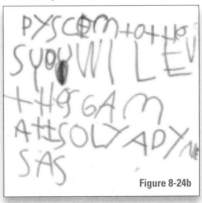

Figure 8-24b

Note to teacher asking her to "Please Come" to see the maze game in the block area, 4 years 10 months.

Figure 8-24c

First page of book "The Fairies."

Figure 8-24d

As is true with most learning, children are proficient at any time with some word-creation strategies, while their grasp of others is fragile. Because fragile strategies take considerably more effort than familiar ones (Siegler & Alibali 2005), children use these when writing only a little, or for just the first page when writing a lot. Children give up scribble writing when they can form letters quickly enough to make this strategy as practical as scribble writing (see Table 8-1 "Preschoolers' Word-Creation Hypotheses").

Table 8-1 Preschoolers' Word Creation Hypotheses

Young children use a variety of strategies to create words, basing each one on an idea about how the writing system works. Because these ideas build on one another, the pattern of hypotheses seen in one child usually resembles fairly closely the pattern seen in other children. But there are variations, because children's experiences vary. When adults understand children's hypotheses, they can interact in ways that move children's understanding forward. Children who enter first grade with a great deal of knowledge about word making have usually benefited from countless hours of informative adult interactions (Durkin 1965; Read 1975).

Children's Hypotheses	Children's Reasoning and Strategies	Moving Their Understanding Forward
Words are physically related to what they represent	• Words capture aspects of the physical appearance of objects they represent. • Words usually have more marks if they are for larger objects and fewer if for smaller ones (Ferreiro & Teberosky 1982; Papandropoulos & Sinclair 1974). For example, a child might use three squiggles for *grasshopper* and seven for *cow*.	• Provide situations that contradict the idea, such as using children's names. The child thus observes that taller children do not always have names with many letters and shorter children do not always have names with few. • Read and underline labels under pictures in books. As a child observes, he obtains key information.
Each word is a stable and arbitrary sequence of letters	• Any sequence of letters is a word. • Each word has its own letters (i.e., children don't know that 26 letters spell all English words). Young children sometimes say, "Hey, that's my name!" when seeing any word beginning with their name's first letter.	• Comment to help children learn that the same letters appear in many different words. For example, "Yes, Juanita, your name starts with J, but so does José's. Your name does not have 's' in the middle. See the 'n' and 't?'"
Letter strings are based on some visual rules	• Every letter string (i.e., mock word) is considered by a child to be a real word if it follows certain rules: (a) has a variety of letters, not multiples of just one	• Sound out children's mock words, if they ask what they say. This demonstrates that letters represent sounds in spoken words

Children's Hypotheses	Children's Reasoning and Strategies	Moving Their Understanding Forward
	(Lavine 1977); (b) is not too long or too short (i.e., has between four and seven characters); and (c) has a unique order of letters, when the same letters are reused in different "words" (i.e., just as *eat* and *tea* are two different words, even though they have the same letters, the mock words ADMA, DDAA, and DMMA are also assumed by the child to be different words) (Clay 1975; Lavine 1977).	and that not every collection of letters is a real word. • Children will then ask for spellings more and create mock words less, except when pretending to write (see Figures 8-23 and 8-24).
Children detect and link large units of sound to letters	• At first only larger speech units (i.e., syllables) are detected. • Letters are used to represent entire syllables. For example, in Figure 8-10 Adam wrote AO for his name, using O for D. When asked to "tell about these two letters," he pointed first to the A and said "A-," and then to O, and said "-dam."	• As children continue to see their names and other words in the environment spelled out, this hypothesis will fade. Children gradually realize syllabic spelling doesn't look right. • Helping children to gain more phonological awareness skill also aids them in giving up this approach (see Chapter 5).
Phoneme-based spellings	• As letter names are learned, children match sounds in spoken words to letters whose names contain the sounds. • Children are able first to segment the first sounds in spoken words. They gradually can segment more sounds in spoken words. • If children cannot link a letter name to a word's isolated first sound, they ask adults how to spell the sound, just as Adam did with "cheese" (see Figure 8-26). • Children gradually learn to segment ending and middle sounds in spoken words, but preschoolers usually need a lot of help.	• Sound out words for children to spell—this helps them develop phoneme-level awareness (Ball & Blachman 1991; Ukrainetz et al. 2000). • Tell children the letter(s) used to write the sounds you have segmented in spoken words. • Later, isolate sounds for children and encourage them to select the letters that are used to write the sounds. • Prompt children to segment sounds in spoken words, as they gain skill, but also help with sounds in the middle and at the end of words, as needed.

Sometimes, younger children also generate spellings (Read 1975). For example, when 45 months old, Adam asked his mom to write words he dictated at home so that he could copy them. After his mother had spelled *cat,* c-a-t, and he had copied it (Figure 8-25a), he rewrote *cat* on a different piece of paper (Figure 8-25b), without looking at his copied version (Figure 8-25a). This time, he used K, not C, as the first letter in cat (Figure 8-25b).

Copied words Adam dictated to his mother to write.

Adam's words copied from mother's paper at home, after he dictated them, 45 months.

Figure 8-25a

Adam's words copied from mother's paper at home, after he dictated them, with CAT spelled KAT here, 45 months.

Figure 8-25b

Perhaps his mother's segmentation of first sounds in this word and others, before writing them for Adam to copy, had an effect (e.g., "Okay, cat. /k/-at; we use C to write the first sound in *cat*"). Apparently, Adam linked the /k/ sound to the first sound in the letter K's name, and wondered why his mother had used C (i.e., this sound is not in C's name). Maybe he wanted to rewrite it, thinking, "This time, I'm going to write it right!"

Following this episode, Adam did not generate any phonemic-based spellings for about a year. Instead, he used syllable-based spellings, asked for spellings, and sometimes created mock words. Often, when he asked for spellings, his preschool teacher segmented the sounds in the words he wanted and matched a letter to them, or Adam selected a letter to go with the sounds. (See Box 8-2 "How Do Children Create Spellings?")

At 4 years and 8 months, when adding *peanuts* and *cheese crackers* to a grocery list (Figure 8-26), Adam first wrote *PE* when spelling *peanuts*, and then asked, "What's next?" His mother said "A" and then segmented /n/ before saying "N." Adam got T and S on his own to finish *peanuts*. Before starting to write *cheese*, he asked how to write /ch/. His mother said that C and H are used together. He wrote 'ch,' represented the next sound with E, and then added S. After writing *CRA* for *crackers*, he asked whether he should use C or K next. His mother said he could use either one. (Today, she would tell him instead that both letters are used together in this word to write the sound. At the time, she didn't want him to become overly

So Much More than the ABCs

Box 8-2 **How Do Children Create Spellings?**

When children create phoneme-based spellings (e.g., **K**AT for *cat*, SA**LE** for *Sally*), adults often wonder why. Invented spellings are actually rule-based decisions, rather similar to some oral language decisions that preschoolers make. For example, although very young children say, "I went . . ." and "I ran . . .," some months later they begin to say, "I goed . . ." and "I runned . . ." (Fenson et al. 1994). These errors emerge after the child has noticed that the past tense for most verbs uses the morpheme *ed*, and applies this general rule to irregular verbs. This behavior—***overregularization***—diminishes gradually as children continue to hear adults use the irregular past tense verbs (e.g., ran, taught, went).

What "rules" are children using to create spellings?

The basis for young children's thoughtful, though incorrect, spelling decisions are discussed in this section.

Code only what you hear

This is a good general rule for spelling in an alphabetic writing system, because alphabet letters (i.e., graphemes) code phonemes in spoken words. The problem in English, however, is that many spellings include letters that do not represent a specific sound heard in the spoken word (e.g., cak**e**, **k**not, e**a**t). When children are unaware of this fact, they spell these words like this: KAK, NT, and ET, respectively.

Use the letter whose name contains the sound

When spelling words, young children also match sounds in letter names to sounds they detect in spoken words, or hear when adults isolate sounds as they assist with spelling. Many sounds are indeed spelled with letters whose names contain them (e.g., B /b/; D /d/; M /m/; T /t/). For example, Adam used this approach when spelling the first and last sounds of *cat* (KAT).

Letter-name matching works well not only for many consonant phonemes, but also for tense vowel phonemes (e.g., **e**at, **E**than). The problem, of course, is that lax vowel phonemes are also spelled with the same letters (e.g., s**e**t, t**e**ll, **e**very), but the letters' names do not contain these sounds. To spell these sounds, young children often search for the letter name whose phonetic features match most closely the vowel sound they hear. For the middle vowel phoneme in *pen* and *mess,* children use the letter A (i.e., *pan* for *pen; mass* for *mess*). If our readers say the names of A and E, and also the lax vowel phoneme in *pen* or *mess*, they can feel a closer resemblance to the speech features in A than in E (Read 1975).

Some sounds are not contained in any letter's name. For example, consider W ("duh-bl-u"), H ("aich"), and Y ("wi-e"). Children sometimes use these letters incorrectly to spell a word, because the sounds in their names are misleading (e.g., *dog* as **W**G; *wind* as **Y**D; *chicken* as **H**KN).

English spelling is also complicated, because some letters can represent more than one sound (e.g., C in **c**ity and **c**andy; Y in **y**es and momm**y**), and different letters can represent the same sound. For example, both C and K are used to write /k/ (e.g., *candy* and *kitten*); both PH and F are used to write /f/ (e.g., **ph**one and **f**unny); and both Ch and Sh are used to write /sh/ (e.g., *Charlene* and *Sharon*). And consider this: in the word, **cri**c**k**et, the very same sound at its beginning and in its middle, is spelled in two different ways.

(Continued on p. 172)

Sounds vary in different contexts

Children make additional spelling errors because the same letter actually represents some sounds that vary somewhat in different word contexts. For example, when /t/ is followed by /r/ (e.g., /t/ in *truck*, *train*, *try*), it has the feature of **affrication** (i.e., slow release of air when saying the sound). When /t/ is not followed by /r/, as in *time*, *talk*, and *tomato*, there is no affrication. Thus, a young child must learn not to spell *truck* as CHK (i.e., 'ch' represents affrication such as in the first sound heard in cherry or chicken). The child learns to ignore the affrication speech feature and focus on the additional speech features in /t/, in words when /t/ is followed by /r/.

Helping young children move toward conventional spellings

Exposing children to conventional spelling found in storybook titles and on classroom signs, labels, and charts helps children move gradually toward conventional spelling. Writing in a group situation, such as when taking dictation for a list of what children learned from having studied something, can also help. In these situations, children learn the most when teachers segment words into some of their constituent sounds, and select the letters that represent these sounds, commenting, as needed, about spellings when they are somewhat unusual.

For example, suppose a child dictates, "I learned that spiders have eight legs." A teacher could say, "Okay, I'll add spiders to our list. Spiders—/s/-piders; we use S to write /s/, the first sound in **s**piders." Continuing, the teacher says *spiders* again, and isolates the next phoneme (i.e., s../p/..iders). "I hear /p/ next in **s**piders. We use P to write /p/." For the next to the last phoneme, the teacher would say, "Spid.. **er**....s. I hear /r/ next, but I'll write a letter E first, because I know E comes before R in this word." After isolating the last sound, the teacher could say, "The last sound in *spiders* is /z/. We use S to write that sound, even though you might think we use Z."

When children create their own spellings, teachers answer their questions honestly, in ways that show respect for their good thinking. For example, if a child asks, "Is that how you spell *cat*?" after writing KT, a teacher could say, "I can read it, because *cat* begins with /k/ and we actually use K to write /k/ in many words. But grown-ups write the first sound in *cat* with C not K. It's kind of tricky." If a child asks "Why?" answer honestly: "I don't know. Somebody decided *cat* should be spelled this way, and that's how grown-ups write it. Grown-ups also put an A in the middle, and you can add that letter, if you'd like." If the child says, "I'm going to leave it this way," the teacher might say, "That's okay. Maybe next time you will want to try writing *cat* with the letters C-A-T."

While we don't want to squelch children's interest in, and attention to, the phonemes in words by insisting on corrections of their early spellings, we also don't want children to see only their own spellings, because many do not contain "legal" letter sequences for English syllables (e.g., CHKN, for *chicken*; KK for *cake*; BK for *bake*; KTN for *kitten*). Because looking at these spellings repeatedly affects children's later spelling, it is important for children to see conventional spellings frequently, throughout this period of creative spelling. A teacher should also explain any violations of children's current assumptions in situations where he is guiding the spelling of words in a group situation.

concerned about which letters to use.) He said, "I'll use both." After writing *C* and *K*, he added *RS* to finish *crackers*.

Tina, Lania, and Kate (older 4-year-olds) generated spellings when they needed just a word or two, and, sometimes, when writing more, if they had time. While playing with a doll in the dramatic play area, Tina pretended that her child, *Flower*, had drawn a picture and needed to write her name on it. When Tina asked for help in spelling *Flower*, the teacher said the word slowly, enunciating each sound. Tina wrote *FLR* to represent the sounds she heard (Figure 8-27a).

At about the same time, Tina and several classmates interviewed the person who ran a food cart to find out what foods she sold. The children wrote down what the lady at the cart told them in little notebooks, as their teacher said each word slowly, enunciating sounds. Tina selected letters to write each sound in each food word to write *hot dogs* (HOIDG), *fruit* (FROT), *muffins* (MFNS), *soup* (SOOO), *salad* (SLD), and *juice* (JOC) (Figure 8-27b).

A few months later, Tina drew a snake and wrote *BOA*. She segmented the word's first sound (/b/) and mapped it to B. She mapped the word's second sound to O. *BOA's* last sound has no letter name match, but Tina knew to represent it with A because the last sound in her name was the same (Figure 8-27c).

Lania (4 years 10 months) wrote KASAL SAV (Castle Save) by herself to label a block building (Figure 8-27d). Kate (4 years 10 months) wrote the chickadee song verses at home, all by herself (Figure 8-27e). Both Lania and Kate were very attuned to sounds in words, perhaps because they had knowledge of more than one language—Lania was trilingual; Kate was bilingual. When they wrote these pieces, they were finishing their second year in an English immersion preschool.

Figure 8-26. Adam's grocery list with peanuts and cheese crackers.

Spellings generated by Tina, Lania, and Kate.

Tina's "FLOWER" signature for pretend child, 4 years 6 months.

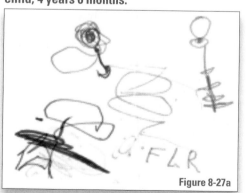

Figure 8-27a

Tina's food list at the food cart, 4 years 6 months.

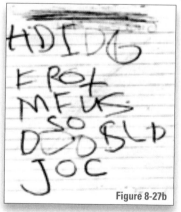

Figure 8-27b

Tina's "BOA," 4 years 10 months.

Figure 8-27c

"Castle Save" by Lania, 4 years 10 months.

Figure 8-27d

Chickadee song at home by Kate, 4 years 10 months.

Figure 8-27e

Box 8-3 Helping Young Children Learn to Form Letters

Although the preschool years are not the time for formal lessons in handwriting, teachers can assist children in ways that will help them develop some skill.

A good visual image

Children gain information about the form of each letter from opportunities to see letters and contrast one with another. Matching alphabet letters using various materials (see Chapter 5), and playing with alphabet puzzles help children to learn the shape of each letter. Some matching materials should use highly confusable letters in a set (e.g., E/F, G/C, B/R, O/Q, N/K), and all alphabet puzzles should have a space for each letter shape, not a letter stamped on jig-saw puzzle pieces.

Line segments

Looking at and comparing letters provide information about each letter's overall design, but not their line segments. Many young children use just one continuous line to make everything but the middle horizontal line of E, because this is how E looks to them. But E is actually comprised of 4 lines, a long vertical line forming its left side, and three horizontal lines out to the right from this line.

When children watch as letters are written, they get information about the lines used to form them. The teacher can provide demonstrations by playing the alphabet clue game (see Box 5-3 in Chapter 5) about once a week after the first month or two of school, focusing on just one or two letters in each game session, which takes no more than 5 to 6 minutes.

The sequence and direction of the lines that form letters

The sequence and direction of drawing the lines to form a letter cannot be discerned from looking at already formed letters nor easily grasped from worksheets with arrows and numbers marking lines in a model letter. The best learning comes from watching demonstrations. The alphabet clue game helps, and teachers can also demonstrate letter formation in authentic tasks—when the class composes a thank-you letter or creates an experience chart following a field trip.

Alphabet letter formation

Skill in letter formation changes quite a lot between 4 and 5 years of age, and also varies considerably from child to child, for a variety of reasons, including wide variations in experiences. Additionally, some alphabet letters are more difficult than others for any preschooler to write. (See Box 8-3 "Helping Young Children Learn to Form Letters.") These include R, K, B, and Y, as we see in the Figure 8-28 samples. Preschoolers also have difficulty making letters uniform in size, and getting the proportions right. For example, Eliot's lowercase 'i' was very long and he crossed 't' a bit lower than is conventional (Figure 8-28). Letter E is interesting because children seem to realize that there is no confusion between E and another letter, no matter how many short horizontal lines they squeeze onto the vertical line. And although the E in *Robert* (Figure 8-28) departs in a different way from a conventional E (i.e., its horizontal lines are bunched high up on the vertical line), there are 3 lines, not 2, which indicate that this is E not F.

The teacher describes the formation of some letters very explicitly as he writes them. Later in the year a teacher can ask, "Okay, what kind of line should I make first for B? Yes, a long vertical line. Should I draw it up like this (moves finger in air), or down like this?"

Teachers can also provide demonstrations individually to children, at the writing center, at the easel when children write names on paintings, or anywhere else that children write and ask for help. While younger preschoolers are usually happy to make a design that resembles the intended letter just a little bit, older 4-year-olds, who sometimes want their letters to look more conventional, might say, "Hey, I can't make a K right! You do it!" The teacher can show the child how or write the letter, judging how in each situation.

When demonstrating, use a separate piece of paper rather than the child's. Make the letter once, line by line and describe the actions. For example, for the letter R, the teacher might say: "To make R, we start with a long vertical line like this. Then, we go to its top, and make a curved line that goes out like this and then comes back to the middle of the vertical line . . . " After writing the letter, start over, this time making one line at a time, as the child writes it after watching you. The child's writing will not be perfect, but demonstrations give children an idea of how to proceed in getting letters to look more as they might wish.

Materials to avoid

Dot-to-dot letters and letter stencils are not helpful, because children cannot learn strokes or the direction and order in which to make them. Worksheets with a model letter and a blank row for children to practice writing a letter multiple times are also of little use, and run the risk of turning writing into a tedious chore.

Large wall charts are not handy as guides to writing letters where children want to write. Small individual letter guides are better resources not only for a writing center, but also for taking to the blocks, the easel, outdoors, and any other area where a child might need one. If the teacher uses one of these as a reference when demonstrating for individual children, some children will learn how to use the reference too.

Figure 8-28. Examples of letter formation and scale in preschoolers' writing.

B

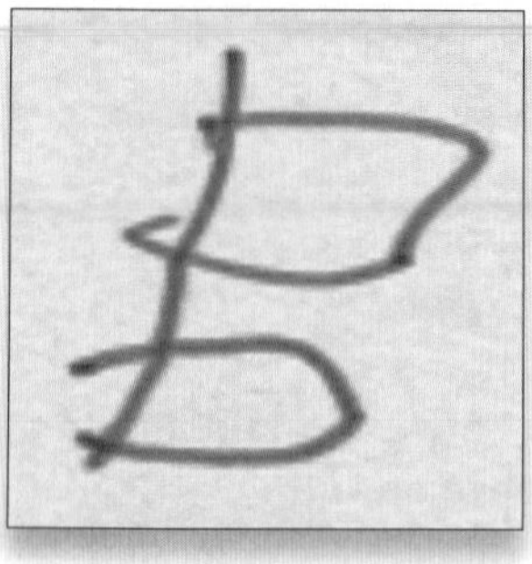

R, Y

K

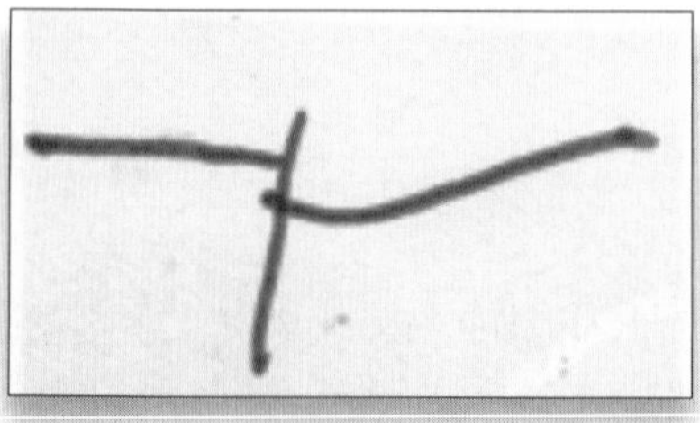

R, B, E

K

T and i

B, Y, R

R E

So Much More than the ABCs

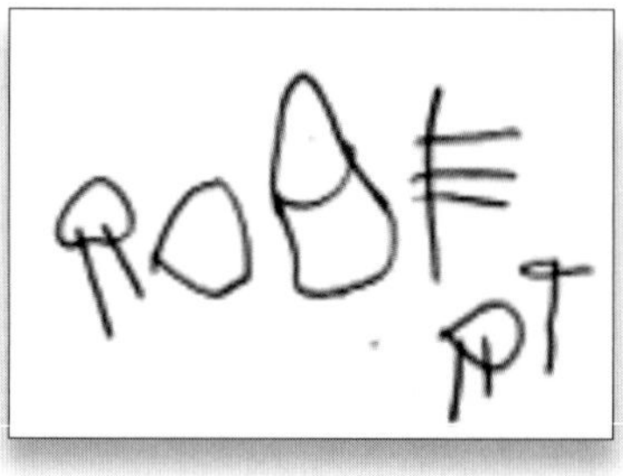

Some children are very skilled in forming letters, including lowercase, by the time they are almost 5, as the samples in Figure 8-29 illustrate. Children whose first language is not English often have little familiarity with English alphabet letters when they start preschool. Of course, their first attempts at forming English alphabet letters will be somewhat awkward.

Figure 8-29. High levels of letter formation skill in older 4-year-olds.

4 years 8 months.

Figure 8-29a

4 years 10 months.

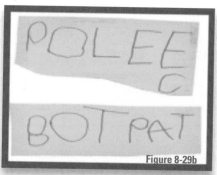

Figure 8-29b

4 years 10 months.

Figure 8-29c

4 years 10 months.

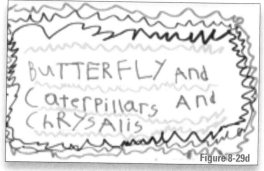

Figure 8-29d

Some samples from a young, bilingual, 4-year-old who wanted restaurant signs for block area play are shown in Figures 8-30a and 8-30b. He asked a teacher for spelling help and to write letters he did not know (e.g., G). He wrote the rest himself and taped the signs to the block structures. The great thing about play is that props created need not be terribly realistic, because children tell their preschool peers what their signs say, anyway, knowing that they are not yet reading.

In all preschoolers, fine motor skills are still developing, and this affects children's writing. (See Box 8-4 "Fine Motor Development.") Children with fine motor issues sometimes have considerable difficulty forming letters, but if teachers accept and respect their efforts, they draw and write, just as much as other children. One child with fairly significant motor delays drew a very interesting picture of her dog lying down, and then wrote his name (mock word) (Figures 8-30c and 8-30d).

Box 8-4 Fine Motor Development

Fine motor development refers to the skilled use of the fingers to manipulate objects. Children use a number of immature grasps as their fine motor skills are maturing (Carlson & Cunningham 1990). Any of these grasps results in larger rather than smaller writing and a lack of precision in creating and connecting lines. Until children have mature fine motor skills, their lines look a bit wobbly, and overruns dominate where lines intersect.

Children first use a fist grasp to hold writing and drawing tools, and use the muscle in the upper arm to move the whole arm and hand. Various overhand and stiff finger grips usually follow before children arrive at a mature grip, using the index and middle fingers, plus their thumb. With a mature grip, the side of the hand rests on the tabletop, which takes the weight off the writing or drawing tool's point and allows its flexible movement by the fingers.

Children vary greatly in fine motor development, which is affected strongly by maturation. Some have a rather mature finger grip at 3 years of age; others do not have a mature group until they are 5 or 6 years old. Children with significant fine motor delays and other motor issues will have different trajectories of fine motor development.

Some children with fine motor issues need assistance from an occupational therapist. Often, such specialists also provide helpful suggestions for classroom teachers. For example, they might recommend providing vertical surfaces (e.g., easel) or covering an entire table with a large piece of paper. These modifications allow a child with fine motor issues to use larger muscles in the arm to move writing or drawing tools, and provide larger surfaces for writing, which accommodates a child's larger marks.

While there are other modifications that might be appropriate for an individual child, children with fine motor issues can still experiment with making letters and will also learn something about their line segments and the order in which they are drawn. Luckily, young children do not need much fine motor skill to enjoy writing and drawing, as long as adults are accepting of the marks they make.

Near the end of the year, she made a thank-you note with a lot of pink paint for the school director whose garden the children had visited to plant flowers. She wrote "For Judy" on her painting (Figure 8-30e).

Writing and drawing are for all children.

English sign for English restaurant, 4 years 4 months.

Figure 8-30a

Japanese sign for Japanese play restaurant, 4 years 4 months.

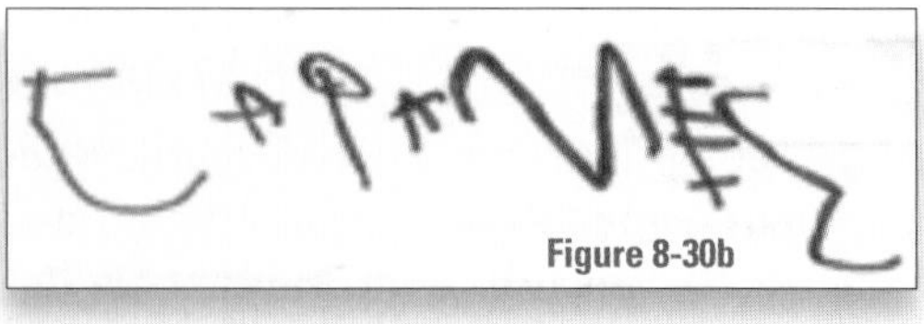

Figure 8-30b

Drawing of dog lying down, 4 years 7 months.

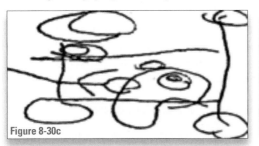

Figure 8-30c

Dog's name (mock word), 4 years 7 months.

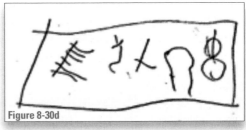

Figure 8-30d

Some children need special assistance and explicit help, and this child received an abundance of both. But most importantly, children need the freedom to draw and write as they wish during center time, in play, and at the writing center. Engagement in meaningful writing experiences not only keeps children interested and motivated to write but also provides

Thank-you note to Judy, 4 years 11 months.

Figure 8-30e

many opportunities for them to learn about writing. Moreover, difficulties with the physical aspects of writing should not provide a barrier to children in generating ideas and in explaining these verbally, when their physical marks for drawing or writing alone cannot convey their full meanings.

More complex pictures

Some pictures that children draw or paint now tell whole stories, or have stories under the surface, if adults probe. For example, one child drew a picture of a boat and explained, "One day, we went on a sailboat and it was cloudy and rained. We had to go back to the dock. Then, we sailed out again" (Figure 8-31a). Another child, who drew a scene at the park, said, "This is mommy, me, and my dog. My dog is barking, 'ruff, ruff, ruff!!' I'm going to pet my dog" (Figure 8-31b).

Pictures that tell a story.

4 years 11 months.

Figure 8-31a

4 years 11 months.

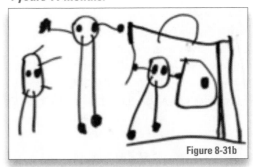

Figure 8-31b

Parents and teachers of older preschoolers can use technology to support children's content knowledge acquisition, provide new ways for children to tell and write both story and informational texts, and nurture their word creation knowledge. Examples of appropriate applications are discussed in Box 8-5 "Preschoolers, Message Composition, and Technology!"

Box 8-5 Preschoolers, Message Composition, and Technology!

Kathleen A. Paciga

Box 7-2 (see Chapter 7) provided information about developmentally appropriate digital marking tools for toddlers. During the preschool years, children can expand their knowledge of technology, especially if it is integrated with the curriculum and supported by adults. The examples here are interactive applications for computers, tablets, or smartphones that build on very young children's knowledge about people and things, from which subsequent mark-making and writing content emerge. The examples expand the content in Box 8-1 (children talking about their pictures) and Box 8-2 (word creation strategies/spellings).

Apps that build content for message creation

These virtual experiences help children develop knowledge about the qualities and behaviors of people and things. Well-designed interactive apps build on children's content knowledge and have characters that replicate human and/ or animal needs and emotions. Of course, the child's interactions should be accompanied by language-rich conversations with an adult.

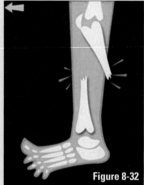
Figure 8-32

- Toca Boca's apps (award-winning) provide playful opportunities that complement and extend traditional dramatic play explorations. For example, in Toca Doctor HD children take care of another person by removing their splinters, cleaning and bandaging a wound, or fixing a broken leg (Figure 8-32).

- In LeapFrog's Leapster Explorer or LeapPad *Pet Pad* (a game loaded on the device), pets can be fed, bathed, entertained, and even petted, much like a real animal. As children explore and play with the digital pet, an adult can make connections to the care of real pets.

Even though children need mostly real experiences with animals and people, virtual experiences can extend a child's real experiences, just as traditional books can, or provide opportunities not available to a child in real life (e.g., a child with allergies might not have a pet). Just as with traditional books, interactions with adults are critical to the child's learning.

Composing messages in the twenty-first century

Many authors and literate adults now use technology in previously unimagined ways. For example, adults today use audio and visual (i.e., media) components in written messages, and document messages in ways that differ from when they were children. Options to explore for composing with preschool and kindergarten children include some of the following:

- Puppet Pals HD also supports storytelling, but its Director's Pass (an in-app purchase) allows use of a child's own photos as character puppets or settings. For example, teachers or children can snap pictures of the events and people involved in a field trip and then import them into Puppet Pals.

So Much More than the ABCs

Summing up Phase 3

Using writing and drawing to communicate and for enjoyment becomes commonplace for some children during the period between 4 and 5 years of age. It is just something they do—*if* adults have been accepting, sensitive, and helpful in response to their previous efforts, and have provided many opportunities. Skill

- With Toontastic, a child selects or draws a setting, inserts characters (from drawings or a menu), presses a start animation button, and then tells a story while moving the characters on screen. Toontastic plays back the child's voice and the characters' movements. Children can add music and share with family or friends around the world. In a screenshot of a cartoon, created by a preschooler with adult assistance (Figure 8-33), a pirate saved a scuba diver by throwing an octopus to distract a shark, which allowed the scuba diver to climb onto the ship to safety.

Figure 8-33

- ShowMe Interactive Whiteboard provides an onscreen drawing canvas in which to insert line drawings, handwritten words, or images, and allows speaking about a drawing. Drawings and spoken explanations can be stored and shared via the Show Me server. For example, after listening to *Snakes: Long, Longer, Longest* by Jerry Pallotta and Van Wallach, a preschooler drew a picture on the screen to show longer and shorter, and recorded explanations about it.

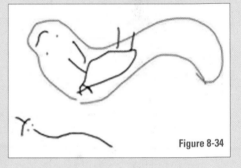

Figure 8-34

  While drawing (Figure 8-34), he said, "This one. Big. Fat. [Ana]conda. Plant [s]nake. He's black and little. Eyes. Mouth. Eyes. And Pig. He eat it." A teacher can view and listen to the drawing as it develops, rather than try to recap a child's story after it's completed.

- Dragon Dictation allows recording and editing of a dictated message, before inserting it into another document (a complex task) or sending it via email. Preschool teachers might listen to a ShowMe recording with its child composer, discuss explanations, and verbally recast and expand the child's language to draft more coherent, connected thoughts, and complete sentences. (Note: Dragon Dictation is sensitive to articulation.)

Technology supports word creation

- Shopping apps help children spell items for a shopping list, much like the grocery store ads that are sometimes available in a dramatic play area. Children can also access Dominick's, Kroger Co., or other grocery store apps to view weekly sale items, select items for purchase, and add these to a shopping list or copy item names to a paper and pencil list.

- There are many apps that focus on letter knowledge and phonological awareness. These are discussed in Box 5-7 in Chapter 5.

Although these apps are useful to support message composition, not all children have access to this technology (Common Sense Media 2011).

increases by leaps and bounds during this year, especially when children have the benefit of preschool teachers who respond genuinely to their ideas and concepts, and help them in ways that support literacy skills learning (e.g., segmenting sounds in words, linking letters to isolated sounds, and noticing the specific features of letters).

With all that is at stake for a child's learning and for a child's knowing that our attention is genuine, parents and teachers should be careful not to slip into responding to children's writing and drawing with quick pat praise (e.g., "Good job," "Good girl," or "Fantastic!"). Because this kind of language is devoid of content, its frequent use limits the diversity of the language that children hear from adults. Less diversity in language used with children limits the vocabulary and content to which children are exposed through conversation, which in turn is related negatively to children's language development (Pan et al. 2005).

There is a need for teacher-guided instruction on literacy skills in preschool classrooms, and some time must be devoted daily to this. But preschoolers also need to use writing in play and for real purposes (e.g., letters, notes, signs, lists). Skilled teachers can work literacy instruction in as they help children meet their goals. (See Box 8-6 "Enhancing Story Creation Skills in Dramatic Play through Teacher Involvement.")

Box 8-6 Enhancing Story Creation Skills in Dramatic Play through Teacher Involvement

Dramatic play involves composing, which is an important aspect of writing, even though such scenarios are not written down. Children's dramatic play provides wonderful opportunities for teachers to support children's ability to create stories, as well as additional literacy-related skills. We provide an example here to illustrate (Schickedanz 1999, 54).

One day, after two children had built a boat in the block area, one child said, "Get in! There are sharks in the water!" A teacher who was listening said, "Oh, my. Maybe you should make a sign to warn people who might be swimming. Signs are often posted at beaches when it isn't safe. Signs say something like, 'Swim at your own risk. Shark-infested waters.'"

Shark Infested Waters sign in block area.

Figure 8-35

The boys jumped out of the boat, got writing materials and tape from the supplies, and one boy wrote BVOVOHR. He also drew two pictures, and then wrote another string of letters beneath them (TOPBIV) (Figure 8-35). Then, he tore off a piece of tape and began taping the sign to the boat, while his friend held it in position.

At this point, the teacher asked, in a worried tone, "What if you go out to sea and people don't see the sign? They won't know they should take precautions." The boys stopped for a moment to think before taking their sign to the block shelves and taping it to one end. "That's a good idea," said the teacher. "Now, it's where everyone can see it."

Teachers might also comment to children's parents at the end of the day when something like this has transpired. A teacher might say, "Oh, be sure to ask Devone about the boat he built today and the sign he made about sharks." The teacher might also place some books about sharks in the book area and encourage the children to take a look. If they engage with the books and learn more about sharks, the teacher might ask if they might like to write a book about what they know.

Teachers have other opportunities to support multiple aspects of writing in dramatic play. Here's a list of some dramatic play contexts, and writing materials and opportunities that teachers can support with them.

Doctor's Office Play

- Child-created signs, such as Doctor Is In, Doctor Is Out; No Smoking; Open and Closed
- Message pad, appointment log (mock computer screen and keyboard), and pencil for receptionist
- Photocopied blank health charts for each patient for child doctor to fill out
- Clipboard for health charts while filling them out
- Index cards (cut into quarters) for appointment cards, which the office receptionist fills in
- Pad of blank prescription forms for the child doctor to fill in

Grocery Store Play

- Message pad and pencils for grocery lists
- Child-created labels for store departments: Dairy, Produce, Bakery, and so on
- Brown paper bags on which children have written the store name
- Child-created signs with store hours

Restaurant Play

- Magnetic letters and board on which children can write and post names of specials
- Place mats made by children from construction paper with restaurant on it (laminated)
- Notepads and pencils for wait staff use in taking orders
- Child-created Open and Closed signs
- Child-created Business Hours sign

Post Office Play

- Child-created Business Hours sign
- Stationery and envelopes in writing center or house play supplies for children to write letters
- Child-created play money
- Cardboard boxes near the house play area, with Post Office written on them by children, for mailing letters

Transportation Play

- Child-created paper tickets
- Poster with arrival and departure times posted
- Child-created play money

Phase 4: More and more of everything

In the period that spans 5 years to 5 years and 9 months, children's writing and drawing change somewhat remarkably, especially in children with a long history of writing and drawing experience. Although children who have not had experiences with marking in infancy and toddlerhood can catch up during preschool, if adequate opportunities and support are provided, children who enter kindergarten without having had a multitude of writing and drawing experiences usually struggle to catch up. As we have seen, the knowledge children gain from early writing and drawing experiences include code-related skills, such as phonological awareness and letter-sound associations, as well as language skills (i.e., from talking with adults about their drawings and paintings).

We do not provide examples here of children who drew and wrote very little before reaching kindergarten. Instead, we show samples that illustrate what children *can* do by this age, if they have had many experiences, starting early in the second year of life or by 3 years of age in an excellent preschool.

The first sample in Figure 8-36a is Jake's sign to advertise a Halloween Puppet Show that he and a friend organized in the block area. Jake had turned 5 when school started in September, and was 5 years and 3 months old when he wrote this sign, with spelling assistance from the teacher. The second sample is a letter Jake wrote when 5 years and 7 months old (Figure 8-36b) to inform the preschool director about the mailbox they had made for her valentine cards.

The next five pictures in Figure 8-36 show the cover and a few pages from an alphabet book made by two girls who turned 5 during their preschool year (Figures 8-36c, d, e, f, and g). Five years and 7 months old at the time, the girls had gotten the idea of making their own little alphabet book after they had participated in making a class alphabet book a few weeks earlier.

Figure 8-36. Examples of writing and drawing in 5-year-olds.

Sign to advertise a Halloween Puppet Show in Block area, 5 years 3 months.

Figure 8-36a

Letter to Judy about a mailbox for her, 5 years 7 months.

Figure 8-36b

Alphabet book cover.

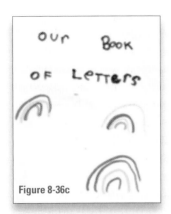

Figure 8-36c

Page of alphabet book.

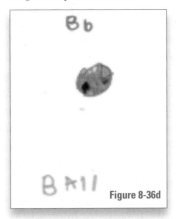

Figure 8-36d

Page of alphabet book.

Figure 8-36e

Page of alphabet book.

Figure 8-36f

Page of alphabet book.

Figure 8-36g

5 years 2 months "Hi, Grandma we will be leaving America."

Figure 8-36h

They drew all of the pictures and wrote all the words, sometimes consulting alphabet books in their classroom library, and sometimes asking a teacher for help. It took them nearly a week. One of the girls spoke Russian at home and was learning English as a second language at her preschool. Her friend, whose home language was English, had a bit more oral language skill, including vocabulary, and suggested many of the items they should draw to accompany each letter. The girls were quite equal in their phonological awareness skill and their alphabet letter writing skill. The book shows what is possible with wonderful teachers who think writing and drawing are important, know how to support their development in young children, and also understand the importance and power of friendships in children's learning, perhaps especially for language learning (Tabors 2008).

A child who was a little past 5 years of age created the last example in this collection (Figure 8-36h). During the period when her family was planning their trip home to South Korea, she wrote a note, all by herself, to her grandmother, saying, "Hi, Grandma. We will be leaving America." Here's how she spelled the words: "Hi, GAMA. WE WILL BE LEVING AMARAC." The family spoke primarily Korean at home, and the child had learned English from an English immersion preschool, which she attended for two years (see Box 8-7 "Invented Spelling Skill in Preschoolers Who Are English Language Learners").

Even children who are in kindergarten when they are between 5 years and 5 years and 9 months of age can benefit from additional writing experiences at home and in after care programs. For example, Adam drew the pictures of a castle, and of a man on a horse with a dog, in November and January, respectively, of his kindergarten year (Figures 8-36i and 8-36j), while attending afternoon family child care. Time was short in his morning-only kindergarten, and many of the writing activities involved drawing and writing about an assigned topic or focus.

Kindergarten typically involves more specific assignments than does preschool for writing and also gives more attention to handwriting and code-related skills. Opportunities to draw and write at home or in an after-school program help children

Box 8-7 Invented Spelling Skill in Preschoolers Who Are English Language Learners

We noted when discussing individual writing samples that some children were bilingual or trilingual. Although we did not conduct systematic studies, it has seemed to us, over the years, that children who were learning more than one language often developed higher levels of phonological awareness, compared to their monolingual peers. Specifically, they often developed skill in creating phonemic-based spellings, independently (e.g., Kasal Sav for "castle save"). We often wondered why.

We have indicated throughout Chapter 8 that many samples were collected in classrooms where English was the language of instruction, and that children created most of the invented samples near the end of their second year of preschool. Additionally, in all of the classrooms from which samples were drawn, teachers scaffolded the spelling of words when children requested help (i.e., segmented the words into their phonemes, and linked these sounds to letters that represent them). They also "talked out loud" in the same way about spellings when writing words in a group situation, such as when children dictated something about a recent field trip or the content for a thank-you note to a classroom volunteer or other guest.

The classrooms also included high levels of language interaction between adults and children, and among the children, in a variety of play settings, and provided a curriculum rich in content and oral language, including vocabulary. As was noted in Chapter 3 (see Box 3-7), children learn vocabulary better when they are provided information about the words, compared to situations in which they are taught only simple labels for objects and actions, without any associated information.

Finally, as discussed in Chapter 5, size of vocabulary is related to phonological awareness skill. One hypothesis about the nature of this relationship suggests that a larger vocabulary prompts reorganization of stored words, based on global sound characteristics, to more segmental features (i.e., smaller units of sound).

All of these features of the social setting, and of the classroom's curriculum and instruction, would likely increase an older preschoolers' skill in creating phonemic-based spellings on their own, but they do not explain why a bilingual or trilingual child in such

Adam's castle with knights, 5 years 4 months at home.

5 years 6 months, afternoon child care.

Figure 8-36i

Figure 8-36j

settings might develop greater skill than their monolingual peers. Recent research on the effects of bilingualism on the brain provides some clues.

Researchers have found that learning a second language actually changes the brain's auditory system (Krizman et al. 2012). Specifically, learning two languages seems to cause children to pay more attention to sounds. Instead of becoming confused by the two (or three) languages they are learning, the researchers concluded that plasticity in the brain allows bilinguals to develop more efficient and flexible auditory systems, which leads to greater auditory attention.

After reading this new research, we also recalled that many of the bilingual and trilingual children watched the teacher's mouth as the words requested were spoken orally and segmented into their phonemes, and as letters needed to write the sounds were named. Monolingual children, on the other hand, did not tend to watch the teacher's mouth, probably because they could simply listen to a word and remember it, and because they could more easily understand exactly what letter the teacher had named. Bilingual children, on the other hand, sometimes checked about the letter's name ("M" when we had said "N") to get clarification.

The monolingual's greater familiarity with English vocabulary led to less attention to the teacher's instructional help, and perhaps elicited less of it. In the long run, looking at the teacher's mouth and listening more attentively to letters named (i.e., to make sure they knew what had been said) might have led to more phonological awareness skill in the bilingual children.

We also wonder whether teachers might have been more explicit, and might have repeated information more often, when assisting bilingual children with spellings, because they thought more explicitness was necessary, or because teachers simply respond with more information when children seem more attentive (e.g., look more often at the teacher, watch the teacher's mouth).

We offer these thoughts as reflections about our experience, because we did not collect data systematically. Based on the new research, we wonder whether there might be a phonological awareness benefit for children whose first language is English, if they, too, had opportunities during the preschool years to learn a second language, such as would occur in a two-way bilingual program.

maintain a high level of motivation while they are supported in kindergarten to develop additional skill.

Concluding thoughts about writing during the preschool years

During the preschool years, children's alphabet letters become better approximations to their conventional forms. Children also develop some understanding of how letters are used to make words, which is informed by the development of phonological awareness (see Chapter 5). When a fairly good grasp of phonological awareness is coupled with the insight that letters function to represent sounds in spoken words (i.e., the alphabetic principle), some older preschoolers start to invent spellings.

Preschoolers' drawings and paintings also begin to resemble the objects and actions that children intend to depict, and their content becomes more and more complex. Because children cannot yet "tell all" with pictures or with writing, it is extremely important for adults to prompt children to relate these meanings more fully with language (see Box 8-1).

As with all aspects of development, children vary greatly in their writing and drawing behavior. Researchers Hart and Risley (1995) estimated a "30 million word gap" by age 3 between children hearing the most language before age 3 and children hearing the least. While we don't know the extent of the "marking gap," we do know that some 3-year-olds enter preschool with about two years of marking experience, while others enter with virtually none. Preschool teachers should *expect* wide variations in children's marking behavior and interest, while not *accepting* low levels of skills as "a given" (i.e., as inborn differences in capacity). If preschool teachers nurture and support writing in all children, no matter the status of their interest and skill when they start, all children will have a chance to learn and thrive in this area.

References

AAP (American Academy of Pediatrics). 2001. "Policy Statement: Children, Adolescents, and Television." *Pediatrics* 101 (2): 423–36.

AAP (American Academy of Pediatrics). 2011. "Policy Statement: Media Use by Children Younger Than 2 Years." *Pediatrics* 128 (5): 1040–45.

Achieve, Inc. 2005. "Rising to the Challenge: Are High School Graduates Prepared for College and Work? A Study of Recent High School Graduates, College Instructors, and Employers." Washington, DC: Author.

Adams, M.J. 1990. *Beginning to Read: Thinking and Learning about Print.* Cambridge, MA: MIT Press.

Anthony, J.L., C.J. Lonigan, K. Driscoll, B.M. Phillips, & S.R. Burgess. 2003. "Preschool Phonological Sensitivity: A Quasi-Parallel Progression of Word Structure Units and Cognitive Operations." *Reading Research Quarterly* 38 (4): 470–87.

Applebee, A.N. 1978. *The Child's Concept of Story: Ages Two to Seventeen.* Chicago: University of Chicago Press.

Armbruster, B.M., M. Lehr, & J. Osborn. 2003. *A Child Becomes a Reader.* Portsmouth, NH: RMC Research Corporation.

Baghban, M. 1984. *Our Daughter Learns to Read and Write: A Case Study from Birth to Three.* Newark, DE: International Reading Association.

Baillargeon, R. 1995. "A Model of Physical Reasoning in Infancy." In *Advances in Psychological Science*, Vol. 9, eds. C. Rovee-Collier & L.P. Lipsitt, 305–71. Norwood, NJ: Ablex.

Baillargeon, R., A. Needham, & J. DeVos. 1992. "The Development of Young Infants' Intuitions about Support." *Early Development and Parenting* 1 (2): 69–78.

Ball, E.W., & B.A. Blachman. 1991. "Does Phoneme Awareness Training in Kindergarten Make a Difference in Early Word Recognition and Developmental Spelling?" *Reading Research Quarterly* 26 (1): 49–66.

Barrera, M.E., & D. Maurer. 1981. "The Perception of Facial Expressions by the Three-Month-Old." *Child Development* 52 (1): 203–06.

Bartlett, F. 1958. *Thinking: An Experimental and Social Study.* London: Allen & Unwin.

Beals, D. 2001. "Eating and Reading: Links between Family Conversations with Preschoolers and Later Language and Literacy." In *Beginning Literacy with Language: Young Children Learning at Home and School*, eds. D.K. Dickinson & P.O. Tabors, 75–92. Baltimore: Brookes.

Beck, I.L., & M.G. McKeown. 2001. "Text Talk: Capturing the Benefits of Read-Aloud Experiences for Young Children." *The Reading Teacher* 55 (1): 10–20.

Beck, I., M. McKeown, & L. Kucan. 2002. *Bringing Words to Life: Robust Vocabulary Instruction.* New York: Guilford.

Bell, M.A., & C.D. Wolfe. 2004. "Emotion and Cognition: An Intricately Bound Developmental Process." *Child Development* 75 (2): 366–70.

Beneke, S.J., M.M. Ostrosky, & L.G. Katz. 2008. "Calendar Time for Young Children: Good Intentions Gone Awry." *Young Children* 63 (3): 12–16.

Benson, M.S. 1997. "Psychological Causation and Goal–Based Episodes: Low-Income Children's Emerging Narrative Skills." *Early Childhood Research Quarterly* 12 (4): 439–457.

Berhenke, A., A.L. Miller, E. Brown, E., R. Seifer, & S. Dickstein. 2011. "Observed Emotional and Behavioral Indicators of Motivation Predict School Readiness in Head Start Graduates." *Early Childhood Research Quarterly* 26 (4): 430–41.

Best, R.M., R.G. Floyd, & D.S. McNamara. 2008. "Differential Competencies Contributing to Children's Comprehension of Narratives and Expository Texts." *Reading Psychology* 29 (2): 137–64.

Biemiller, A., & C. Boote. 2006. "An Effective Method for Building Meaning Vocabulary in Primary Grades." *Journal of Educational Psychology* 98 (1): 44–57.

Birckmayer, J., A. Kennedy, & A. Stonehouse. 2008. *From Lullabies to Literature: Stories in the Lives of Infants and Toddlers.* Washington, DC: NAEYC; Castle Hill, Australia: Pademelon Press.

Blair, C. 2002. "Integrating Cognition and Emotion in a Neurobiological Conceptualization of Children's Functioning at School Entry." *American Psychologist* 57 (2): 111–27.

Blake, J., S. Macdonald, L. Bayrami, V. Agosta, & A. Milian. 2006. "Book Reading Styles in Dual-Parent and Single-Mother Families." *British Journal of Educational Psychology* 76 (3): 501–15.

Bloodgood, J.W. 1999. "What's in a Name? Children's Name Writing and Literacy Acquisition." *Reading Research Quarterly* 34 (3): 342–67.

Bloom, K. 1977. "Patterning of Infant Vocal Behavior." *Journal of Experimental Child Psychology* 23 (3): 367–77.

Booth, A.E. 2009. "Causal Supports for Early Word Learning." *Child Development* 80 (4): 1234–50.

Bornstein, M.H., M.E. Arterberry, C. Mash, & N. Manian. 2011. "Discrimination of Facial Expressions by 5-Month-Old Infants of Nondepressed and Clinically Depressed Mothers." *Infant Behavior & Development* 34 (1): 100–106.

Bourgeois, K.S., A.W. Khawar, S.A. Neal, & J.J. Lockman. 2005. "Infant Manual Exploration of Objects, Surfaces, and Their Interrelations." *Infancy* 8 (3): 233–52.

Brazelton, T.B., E. Tronick, L. Adamson, H. Als, & S. Weise. 1975. "Early Mother-Infant Reciprocity." In *Parent-Infant Interaction* (Ciba Foundation Symposium. No. 33). Amsterdam: Elsevier.

Bretherton, I. 1984. "Representing the Social World in Symbolic Play." In *Symbolic Play: The Development of Social Understanding*, ed. I. Bretherton, 3–41. New York: Academic Press.

Bretherton, I., & M. Beeghly. 1982. "Talking about Internal States: The Acquisition of an Explicit Theory of Mind." *Developmental Psychology* 18 (6): 906–21.

Britto, P.R., J. Brooks-Gunn, & T.M. Griffin. 2006. "Maternal Reading and Teaching Patterns: Associations with School Readiness in Low-Income African American Families." *Reading Research Quarterly* 41 (1): 68–89.

Broerse, J., & G. Elias. 1994. "Changes in the Content and Timing of Mothers' Talk to Infants." *British Journal of Developmental Psychology* 12 (1): 131–45.

Brooks, R., & A.N. Meltzoff. 2008. "Infant Gaze Following and Pointing Predict Accelerated Vocabulary Growth through Two Years of Age: A Longitudinal, Growth Curve Modeling Study." *Journal of Child Language* 35 (1): 207–20.

Brown, R. 1973. *A First Language: The Early Stages*. Cambridge, MA: Harvard University Press.

Bryant, G.A., & H.C. Barrett. 2007. "Recognizing Intentions in Infant-Directed Speech: Evidence for Universals." *Psychological Science* 18 (8): 746–51.

Bus, A., M.H. van IJzendoorn, & A.D. Pellegrini. 1995. "Joint Book Reading Makes for Success in Learning to Read: A Meta-Analysis on Intergenerational Transmission of Literacy." *Review of Educational Research* 65 (1): 1–21.

Bushnell, E.W., & J.P. Boudreau. 1993. "Motor Development and the Mind: The Potential Role of Motor Abilities as a Determinant of Aspects of Perceptual Development." *Child Development* 64 (4): 1005–21.

Butterworth, G.E., & N. Jarrett. 1991. "What Minds Have in Common in Space: Spatial Mechanisms Serving Joint Visual Attention in Infancy." *British Journal of Developmental Psychology* 9 (1): 55–72.

Campos, J., C. Frankel, & L. Camras. 2004. "On the Nature of Emotional Regulation." *Child Development* 75 (2): 377–94.

Carlson, K., & J.L. Cunningham. 1990. "Effects of Pencil Diameter on the Grapho-Motor Skills of Preschoolers." *Early Childhood Research Quarterly* 5: 279–93

Carey, S. 1978. "The Child as Word Learner." In *Linguistic Theory and Psychological Reality*, eds. M. Halle, J. Bresnan, & G.A. Miller, 359–73. Cambridge, MA: MIT Press.

Carey, S. 1985. *Conceptual Change in Childhood*. Cambridge, MA: MIT Press.

Caswell, L.J., & N.K. Duke. 1998. "Non-Narrative as a Catalyst for Literacy Development." *Language Arts* 75 (2): 108–17.

Chall, J.S., & V.A. Jacobs. 2003. "Poor Children's Fourth-Grade Slump." *American Educator* 27 (1): 14–15, 44.

Christ, T., & X.C. Wang. 2012. "Supporting Preschoolers' Vocabulary Learning: Using a Decision-Making Model to Select Appropriate Words and Methods." *Young Children* 67 (2): 74–80.

Cioffi, G. 1984. "Observing Composing Behaviors of Primary-Age Children: The Interaction of Oral and Written Language." In *New Directions in Composition Research*, eds. R. Beach & L.S. Bridwell, 171–90. New York: Guilford.

Clay, M.M. 1975. *What Did I Write?* Auckland, New Zealand: Heinemann.

Cohen, L.B., & B.A. Younger. 1984. "Infant Perception of Angular Relations." *Infant Behavior & Development* 7 (1): 37–47.

Cole, P.M., S.E. Martin, & T.A. Dennis. 2004. "Emotion Regulation as a Scientific Construct: Methodological Challenges and Directions for Child Development Research. *Child Development* 74 (2): 317–33.

Collins, M.F. 2004. "ELL Preschoolers' English Vocabulary Acquisition and Story Comprehension from Storybook Reading." (Unpublished doctoral dissertation.) Boston University, Boston, MA.

Collins, M.F. 2010. "ELL Preschoolers' English Vocabulary Acquisition from Storybook Reading." *Early Childhood Research Quarterly* 25 (1): 84–97. doi:10.1016/j.ecresq.2009.07.009.

Collins, M.F. 2011. "Supporting Vocabulary and Comprehension in Young Children: Multiple Goals for Storybook Reading." Paper presented at the annual conference of the Literacy Research Association, Jacksonville, FL.

Colonnesi, C., G.J.J.M. Stams, I. Koster, & M.J. Noom. 2010. "The Relation between Pointing and Language Development: A Meta-Analysis." *Developmental Review* 30 (4): 352–66.

Common Sense Media. 2011. "Zero to Eight: Children's Media Use in America." A Common Sense Media Research Study. Retrieved from www.commonsensemedia.org/research/zero-eight-childrens-media-use-america/key-finding-4%3A-tv-dominates-young-child-media-time.

Condon, S. 1979. "Neonatal Entrainment and Enculturation." In *Before Speech: The Beginning of Interpersonal Communication*, ed. M. Bullowa, 131–48. Cambridge: Cambridge University Press.

Connolly, K., & M. Dalgleish. 1989. "The Emergence of Tool-Using Skill in Infancy." *Developmental Psychology* 25 (6): 894–912.

Cooper, R.P., & R.N. Aslin. 1990. "Preference for Infant-Directed Speech in the First Month after Birth." *Child Development* 61 (5): 1584–95.

Copeland, K.A., S. Sherman, C.A. Kendeigh, H.J. Kalkwarf, & B.E. Saelens. 2012. "Societal Values and Policies May Curtail Preschool Children's Physical Activity in Child Care Centers." *Pediatrics* 129 (2): 265–74.

Copple, C., ed. 2012. *Growing Minds: Building Strong Cognitive Foundations in Early Childhood.* Washington, DC: NAEYC.

Copple, C., & S. Bredekamp, eds. 2009. *Developmentally Appropriate Practice in Early Childhood Programs Serving Children from Birth through Age 8.* 3rd. ed. Washington, DC: NAEYC.

Correia, M.P. 2011. "Fiction vs. Informational Texts: Which Will Kindergartners Choose?" *Young Children* 66 (6): 100–104.

Corkum, V., & C. Moore. 1995. "Development of Joint Visual Attention in Infants." In *Joint Attention: Its Origins and Role in Development*, eds. C. Moore & P. Dunham, 61–83. Hillsdale, NJ: Erlbaum.

Council of Chief State School Officers. 2012. "Framework for English Language Proficiency Development Standards Corresponding to the Common Core State Standards and the Next Generation Science Standards." Washington, DC: Author.

Coyne, M., D.B. McCoach, S. Loftus, R. Zipoli, & S. Kapp. 2009. "Direct Vocabulary Instruction in Kindergarten: Teaching for Breadth vs. Depth." *Elementary School Journal* 110 (1): 1–18.

Crain-Thoreson, C., & P.S. Dale. 1992. "Do Early Talkers Become Early Readers? Linguistic Precocity, Preschool Language, and Emergent Literacy." *Developmental Psychology* 28 (3): 521–429.

Crosson, A.C., & N.K. Lesaux. 2010. "Revisiting Assumptions about the Relationship of Fluent Reading to Comprehension: Spanish Speakers' Text-Reading Fluency in English." *Reading and Writing* 23 (5): 475–94.

Cunningham, A., & J. Zibulsky. 2011. "Tell Me a Story: Examining the Benefits of Shared Reading." In *Handbook of Early Literacy Research*, Vol. 3, eds. S.B. Neuman & D.K. Dickinson, 396–411. New York: Guilford.

Dahl, K., & P. Freppon. 1995. "A Comparison of Inner-City Children's Interpretations of Reading and Writing Instruction in the Early Grades in Skills-Based and Whole Language Classrooms." *Reading Research Quarterly* 31 (1): 50–74.

De Jong, M.T., & A.G. Bus. 2002. "Quality of Book-Reading Matters for Emergent Readers: An Experiment with the Same Book in a Regular or Electronic Format." *Journal of Educational Psychology* 94 (1): 145–55.

De Jong, M.T., & A.G. Bus. 2004. "The Efficacy of Electronic Books in Fostering Kindergarten Children's Emergent Story Understanding." *Reading Research Quarterly* 39 (4): 378–93.

Deckner, D.F., L.B. Adamson, & R. Bakeman. 2006. "Child and Maternal Contributions to Shared Reading: Effects on Language and Literacy Development." *Journal of Applied Developmental Psychology* 27 (1): 31–41.

DeLoache, J.S., & O.A.P. DeMendoza. 1987. "Joint Picturebook Interactions of Mothers and 1-Year-Old Children." *British Journal of Developmental Psychology* 5 (2): 111–23.

Dickinson, D.K., R.M. Golinkoff, & K. Hirsh-Pasek. 2010. "Speaking Out for Language: Why Language Is Central to Reading Development." *Educational Researcher* 39 (4): 305–15.

Dickinson, D.K., A. McCabe, N. Clark-Chiarelli, & A. Wolf. 2004. "Cross-Language Transfer of Phonological Awareness in Low-Income Spanish and English Bilingual Children." *Applied Psycholinguistics* 25 (3): 323–47.

Dickinson, D.K., & M.V. Porche. 2011. "Relation between Language Experiences in Preschool Classrooms and Children's Kindergarten and Fourth-Grade Language and Reading Abilities." *Child Development* 82 (3): 870–86.

Dickinson, D.K., & M.W. Smith. 1994. "Long-Term Effects of Preschool Teachers' Book Readings on Low-Income Children's Vocabulary and Story Comprehension." *Reading Research Quarterly* 29 (2): 105–22.

Duke, N. 2000. "3.6 Minutes per Day: The Scarcity of Informational Texts in First Grade." *Reading Research Quarterly* 35 (2): 202–24.

Duke, N.K. 2004. "The Case for Informational Text." *Educational Leadership* 61 (6): 40–44.

Duke, N.K., & V.S. Bennett-Armistead, with A. Huxley, M. Johnson, D. McLurkin, E. Roberts, C. Rosen, & E. Vogel. 2003. *Reading and Writing Informational Text in the Primary Grades: Research-Based Practices.* New York: Scholastic.

Duke, N.K., & J. Carlisle. 2011. "The Development of Comprehension." In *Handbook of Reading Research,* Vol. IV, eds. M.L. Kamil, P.D. Pearson, E.B. Moje, & P.P. Afflerbach, 199–228. New York: Routledge.

Duke, N.K., & J. Kays. 1998. "'Can I Say Once upon a Time?': Kindergarten Children Developing Knowledge of Information Book Language." *Early Childhood Research Quarterly* 13 (2): 295–318.

Duke, N.K., K.L. Roberts, R.R. Norman, N.M. Martin, J.A. Knight, P.M. Morsink, & S.L. Calkins. 2010. "What We've Been Learning about Children's Visual Literacy and What It Might Mean for Assessment and Instruction." Paper presented at the annual meeting of the International Reading Association.

Dunn, J. 1998. "Young Children's Understanding of Other People: Evidence from Observation within the Family." In *Cultural Worlds of Early Childhood*, eds. Woodhead, D. Faulkner, & K. Littleton, 101–16. New York: The Open University.

Dunn, J., I. Bretherton, & P. Munn. 1987. "Conversations about Feeling States between Mothers and Their Young Children." *Developmental Psychology* 23 (1): 132–39.

Durkin, D. 1966. *Children Who Read Early: Two Longitudinal Studies.* New York: Teachers College Press.

Dyson, A.H. 2000. "Writing and the Sea of Voices: Oral Language in, around, and about Writing." In *Perspectives on Writing: Research, Theory, and Practice*, eds. R. Indrisano & James Squire, 45–65. Newark, DE: International Reading Association.

Ehri, L.C., & J. Sweet. 1991. "Fingerpoint-Reading of Memorized Text: What Enables Beginners to Process the Print?" *Reading Research Quarterly* 26 (4): 443–62.

Elley, W.B. 1989. "Vocabulary Acquisition from Listening to Stories." *Reading Research Quarterly* 24 (2): 174–87. doi:10.2307/747863.

Fang, Z. 2008. "Going beyond the Fab Five: Helping Students Cope with the Unique Linguistic Challenges of Expository Reading in Intermediate Grades." *Journal of Adolescent & Adult Literacy* 51 (6): 476–87.

Fantozzi, V.B. 2012. "Exploring Elephant Seals in New Jersey: Preschoolers Use Collaborative Multimedia Albums." *Young Children* 67 (3): 42–49.

Fantz, R.L. 1963. "Pattern Vision in Newborn Infants." *Science* 140 (3564): 296–97.

Fein, G.G. 1975. "A Transformational Analysis of Pretending." *Developmental Psychology* 11 (3): 291–96.

Fein, G.G. 1984. "The Self-Building Potential of Make-Believe Play, or 'I Got a Fish, All by Myself.'" In *Child's Play: Developmental and Applied*, eds. T.D. Yawkey & A.D. Pellegrini, 125–42. Hillsdale, NJ: Lawrence Erlbaum.

Fenson, L. 1984. "Developmental Trends for Action and Speech in Pretend Play." In *Symbolic Play: The Development of Social Understanding*, ed. I. Bretherton, 249–70. New York: Academic Press.

Fenson, L., & D.S. Ramsay. 1980. "Decentration and Integration of the Child's Play in the Second Year." *Child Development* 51 (1): 171–78.

Fenson, L., P.S. Dale, J.S. Reznick, E. Bates, D.J. Thal, & S.J. Pethick. 1994. "Variability in Early Communicative Development." *Monographs of the Society for Research in Child Development* 59 (5): Serial No. 242.

Fenson, L., J. Kagan, R. Kearsley, & P. Zelazo. 1976. "The Developmental Progression of Manipulative Play in the First Two Years." *Child Development 47* (1): 232–36.

Fernald, A., & T. Simon. 1984. "Expanded Intonation Contours in Mothers' Speech to Newborns." *Developmental Psychology* 10 (1): 104–13.

Ferreiro, E. 1986. "The Interplay between Information and Assimilation in Beginning Literacy." In *Emergent Literacy: Writing and Reading*, eds. W.H. Teale & E. Sulzby, 15–49. Norwood, NJH: Ablex.

Ferreiro, E., & A. Teberosky. 1982. *Literacy before Schooling*. Translated by K.G. Castro. Portsmouth, NH: Heinemann.

Fisch, S.M., J.S. Shulman, A. Akerman, & G.A. Levin. 2002. "Reading between the Pixels: Parent–Child Interaction While Reading Online Storybooks." *Early Education and Development* 12 (4): 435–51.

Fivush, R. 1991. "The Social Construction of Personal Narratives." *Merrill-Palmer Quarterly* 37 (1): 59–81.

Fletcher, K.L., & B. Jean-Francois. 1998. "Spontaneous Responses to Repeated Reading in Young Children from At Risk Backgrounds." *Early Childhood Development and Care* 146 (1): 53–68.

Fletcher, K.L., A. Perez, C. Hooper, & A.H. Claussen. 2005. "Responsiveness and Attention during Picture-Book Reading in 18-Month-Old to 24-Month-Old Toddlers At Risk." *Early Child Development & Care* 175 (1): 63–83.

Fletcher, K.L., & E. Reese. 2005. "Picture Book Reading with Young Children: A Conceptual Framework." *Developmental Review* 25 (1): 64–103.

Flom, R., G.O. Deak, C.G. Phill, & A.D. Pick. 2004. "Nine-Month-Olds' Shared Visual Attention as a Function of Gesture and Object Location." *Infant Behavior & Research* 27 (1): 181–94.

Gambrell, L.B. 2011. "Seven Rules of Engagement: What's Most Important to Know about Motivation to Read." *The Reading Teacher* 65 (3): 172–82.

Gardner, H. 1980. *Artful Scribbles: The Significance of Children's Drawings.* New York: Basic Books.

Geangu, E., O. Benga, D. Stahl, & T. Striano. 2010. "Contagious Crying beyond the First Days of Life." *Infant Behavior and Development* 33 (3): 279–88.

Gelman, R., & K. Brenneman. 2004. "Science Learning Pathways for Young Children." *Early Childhood Research Quarterly* 19 (1): 150–58.

Gelman, S.A., & J.D. Coley. 1990. "The Importance of Knowing a Dodo Is a Bird: Categories and Inferences in 2-Year-Old Children." *Developmental Psychology* 26 (5): 796–804.

Genishi, C., & A.H. Dyson. 2009. *Children, Language, and Literacy: Diverse Learners in Diverse Times.* New York: Teachers College Press; Washington, DC: NAEYC.

Gesell, A., & F.L. Ilg. 1937. *Feeding Behavior of Infants.* Philadelphia: Lippincott.

Gibson, E. J. 1975. "Theory-Based Research on Reading and Its Implications for Instruction." In *Toward a Literate Society*, eds. J.B. Carroll & J.S. Chall, 288–321. New York: McGraw-Hill.

Gola, A.A.H. 2012. "Mental Verb Input for Promoting Children's Theory of Mind: A Training Study. *Cognitive Development* 27 (1): 64–76.

Goncu, A. 1998. "Development of Intersubjectivity in Social Play." In *Cultural Worlds of Early Childhood*, eds. M. Woodhead, D. Faulkner, & K. Littleton, 117–32. New York: The Open University.

Graham, S., & D. Perin. 2007. "A Meta-Analysis of Writing Instruction for Adolescent Students." *Journal of Educational Psychology* 99 (3): 445–76.

Gratier, M., & E. Devouche. 2011. "Imitation and Repetition of Prosodic Contour in Vocal Interaction at 3 Months." *Developmental Psychology* 47 (1): 67–76.

Graves, D. 1981. "A Case Study Observing the Development of Primary Children's Composing, Spelling, and Motor Behavior during the Writing Process." (Final report, NIE Grant No. G-78-0174. ED 218–653.) Durham, NH: University of New Hampshire.

Grieser, D.L. & P.K. Kuhl. 1988. "Maternal Speech to Infants in a Tonal Language: Support for Universal Prosodic Features in Motherese. *Developmental Psychology* 24 (1): 14–20.

Guthrie, J.T., W.D. Schafer, & C. Huang. 2001. "Benefits of Opportunity to Read and Balanced Reading Instruction for Reading Achievement and Engagement: A Policy Analysis of State NAEP in Maryland." *Journal of Educational Research* 94 (3): 145–62.

Guthrie, J.T., & A. Wigfield. 2000. "Engagement and Motivation in Reading." In *Handbook of Reading Research,* Vol. III, eds. M.L. Kamil, P.B. Mosenthal, P.D. Pearson, & R. Barr, 403–22. New York: Lawrence Erlbaum.

Hakuta, K., & R. Diaz. 1985. "The Relationship between Degree of Bilingualism and Cognitive Ability: A Critical Discussion and Some New Longitudinal Data." In *Children's Language*, Vol. 5, ed. K.E. Nelson, 319–44. Hillsdale, NJ: Erlbaum.

Hamlin, J.K., K. Wynn, & P. Bloom. 2007. "Social Evaluations by Preverbal Infants." *Nature* 450 (7169): 557–60.

Hammer, C.S., S. Scarpino, & M.D. Davison. 2011. "Beginning with Language: Spanish-English Bilingual Preschoolers' Early Literacy Development." In *Handbook of Early Literacy Research*, Vol. 3, eds. S.B. Neuman & D.K. Dickinson, 118–35. New York: Guilford.

Hart, B., & T.R. Risley. 1995. *Meaningful Differences in the Everyday Experience of Young American Children.* Baltimore: Brookes.

Hay, D.F., F. Nash, & J. Pederson. 1981. "Responses of Six-Month-Olds to the Distress of Their Peers." *Child Development 52* (3): 1071–75.

Hayes, J.R. 2000. "A New Framework for Understanding Cognition and Affect in Writing." In *Perspectives on Writing: Research, Theory, and Practice*, eds. R. Indrisano & J.R. Squire, 6–41. Newark, DE: International Reading Association.

Hayes, J.R., L.S. Flowers, K.A. Schriver, J. Stratman, & L. Carey. 1987. "Cognitive Processes in Revision." In *Advances in Applied Psycholinguistics: Volume 2, Reading, Writing, and Language Learning*, ed. S. Rosenberg, 176–240. New York: Cambridge University Press.

Heath, S.B. 1983. *Ways with Words: Language, Life, and Work in Communities and Classrooms.* New York: Cambridge University Press.

Hepburn, E., B. Egan, & N. Flynn. 2010. "Vocabulary Acquisition in Young Children: The Role of the Story." *Journal of Early Childhood Literacy* 10 (2): 159–82.

Hirsh-Pasek, K., & R.M. Golinkoff. 2007. *Celebrate the Scribble: Appreciating Children's Art.* Easton, PA: Crayola Beginnings Press.

Holland, J.W. 2008. "Reading Aloud with Infants: The Controversy, the Myth, and a Case Study." *Early Childhood Education Journal* 35 (4): 383–85.

Hollich, G.J., K. Hirsh-Pasek, R. Golinkoff, R.J. Brand, E. Brown, H.L. Chung, E. Hennon, C. Rocroi, & L. Bloom. 2000. "Breaking the Language Barrier: An Emergentist Coalition Model for the Origins of Word Learning." *Monographs of the Society for Research in Child Development* 65 (3): 1–135.

Hood, M., E. Conlon, & G. Andrews. 2008. "Preschool Home Literacy Practices and Children's Literacy Development: A Longitudinal Analysis." *Journal of Educational Psychology* 100 (2): 252–71.

Horner, S.L. 2004. "Observational Learning during Shared Book Reading: The Effects on Preschoolers' Attention to Print and Letter Knowledge." *Reading Psychology* 25 (3): 167–88. doi: 10.1080/027027109084714.

Hughes, F.P. 1999. *Children, Play, and Development.* 3rd ed. Boston: Allyn & Bacon.

Huttenlocher, J., W. Haight, A. Bryk, M. Seltzer, & T. Lyons. 1991. "Early Vocabulary Growth: Relation to Language Input and Gender." *Developmental Psychology* 27 (2): 236–48.

Johnson, D.D. 2000. "Just the Right Word: Vocabulary and Writing." In *Perspectives on Writing: Research, Theory, and Practice*, eds. R. Indrisano & J.R. Squire, 162–86. Newark, DE: The International Reading Association.

Johnson, M.H., S. Dziurawiec, H. Ellis, & J. Morton. 1991. "Newborns' Preferential Tracking of Face-Like Stimuli and Its Subsequent Decline." *Cognition* 40 (1-2): 1–19.

Juel, C. 1988. "Learning to Read and Write: A Longitudinal Study of 54 Children from First through Fourth Grade." *Journal of Educational Psychology* 80 (4): 437–47.

Justice, L.M., & H.L. Ezell. 2002. "Use of Storybook Reading to Increase Print Awareness in At-Risk Children. *American Journal of Speech-Language Pathology* 11 (1): 17–29.

Justice, L.M., J. Meier, & S. Walpole. 2005. "Learning New Words from Storybooks: An Efficacy Study with At-Risk Kindergartners." *Language, Speech, and Hearing Services in Schools* 36 (1): 17–32.

Justice, L.M., K. Pence, R. Bowles, & A.K. Wiggins. 2006. "An Investigation of Four Hypotheses Concerning the Order by Which 4-Year-Old Children Learn the Alphabet Letters." *Early Childhood Research Quarterly* 21 (3): 374–89.

Justice, L.M., Y. Petscher, C. Schatschgneider, & A. Mashburn. 2011. "Peer Effects in Preschool Classrooms: Classmates' Abilities Are Associated with Children's Language Growth." *Child Development* 82 (6): 1768–77.

Karniol, R. 1989. "The Role of Manual Manipulation Stages in the Infant's Acquisition of Perceived Control over Objects." *Developmental Review* 9 (3): 205–33.

Karrass, J., & J.M. Braungart-Rieker. 2005. "Effects of Shared Parent-Infant Book Reading on Early Language Acquisition." *Journal of Applied Developmental Psychology: An International Lifespan Journal* 26 (2): 133–48.

Karweit, N., & B. Wasik. 1996. "The Effects of Story Reading Programs on Literacy and Language Development of Disadvantaged Preschoolers." *Journal of Education for Students Placed at Risk* 1 (4): 319–48.

Kaye, K. 1982. *The Mental and Social Life of Babies: How Parents Create Persons*. Chicago: University of Chicago Press.

Kaye, K., & A. Fogel. 1980. "The Temporal Structure of Face-to-Face Communication between Mothers and Infants." *Developmental Psychology* 16 (5): 454–64.

Kelley, J.G., N.K. Lesaux, M.J. Kieffer, & S.E. Faller. 2010. "Effective Academic Vocabulary Instruction in the Urban Middle School." *The Reading Teacher* 64 (1): 5–14.

Kellogg, R., & S. O'Dell. 1967. *The Psychology of Children's Art*. New York: Random House Publications.

Kim, J.E., & J. Anderson. 2008. "Mother-Child Shared Reading with Print and Digital Texts." *Journal of Early Childhood Literacy* 8 (2): 213–45.

Kim, K., & E.S. Spelke. 1992. "Infants' Sensitivity to Effects of Gravity on Visible Object Motion." *Journal of Experimental Psychology: Human Perception and Performance* 18 (3): 385–93.

Kotovsky, L., & R. Baillargeon. 1994. "Calibration-Based Reasoning about Collision Events in 11-Month-Old Infants." *Cognition* 51 (2): 107–29.

Kotovsky, L., & R. Baillargeon. 1998. "The Development of Calibration-Based Reasoning about Collision Events in Young Infants." *Cognition* 67 (3): 311–51.

Kotovsky, L., & R. Baillargeon. 2000. "Reasoning about Collision Events Involving Inert Objects in 7.5-Month-Old Young Infants." *Developmental Science* 3 (3): 344–59.

Krashen, S.D. 1985. *The Input Hypothesis: Issues and Implications*. London: Longman.

Krashen, S.D. 2003. *Explorations in Language Acquisition and Use*. Portsmouth, NH: Heinemann.

Krizman, J., V. Marian, A. Shook, E. Skoe, & N. Krause. 2012. "Subcortical Encoding of Sound Is Enhanced in Bilinguals and Relates to Executive Function Advantages." *Proceedings of the National Academy of Sciences* 109 (20): 7877–81. doi: 10.1073/pnas.120575109.

LaBarbera, J.D., C.E. Izard, P. Vietze, & S.A. Parisi. 1976. "Four- and Six-Month-Old Infants' Visual Response to Joy, Anger and Neutral Expressions." *Child Development* 47 (2): 535–38.

Labbo, L.D. 2009. "'Let's Do the Computer Story Again, Nana': A Case Study of How a 2-Year-Old and His Grandmother Shared Thinking Spaces during Multiple Readings of an Electronic Story." In *Multimedia and Literacy Development: Improving Achievement for Young Learners*, eds. A.G. Bus & S.B. Neuman, 196–210. New York: Routledge.

Labbo, L.D. 1996. "Computers Real and Make-Believe: Providing Opportunities for Literacy Development in an Early Childhood Sociodramatic Play Center." *Instructional Resource* No. 26 (pp. Report ED396254. 396225).

Labbo, L.D., & M.R. Kuhn. 2000. "Weaving Chains of Affect and Cognition: A Young Child's Understanding of CD-ROM Talking Books." *Journal of Literacy Research* 32 (2): 187–210.

LaBerge, D., & S.J. Samuels. 1974. "Toward a Theory of Automatic Information Processing in Reading." *Cognitive Psychology* 6 (2): 293–323.

Landry, S.H., K.E. Smith, P.R. Swank, M.A. Assel, & S. Vellet. 2001. "Does Early Responsive Parenting Have a Special Importance for Children's Development or Is Consistency across Early Childhood Necessary?" *Developmental Psychology* 37 (3): 387–403.

Lavine, L. 1977. "Differentiation of Letter-Like Forms in Prereading Children." *Developmental Psychology* 13 (2): 89–94.

Lee, Y., J. Lee, M. Han, & J.A. Schickedanz. 2011. "Narratives, the Classroom Book Environment, and Teacher Attitudes toward Literacy Practices in Korea and the United States." *Early Education and Development* 22 (2): 234–55.

Legerstee, M. 1991. "Changes in the Quality of Infant Sounds as a Function of Social and Nonsocial Stimulation." *First Language* 11 (33): 327–43.

Legerstee, M. 1992. "A Review of the Animate-Inanimate Distinction in Infancy: Implications for Models of Social and Cognitive Knowing." *Early Development and Parenting* 1 (1): 59–67.

Legerstee, M., C. Corter, & K. Kienapple. 1990. "Hand, Arm, and Facial Actions of Young Infants to a Social and Nonsocial Stimulus." *Child Development* 61 (3): 774–84.

Lesaux, N.K., & M.J. Kieffer. 2010. "Exploring Sources of Reading Comprehension Difficulties among Language Minority Learners and Their Classmates in Early Adolescence." *American Educational Research Journal* 47 (3): 596–632.

Leung, C.B. 2008. "Preschoolers' Acquisition of Scientific Vocabulary through Repeated Read-Aloud Events, Retellings, and Hands-On Science Activities." *Reading Psychology* 29 (2): 165–93.

Lewis, M., S.M. Alessandri, & M.W. Sullivan. 1992. "Differences in Shame and Pride as a Function of Children's Gender and Task Difficulty." *Child Development* 63 (3): 630–38.

Lewis, M., & L. Rosenblum. 1974. *The Origins of Fear*. New York: Wiley.

Lewis, M., M.W. Sullivan, C. Stanger, & M. Weiss. 1989. "Self Development and Self-Conscious Emotions." *Child Development 60* (1): 146–56.

Lieven, E.V.M. 1994. "Crosslinguistic and Crosscultural Aspects of Language Addressed to Children." In *Input and Interaction in Language Acquisition*, eds. C. Gallaway & B. J. Richards, 56–73. Cambridge: Cambridge University Press.

Liu, H.M., F.M. Tsao, & P.K. Kuhl. 2007. "Acoustic Analysis of Lexical Tone in Mandarin Infant-Directed Speech." *Developmental Psychology* 43 (4): 912–17.

Lonigan, C.J. 2006. "Conceptualizing Phonological Processing Skills in Preschoolers." In *Handbook of Early Literacy Research*, Vol. 2, eds. D.K. Dickinson & S.B. Neuman, 77–89. New York: Guilford.

Lundberg, I., J. Frost, & O. Petersen. 1988. "Effects of an Extensive Program for Stimulating Phonological Awareness in Preschool Children." *Reading Research Quarterly* 23 (3): 263–84.

Makin, L. 2006. "Literacy 8-12 Months: What Are Babies Learning?" *Early Years: An International Journal of Research and Development* 26 (3): 267–77.

Mandler, J.M., & L. McDonough. 1998. "Studies in Inductive Inference in Infancy." *Cognitive Psychology* 37 (1): 60–80.

Martin, L.E. 1998. "Early Book Reading: How Mothers Deviate from Printed Text for Young Children." *Reading Research and Instruction* 37 (2): 137–60.

Martinez, M., & N. Roser. 1985. "Read It Again: The Value of Repeated Readings during Storytime." *The Reading Teacher 40* (5): 444–51.

Martinez, M.G., & W.H. Teale. 1989. "Children's Book Selections in a Kindergarten Classroom Library." Unpublished raw data. (Cited in J.S. Fractor, M.C. Woodruff, M.G. Martinez, & W.H. Teale. 1993. "Let's Not Miss Opportunities to Promote Voluntary Reading: Classroom Libraries in the Elementary School." *The Reading Teacher* 46 (6): 476–84.)

Mashburn, A., L.M. Justice, J.T. Downer, & R.C. Pianta. 2009. "Peer Effects on Children's Language Achievement during Pre-Kindergarten." *Child Development* 80 (3): 686–702.

Masonheimer, P.E., P.A. Drum, & L.C. Ehri. 1984. "Does Environmental Print Identification Lead Children into Word Reading?" *Journal of Reading Behavior* 16 (4): 257–71.

McArthur, D., L.B. Adamson, & D.F. Deckner. 2005. "As Stories Become Familiar: Mother-Child Conversations during Shared Reading." *Merrill Palmer Quarterly: Journal of Developmental Psychology* 51 (4): 389–411.

McCune-Nicolich, I. 1981. "Toward Symbolic Functioning: Structure of Early Pretend Games and Potential Parallels with Language." *Child Development* 52 (3): 785–97.

McDonough, L., & J.M. Mandler. 1998. "Inductive Generalization in 9- and 11-Month-Olds." *Developmental Science* 1 (2): 227–32.

McGee, L., & D.J. Richgels. 1989. "'K is Kristen's': Learning the Alphabet from a Child's Perspective." *The Reading Teacher* 39 (2): 216–25.

McGee, L., & J.A. Schickedanz. 2007. "Repeated Interactive Read-Alouds in Preschool and Kindergarten." *The Reading Teacher* 60 (8): 742–51.

Meltzoff, A.N. 1995. "Understanding the Intentions of Others: Re-enactment of Intended Acts by 18-Month-Old Children." *Developmental Psychology* 31 (5): 838–50.

Mercer, N. 1995. *The Guided Construction of Knowledge Talk amongst Teachers and Learners*. Clevedon, Avon, England: Multilingual Matters.

Metsala, J.L. 1997. "An Examination of Word Frequency and Neighborhood Density in the Development of Spoken-Word Recognition." *Memory & Cognition 25* (1): 47–56.

Metsala, J.L. 1999. "Young Children's Phonological Awareness and Nonword Repetition as a Function of Vocabulary Development." *Journal of Educational Psychology* 91 (1): 3–19.

Metsala, J.L., & A.C. Walley. 1998. "Spoken Vocabulary Growth and the Segmental Restructuring of Lexical Representations: Precursors to Phonemic Awareness and Early Reading Ability." In *Word Recognition in Beginning Literacy*, eds. J.L. Metsala & L.C. Ehri, 89–120. Hillsdale, NJ: Erlbaum.

Mills, C.M., J.H. Danovitch, M.G. Grant, & F.B. Elashi. 2012. "Little Pitchers Use Their Big Ears: Preschoolers Solve Problems by Listening to Others Ask Questions." *Child Development* 83 (2): 568–80.

Milteer, K.R. Ginsburg, & D.A. Mulligan. 2012. "The Importance of Play in Promoting Healthy Child Development and Maintaining Strong Parent-Child Bond: Focus on Children in Poverty." *Pediatrics* 129 (1): 204–13.

Morgante, J.D., & R. Keen. 2008. "Vision and Action: The Effect of Visual Feedback on Infants' Exploratory Behaviors." *Infant Behavior and Development* 31 (4): 729–33.

Morris, A.S., J.S. Silk, M.D. Morris, & L. Steinberg. 2011. "The Influence of Mother-Child Emotion Regulation Strategies on Children's Expression of Anger and Sadness." *Developmental Psychology* 47 (1): 213–25.

Morrow, L. 1985. "Reading and Retelling Stories: Strategies for Emergent Readers." *The Reading Teacher* 38 (9): 870–75.

Myowa-Yamakoshi, M., Y. Kawakita, M. Okanda, & H. Takeshita. 2011. "Visual Experience Influences 12-Month-Old Infants' Perception of Goal-Directed Actions of Others." *Developmental Psychology* 47 (4): 1042–49.

NAEYC. 2009. "Developmentally Appropriate Practice in Early Childhood Programs Serving Children from Birth through Age 8." Position statement. Washington, DC: Author.

NAEYC & Fred Rogers Center for Early Learning and Children's Media. 2012. "Technology and Interactive Media as Tools in Early Childhood Programs Serving Children from Birth through Age 8." Joint position statement. Washington, DC: NAEYC; Latrobe, PA: Fred Rogers for Early Learning at Saint Vincent College.

Nagell, K. 1995. "Joint Attention and Gestural and Verbal Communication in 9- to 15-Month-Olds." Paper presented at the Bienniel Meeting of the Society for Resarch in Child Development, Indianapolis, IN.

Nagy, W.E., R.C. Anderson, & P.A. Herman. 1987. "Learning Words from Context during Normal Reading." *American Educational Research Journal* 24 (2): 237–70.

Nagy, W., & E.H. Hiebert. 2011. "Toward a Theory of Word Selection." In *Handbook of Reading Research,* Vol. IV, eds. M.L. Kamil, P.D. Pearson, E.B. Moje, & P.P. Afflerbach, 388–404. New York: Routledge.

Nagy, W., & D. Townsend. 2012. "Words as Tools: Learning Academic Vocabulary as Language Acquisition." *Reading Research Quarterly* 47 (1): 91–108.

National Governors Association Center for Best Practices, Council of Chief State School Officers. 2010. "Common Core State Standard (English Language Arts)." Washington, DC: Authors. Retrieved from www.corestandards.org/the-standards.

National Reading Panel. 2000. "Report of the National Reading Panel." Washington, DC: National Institute for Literacy.

NCES (National Center for Education Statistics). 2011. "NAEP 2011 Trends in Academic Progress: The Nation's Report Card." Retrieved from http://nces.ed.gov/nationsreportcard/pdf/main2011/2012457.pdf.

NELP (National Early Literacy Panel). 2008. "Developing Early Literacy: Report of the National Early Literacy Panel." Washington, DC: National Institute for Literacy. Retrieved from http://www.nifl.gov/earlychildhood/NELP/NELPreport.html.

NICHD (National Institute of Child Development) Early Child Care Research Network. 2005. "Pathways to Reading: The Role of Oral Language in the Transition to Reading." *Developmental Psychology* 41 (2): 428–42.

Nelson, C.A., P.A. Morse, & L.A. Leavitt. 1979. "Recognition of Facial Expressions by Seven-Month-Old Infants." *Child Development* 50 (4): 1239–42.

Nelson, D.G.K., K.A. O'Neil, & Y.M. Asher. 2008. "A Mutually Facilitative Relationship between Learning Names and Learning Concepts in Preschool Children: The Case of Artifacts." *Journal of Cognition and Development* 9 (2): 171–93.

Neuman, S.B. 2010. "Lessons from My Mother: Reflections on the National Early Literacy Panel Report." *Educational Researcher* 39 (4): 301–04.

Neuman, S.B., & D.C. Celano. 2013. *Giving Our Children a Fighting Chance: Poverty, Literacy, and the Development of Informational Capital.* New York: Teachers College Press.

Ninio, A., & J. Bruner. 1978. "The Achievement and Antecedents of Labelling." *Journal of Child Language* 5 (1): 1–15.

Ninio, A., & P. Wheeler. 1984. "Functions of Speech in Mother-Infant Interaction." In *The Origins and Growth of Communication*, eds. L. Feagans, G.J. Garvey, & R. Golinkoff, 196–207. Norwood, NJ: Ablex.

Ortiz, C., R.M. Stowe, & D.H. Arnold. 2001. "Parental Influence on Child Interest in Shared Picture Book Reading." *Early Childhood Research Quarterly* 16 (2): 263–81.

Ouellette, G.P. 2006. "What's Meaning Got to Do with It: The Role of Vocabulary in Word Reading and Reading Comprehension." *Journal of Educational Psychology* 98 (3): 554–66.

Paciga, K.A., J.L. Hoffman, & W.H. Teale. 2011. "The National Early Literacy Panel and Preschool Literacy Instruction: Green Lights, Caution Lights, and Red Lights." *Young Children* 66 (6): 50–57.

Palmer, C.F. 1989. "The Discriminating Nature of Infants' Exploratory Actions." *Developmental Psychology* 25 (6): 885–93.

Pan, B.A., M.L. Rowe, J.D. Singer, & C.E. Snow. 2005. "Maternal Correlates of Growth in Toddler Vocabulary Production in Low-Income Families." *Child Development* 76 (4): 763–82.

Papandropoulos, I., & H. Sinclair. 1974. "What's a Word? Experimental Study of Children's Ideas on Grammar." *Human Development* 17 (2): 241–258.

Paratore, J.R., C.M. Cassano, & J.A. Schickedanz. 2011. "Supporting Early (and Later) Literacy Development at Home and at School: The Long View." In *Handbook of Reading Research*, Vol. IV, eds. M.L. Kamil, P.D. Pearson, E.B. Moje, & P.P Afflerbach, 106–35. New York: Routledge.

Paris, A.H., & S.G. Paris. 2003. "Assessing Narrative Comprehension in Young Children." *Reading Research Quarterly* 38 (1): 36–76.

Penuel, W.R., S. Pasnik, L. Bates, E. Townsend, L.P. Gallagher, C. Llorente, & N. Hupert. 2009. *Preschool Teachers Can Use a Media-Rich Curriculum to Prepare Low-Income Children for School Success: Results of a Randomized Controlled Trial*. Newton, MA: Education Development Center and SRI.

Persky, H.R., M.C. Daane, & Y. Jin. 2003. The Nation's Report Card: Writing 2002. (NCES 2003-529). U.S. Department of Education. Institute of Education Sciences. National Center for Educational Statistics. Washington, DC: Government Printing Office.

Peterson, C.L., & A. McCabe. 1994. "A Social Interactionist Account of Developing Decontextualized Narrative Skill." *Developmental Psychology* 30 (6) 937–48.

Peterson, C.L., B. Jesso, & A. McCabe. 1999. "Encouraging Narratives in Preschoolers: An Intervention Study." *Journal of Child Language* 26 (1): 49–97.

Phillips, L.B, & S. Twardosz. 2003. "Group Size and Storybook Reading: Two-Year-Old Children's Verbal and Nonverbal Participation with Books." *Early Education & Development* 14 (4): 453–78.

Piasta, S.B., Y. Petscher, & L.M. Justice. 2012. "How Many Letters Should Preschoolers in Public Programs Know? The Diagnostic Efficiency of Various Preschool Letter-Naming Benchmarks for Predicting First-Grade Literacy Achievement." *Journal of Educational Psychology* doi: 10.1037/a0027757.

Pikulski, J.J. 2006. "Fluency: A Developmental and Language Perspective." In *What Research Has to Say about Fluency Instruction*, eds. S.J. Samuels & A.E. Farstrup, 70–93. Newark, DE: International Reading Association.

Pikulski, J.J., & D. Chard. 2005. "Fluency: The Bridge between Decoding and Reading Comprehension." *The Reading Teacher* 58 (6): 510–21.

Pollard-Durodola, S.D., J.E. Gonzalez, D.C. Simmons, M.J. Davis, L. Simmons, & M. Nava-Walichowski. 2011. "Using Knowledge Networks to Develop Preschoolers' Content Vocabulary." *The Reading Teacher* 65 (4): 265–74.

Poulin-Dubois, D., & J.N. Forbes. 2006. "Word, Intention, and Action: A Two-Tiered Model of Action Word Learning." In *Action Meets Word: How Children Learn Verbs*, eds. K. Hirsh-Pasek & R.M. Golinkoff, 262–85. New York: Oxford University Press.

Poulin-Dubois, D., & T.R. Shultz. 1990. "The Infant's Concept of Category: The Distinction between Social and Nonsocial Objects." *Journal of Genetic Psychology* 151 (1): 77–90.

Pulverman, R., K. Hirsh-Pasek, R.M. Golinkoff, S. Pruden, & S.J. Salkind. 2006. "Conceptual Foundations for Verb Learning: Celebrating the Event." In *Action Meets Word: How Children Learn Verbs*, eds. K. Hirsh- Pasek & R.M. Golinkoff, 134–59. New York: Oxford University Press.

Purcell-Gates, V. 1996. "Stories, Coupons, and the TV Guide: Relationships between Home Literacy Experiences and Emergent Literacy Knowledge." *Reading Research Quarterly* 31 (4): 406–28.

Quinn, P.C., P.D. Eimas, & S.L. Rosenkrantz. 1993. "Evidence for Representations of Perceptually Similar Natural Categories by 3-Month-Old and 4-Month-Old Infants." *Perception* 22 (4): 463–75.

Raver, C. 2002. "Emotions Matter: Making the Case for the Role of Young Children's Emotional Development for Early School Readiness." *SRCD Social Policy Report* 16 (3): 3–14.

Read, C. 1975. *Children's Categorization of Speech Sounds in English*. Urbana, IL: National Council of Teachers of English.

Repacholi, B.M., & A. Gopnik. 1997. "Early Reasoning about Desires: Evidence from 14- and 18-Month-Olds." *Developmental Psychology* 33 (1): 12–21.

Reutzel, R., P. Fawson, J. Young, T. Morison, & B. Wilcox. 2003. "Reading Environmental Print: What Is the Role of Concepts about Print in Discriminating Young Readers' Responses?" *Reading Psychology* 24 (2) 123–62.

Richman, W.A., & J. Colombo. 2007. "Joint Book Reading in the Second Year and Vocabulary Outcomes." *Journal of Research in Childhood Education* 21 (3): 242–53.

Roberts, T.A. 2008. "Home Storybook Reading in Primary or Second Language with Preschool Children: Evidence of Equal Effectiveness for Second-Language Vocabulary Acquisition." *Reading Research Quarterly* 43 (2): 103–30.

Rochat, P. 1989. "Object Manipulation and Exploration in 2-to 5-Month-Old Infants." *Developmental Psychology* 25 (6): 871–84.

Roskos, K., K. Burstein, Y. Byeong-Keun, J. Brueck, & C. O'Brien. 2011. "A Formative Study of an E-Book Instructional Model in Early Literacy." *Creative Education* 2 (1): 10–17.

Roskos, K., & S.B. Neuman. 2011. "The Classroom Environment: First, Last, and Always." *The Reading Teacher* 65 (2): 110–14.

Roth-Hanania, R., M. Davidov, & C. Zahn-Waxler. 2011. "Empathy Development from 8-16 Months: Early Signs of Concern for Others." *Infant Behavior and Development* 34 (3): 447–58.

Rowe, D.W. 2008. "Social Contracts for Writing: Negotiating Shared Understandings about Text in the Preschool Years." *Reading Research Quarterly* 44 (1): 66–95.

Ruff, H.A. 1984. "Infants' Manipulative Exploration of Objects: Effects of Age and Object Characteristics." *Developmental Psychology* 20 (1): 9–20.

Rutter, D.R., & K. Durkin. 1987. "Turn-Taking in Mother-Infant Interaction: An Examination of Vocalization and Gaze." *Developmental Psychology* 23 (1): 54–61.

Salahu-Din, D., H. Persky, & J. Miller. 2008. "The Nation's Report Card: Writing 2007." (NCES 2008-468). National Center for Educational Statistics, Institute of Education Sciences, U.S. Department of Education, Washington, DC.

Salapatek, P., & W. Kessen. 1966. "Visual Scanning of Triangles by the Human Newborn." *Journal Of Experimental Child Psychology* 3 (2): 155–67.

Scarborough, H. & W. Dobrich. 1994. "On the Efficacy of Reading to Preschoolers." *Developmental Review* 14 (3): 245–302.

Schickedanz, J.A. 1990. *Adam's Righting Revolutions: One Child's Literacy Development from Infancy through Grade One*. Portsmouth, NH: Heinemann.

Schickedanz, J. 1999. "Setting the Stage for Literacy Events in the Classroom." *Child Care Information Exchange* 123: 53–57.

Schickedanz, J.A., & R.M. Casbergue. 2009. *Writing in Preschool: Learning to Orchestrate Meaning and Marks*. 2nd ed. Newark, DE: The International Reading Association.

Schickedanz, J.A., & M.F. Collins. 2012. "For Young Children, Pictures in Storybooks Are Rarely Worth a Thousand Words." *The Reading Teacher* 65 (8): 539–49.

Schickedanz, J.A., & L.M. McGee. 2010. "The NELP Report on Shared Story Reading Interventions (Chapter 4): Extending the Story." *Educational Researcher* 39 (4): 323–29.

Sénéchal, M. 1997. "The Differential Effect of Storybook Reading on Preschoolers' Acquisition of Expressive and Receptive Vocabulary." *Journal of Child Language* 24 (1): 123–38.

Sénéchal, M., E.H. Cornell, & L.S. Broda. 1995. "Age-Related Changes in the Organization of Parent-Infant Interactions during Picture-Book Reading." *Early Childhood Research Quarterly* 10 (3): 317–37.

Sénéchal, M., & J. LeFevre. 2002. "Parental Involvement in the Development of Children's Reading Skill: A Five-Year Longitudinal Study." *Child Development* 73 (2): 445–60.

Sénéchal, M., G. Ouellette, & D. Rodney. 2006. "The Misunderstood Giant: On the Predictive Value of Early Vocabulary to Future Reading." In *Handbook of Early Literacy Research*, Vol. 2, eds. D.K. Dickinson & S.B. Neuman, 173–82. New York: Guilford.

Serafini, F. 2011. "When Bad Things Happen to Good Books." *The Reading Teacher* 65 (4): 238–41.

Share, D.L. 1999. "Phonological Recoding and Orthographic Learning: A Direct Test of the Self-Teaching Hypothesis." *Journal of Experimental Child Psychology* 72 (1): 95–129.

Shuler, C. 2009. "iLearn: A Content Analysis of the iTunes App Store's Education Section." New York: The Joan Ganz Cooney Center at Sesame Workshop. Retrieved from http://joangan-zcooneycenter.org/upload_kits/ilearn_1_.pdf.

Shuler, C. 2012. "iLearn II: An Analysis of the Education Category of the Apple's App Store." New York : The Joan Ganz Cooney Center at Sesame Workshop. Retrieved from http://joangan-zcooneycenter.org/upload_kits/ilearnii.pdf.

Siegler, R.S., & M.W. Alibali. 2005. *Children's Thinking.* 4th ed. Upper Saddle River, NJ: Prentice Hall.

Simcock, G., & J.S. DeLoache. 2008. "The Effect of Repetition on Infants' Imitation from Picture Books Varying in Iconicity." *Infancy* 13 (6): 687–97.

Simion, F., V. Macchi Cassia, C. Turati, & E. Valenza. 2001. "The Origins of Face Perception: Specific Versus Non-Specific Mechanisms." *Infant and Child Development* 10 (1-2): 59–65.

Sipe, L.R. 2000. "The Construction of Literary Understanding by First and Second Graders in Oral Response to Picture Storybook Read-Alouds." *Reading Research Quarterly* 35 (2): 252–75.

Smith, C.R. 2001. "Click and Turn the Page: An Exploration of Multiple Storybook Literacy." *Reading Research Quarterly* 36 (2): 152.

Smith, M.W., J.P. Brady, & L. Anastasopoulos. 2008. *Early Language and Literacy Classroom Observation Toolkit.* Baltimore: Brookes Publishing.

Snow, C. 1972. "Mothers' Speech to Children Learning Language." *Child Development* 43 (2): 549–65.

Snow, C.E. 1977. "The Development of Conversation between Mothers and Babies." *Journal of Child Language* 4 (1): 1–22.

Snow, C., W. Barnes, J. Chandler, L. Hemphill, & I. Goodman. 1991. *Unfulfilled Expectations: Home and School Influences on Literacy.* Cambridge, MA: Harvard University Press.

Sorce, J., R. Emde, J. Campos, & M. Klinnert. 1985. "Maternal Emotional Signaling: Its Effect on the Visual-Cliff Behavior of 1-Year-Olds." *Developmental Psychology* 21 (1): 195–200.

Spelke, E.S., A. Phillips, & A.L. Woodward. 1995. "Infants' Knowledge of Objects in Motion and Human Action. In *Causal Cognition: A Multidisciplinary Debate*, eds. A.J. Premack, D. Premack, & D. Sperber, 44–77. Oxford: Clarendon Press.

Sperry, L.L., & D.E. Sperry. 1996. "The Early Development of Narrative Skills." *Cognitive Development* 11 (3): 443–66.

Spira, E.G., S.S. Bracken, & J. Fischel. 2005. "Predicting Improvement after First-Grade Reading Difficulties: The Effects of Oral Language, Emergent Literacy and Behavior Skills." *Developmental Psychology* 41 (1): 225–34.

Sroufe, LA., & J.P. Wunsch. 1972. "The Development of Laughter in the First Year of Life." *Child Development* 43 (4): 1326–44.

Stahl, K.A.D. 2012. "Applying New Visions of Reading Development in Today's Classrooms." *The Reading Teacher 65* (1): 52–56.

Stein, N.L. 1988. "The Development of Children's Storytelling Skill." In *Child Language: A Reader*, eds. M.B. Franklin & S.S. Barten, 282–98. New York: Oxford University Press.

Stern, D., J. Jaffe, B. Beebe, & S.L. Bennett. 1975. "Vocalizing in Unison and in Alternation: Two Modes of Communication within the Mother-Infant Dyad." *Annals of the New York Academy of Sciences* 263 (1): 89–100.

Stevens, R., & W.R. Penuel. 2010. "Studying and Fostering Learning through Joint Media Engagement." Paper presented at the Principal Investigators Meeting of the National Science Foundation's Science of Learning Centers, Arlington, VA.

Storch, S.A. & G.J. Whitehurst. 2002. "Oral Language and Code-Related Precursors to Reading: Evidence from a Longitudinal Structural Model." *Developmental Psychology* 38 (6): 934–47.

Sulzby, E. 1985. "Children's Emergent Reading of Favorite Storybooks: A Developmental Study." *Reading Research Quarterly* 20 (4): 458–81.

Swain, M. 2005. "The Output Hypothesis: Theory and Research." In *Handbook of Research in Second Language Teaching and Learning*, ed. E. Hinkel, 471–84. Mahwah, NJ: Erlbaum.

Sweet, A.P., & C. Snow. 2002. "Reconceptualizing Reading Comprehension." In *Improving Comprehension Instruction: Rethinking Research*, eds. C.C. Block, L.B. Gambrell, & M. Pressley, 54–79. Newark, DE, International Reading Association.

Tabors, P.O. 2008. *One Child, Two Languages: A Guide for Early Childhood Educators of Children Learning English as a Second Language.* 2nd ed. Baltimore, MD: Brookes.

Takeuchi, L. 2011. *Families Matter: Designing Media for a Digital Age.* New York.

Takeuchi, L., & R. Stevens. 2011. "The New Coviewing: Designing Learning through Joint Media Engagement." New York: Joan Ganz Cooney Center Sesame Workshop and LIFE Center. Retrieved from http://joanganzcooneycenter.org/Reports-32.html.

Taumoepeau, M., & T. Ruffman. 2006. "Mother and Infant Talk about Mental States Relates to Desire Language and Emotional Understanding." *Child Development* 77 (3): 465–81.

Taumoepeau, M., & T. Ruffman. 2008. "Stepping Stones to Others' Minds: Maternal Talk Related to Child Mental Language and Emotion Understanding at 15, 24, and 33 Months." *Child Development* 79 (2): 284–302.

Taylor, D., & C. Dorsey-Gaines. 1988. *Growing Up Literate.* Portsmouth, NH: Heinemann.

Taylor, H. B., J.L. Anthony, R. Aghara, K.E. Smith, & S.H. Landry. 2008. "The Interaction of Early Maternal Responsiveness and Children's Cognitive Abilities on Later Decoding and Reading Comprehension Skills." *Early Education and Development* 19 (1): 188–207.

Taylor, I. 1981. "Writing Systems and Reading." In *Reading Research: Advances in Theory and Practice,* Vol. 2, eds. G.E. MacKinnon & T.G. Waller, 1–51. New York: Academic Press.

Teale, W.H., J.L. Hoffman, & K.A. Paciga. 2010. "Where Is NELP Leading Preschool Literacy Instruction? Potential Positives and Pitfalls." *Educational Researcher 39* (4): 311–15.

Teale, W.H. 1986. "Home Background and Children's Literacy Development." In *Emergent Literacy: Writing and Reading,* eds. W.H. Teale & E. Sulzby, 173–206. Norwood, NJ: Ablex.

Teale, W.H., & E. Sulzby, eds. 1986. *Emergent Literacy: Writing and Reading.* Norwood, NJ: Ablex.

Termine, N.T., & C.E. Izard. 1988. "Infants' Responses to Their Mothers' Expressions of Joy and Sadness." *Developmental Psychology* 24 (2): 223–29.

Tomasello, M., & M.J. Farrar. 1986. "Joint Attention and Early Language." *Child Development* 57 (6): 1454–63.

Treiman, R., & V. Broderick. 1998. "What's in a Name: Children's Knowledge about the Letters in Their Own Names." *Journal of Experimental Child Psychology* 70 (2): 97–116.

Treiman, R., J. Cohen, K. Mulqueeny, B. Kessler, & S. Schechtman. 2007. "Young Children's Knowledge about Printed Names." *Child Development* 78 (5): 1458–71.

Turbill, J. 2001. "A Researcher Goes to School: Using Technology in the Kindergarten Literacy Curriculum." *Journal of Early Childhood Literacy* 1 (3): 255–79. doi: 10.1177/14687984010013002.

Ukrainetz, T.A., M.H. Cooney, S.K. Dyer, A.J. Kysar, & T.J. Harris. 2000. "An Investigation into Teaching Phonemic Awareness through Shared Reading and Writing." *Early Childhood Research Quarterly* 15 (2): 331–35.

Ukrainetz, T.A., J.J. Nuspl, K. Wilkerson, & S.R. Beddes. 2011. "The Effects of Syllable Instruction on Phonemic Awareness in Preschoolers." *Early Childhood Research Quarterly* 26 (1): 50–60.

Ungerer, J.A., R. Dolby, W. Brent, B. Barnett, N. Kelk, & V. Lewin. 1990. "The Early Development of Empathy: Self-Regulation and Individual Differences in the First Year." *Motivation and Emotion* 14 (1): 93–106.

Ungerer, J.A., P.R. Zelazo, R.B. Kearsley, & K. O'Leary. 1981. "Developmental Changes in the Representation of Objects in Symbolic Play from 18 to 35 Months of Age." *Child Development* 52 (1): 186–95.

Unsworth, L. 2006. *E-Literature for Children: Enhancing Digital Literacy Learning.* New York: Routledge.

U.S. Department of Education. 2008. *Early Reading First Performance.* Retrieved from www2.ed.gov/programs/earlyreading/performance.html.

Vaish, A., & T. Sriano. 2004. "Is Visual Reference Necessary? Contributions of Facial versus Vocal Cues in 12-Month-Olds' Social Referencing Behavior." *Developmental Science* 7 (3): 261–69.

van Kleeck, A., J. Vander Woude, & L. Hammett. 2006. "Fostering Literal and Inferential Language Skills in Head Start Preschoolers with Language Impairment Using Scripted Book-Sharing Discussions." *American Journal of Speech-Language Pathology* 15 (1): 85–95.

Verhallen, M.J.A.J., A.G. Bus, & M.T. De Jong. 2006. "The Promise of Multimedia Stories for Kindergarten Children at Risk." *Journal of Educational Psychology* 98 (2): 410–19.

Vukelich, C., & J. Christie. 2009. *Building a Foundation for Preschool Literacy.* 2nd ed. Newark, DE: International Reading Association.

Wang, S., L. Kaufman, & R. Baillargeon. 2003. "Should All Stationery Objects Move When Hit? Development of Infants' Causal and Statistical Expectations about Collisions Events." *Infant Behavior & Development* 26 (3): 529–67.

Wasik, B.A., & MA. Bond. 2001. "Beyond the Pages of a Book: Interactive Book Reading and Language Development in Preschool Classrooms." *Journal of Educational Psychology* 93 (2): 243–50.

Weinberg, M.K., & E.Z. Tronick. 1996. "Infant Affective Reactions to the Resumption of Maternal Interaction after the Still-Face." *Child Development* 67 (3): 905–14.

Weizman, Z.O., & C.E. Snow. 2001. "Lexical Input as Related to Children's Vocabulary Acquisition: Effects of Sophisticated Exposure and Support for Meaning." *Developmental Psychology* 37 (2): 265–279.

Werker, J.F., & S. Curtin. 2005. "PRIMIR: A Developmental Framework of Infant Speech Processing." *Language Learning & Development* 1 (2): 197–234.

Whitehead, M.R. 2002. "Dylan's Routes to Literacy: The First Three Years with Picture Books." *Journal of Early Childhood Literacy* 2 (3): 269–89.

Whitehurst, G. J., F.L. Falco, C.J. Lonigan, J.E. Fischel, B.D. DeBaryshe, M.C. Valdez-Menchaca, & M. Caulfield. 1988. "Accelerating Language Development through Picture Book Reading." *Developmental Psychology* 24 (4): 552–59.

Willingham, D.T. 2009. *Why Don't Students Like School? A Cognitive Scientist Answers Questions about How the Mind Works and What it Means for the Classroom.* San Francisco: Jossey-Bass.

Wong Fillmore, L. 1976. "The Second Time Around: Cognitive and Social Strategies in Second Language Acquisition." Unpublished PhD dissertation, Stanford University.

Wong Fillmore, L. 1991. "Second Language Learning in Children: A Model of Language Learning in Social Context." In *Language Processing in Bilingual Children*, ed. E. Bialystok, 49–69. Cambridge, England: Cambridge University Press.

Wood, D.J., J. Bruner, & G. Ross. 1976. "The Role of Tutoring in Problem Solving." *Journal of Child Psychology and Psychiatry* 17 (2): 89–100.

Yaden, D. B., Jr. 1988. "Understanding Stories through Repeated Read-Alouds: How Many Does It Take?" *The Reading Teacher* 41 (6): 556–61.

Yesil-Dagli, U. 2011. "Predicting ELL Students' Beginning First Grade English Oral Reading Fluency from Initial Kindergarten Vocabulary, Letter Naming, and Phonological Awareness Skills." *Early Childhood Research Quarterly* 26 (1): 15–29.

Yopp, H.K., & R.H. Yopp. 2009. "Phonological Awareness Is Child's Play." *Young Children* 64 (1): 12–21.

Young-Browne, G., H.M. Rosenfeld, & F.D. Horowitz. 1977. "Infant Discrimination of Facial Expressions." *Child Development* 48 (2): 555–62.

Zahn-Waxler, C., M. Radke-Yarrow, E. Wagner, & M. Chapman. 1992. "Development of Concern for Others." *Developmental Psychology* 28 (1): 126–36.

Zambo, D., & C.C. Hansen. 2007. "Love, Language, and Emergent Literacy." *Young Children* 62 (3): 32–37.

List of Children's Literature Cited

Chapter 1

Gilberto and the Wind, by Marie Hall Ets. 1978. Puffin Books.

One Dark Night, by Hazel Hutchins. Illus. Susan Kathleen Hartung. 2001. Viking.

The Snowy Day, by Ezra Jack Keats. 1962. Viking Children's.

Whistle for Willie, by Ezra Jack Keats. 1964. Viking Children's.

Chapter 2

Baby Dance, by Ann Taylor. Illus. Marjorie van Heerden. 1998. HarperFestival.

Baby EyeLike series. PlayBac.

Baby Faces, by Margaret Miller. 1998. Little Simon.

Black on White, by Tana Hoban. 1993. Greenwillow Books.

Boats, by Byron Barton. 1998. HarperFestival.

Brown Bear, Brown Bear, What Do You See?, by Bill Martin Jr. Illus. Eric Carle. 1992. Holt, Rinehart, & Wilson.

Dog, by Matthew Van Fleet. Photography by Brian Stanton. 2007. Simon & Schuster.

Fiesta Babies, by Carmen Tafolla. Illus. Amy Córdova. 2010. Tricycle Press.

Freight Train, by Donald Crews. 1978. Greenwillow Books.

Go Baby!, by Richard Steckel & Michele Steckel. 2008. Tricycle Press.

Go, by Dwell Studio. 2010. Blue Apple Books.

The Going to Bed Book, by Sandra Boynton. 1982. Little Simon.

Goodnight Moon, by Margaret Wise Brown. Illus. Clement Hurd. 1947. Harper & Row.

Gossie, by Olivier Dunrea. 2002. Houghton Mifflin.

How Do Dinosaurs Say Goodnight?, by Jane Yolen. Illus. Mark Teague. 2000. Blue Sky Press.

Hugs & Kisses, by Robert Grobel Intrater. 2002. Scholastic.

Hush! A Thai Lullaby, by Minfong Ho. Illus. Holly Meade. 1996. Orchard Books.

In My Pond, by Sara Gillingham. Illus. Lorena Siminovich. 2009. Chronicle Books.

In the Tall, Tall Grass, by Denise Fleming. 1991. Henry Holt.

Little Blue Truck, by Alice Schertle. Illus. Jill McElmurry. 2008. Harcourt.

Little Feet Love, by Anthony Nex. 2009. Piggy Toes Press.

Max and Ruby series, by Rosemary Wells. Viking Children's.

The Mitten, by Jan Brett. 1989. Putnam Juvenile.

Moo, Baa, La La La!, by Sandra Boynton. 1982. Little Simon.

"More More More," Said the Baby, by Vera B. Williams. 1990. Greenwillow.

Mrs. Mustard's Baby Faces, by Jane Wattenberg. 2007. Chronicle Books.

My Big Animal Book, by Roger Priddy. 2002. St. Martin's Press by Priddy Brinknell.

Oh, David!, by David Shannon. 2005. Blue Sky Press.

On Mother's Lap, by Ann Herbert Scott. Illus. Glo Coalson. 1992. Clarion Books.

Owl Babies, by Martin Waddell. Illus. Patrick Benson. 1992. Candlewick Press.

Peek-a Who?, by Nina Laden. 2000. Chronicle Books.

Peekaboo Morning, by Rachel Isadora. 2002. Putnam.

Pumpkin Day, Pumpkin Night, by Anne Rockwell. Illus. Megan Halsey. 1999. Walker Children's.

The Snowy Day, by Ezra Jack Keats. 1962. Viking.

Ten Little Fingers and Ten Little Toes, by Mem Fex. Illus. Helen Oxenbury. 2008. Houghton Mifflin Harcourt.

That's Not My Teddy. . . Its Paws Are Too Woolly, by Fiona Watt. Illus. Rachel Wells. 1999. EDC Publishing.

Toddler Two/Dos Años, by Anastasia Suen. Illus. Winnie Cheon. 2000. Lee & Low Books.

Toes, Ears, & Nose!, by Marion Dane Bauer. Illus. Karen Katz. 2003. Little Simon.

Trucks, by Byron Barton. 1986. HarperFestival.

The Wheels on the Bus, by Raffi. Illus. Sylvie Kantorovitz Wickstrom. 1988. Crown Books for Young Readers.

White on Black, by Tana Hoban. 1993. Greenwillow Books.

Chapter 3

Alphabet Under Construction, by Denise Fleming. 2002. Henry Holt.

Amos & Boris, by William Steig. 1971. Farrar, Straus and Giroux.

Caps for Sale: A Tale of a Peddler, Some Monkeys and Their Monkey Business, by Esphyr Slobodkina. 1947. HarperCollins.

Corduroy, by Don Freeman. 1968. Viking Children's.

Dog's Colorful Day: A Messy Story about Colors and Counting, by Emma Dodd. 2001. Puffin Books.

Dreams, by Ezra Jack Keats. 1974. Puffin Books.

Duck in the Truck, by Jez Alborough. 1999. HarperCollins.

Farmer Duck, by Martin Waddell. Illus. Helen Oxenbury. 1992. Candlewick Press.

Feast for 10, by Cathryn Falwell. 1993. Clarion.

Fish Is Fish, by Leo Lionni. 1974. Dragonfly Books.

Gilberto and the Wind, by Marie Hall Ets.1978. Puffin.

Goodnight Moon, by Margaret Wise Brown. Illus. Clement Hurd. 1947. Harper & Row.

A Hat for Minerva Louise, by Janet Morgan Stoeke. 1994. Puffin Books.

Henny Penny, by Paul Galdone. 1968. Clarion Books.

Henry's Happy Birthday, by Holly Keller. 1993. Walker Books Ltd.

Inch by Inch, by Leo Lionni. 1995. HarperCollins.

The Little Red Hen (Makes a Pizza), by Philemon Sturges. Illus. Amy Walrod. 1999. Puffin Books.

Max's Dragon Shirt, by Rosemary Wells. 2000. Puffin Books.

Mouse Paint, by Ellen Stoll Walsh. 1989. Harcourt.

One Dark Night, by Hazel Hutchins. Illus. Susan Kathleen Hartung. 2001. Viking.

One Gorilla, by Atsuko Morozumi. 1990. Mathew Price.

Peter's Chair, by Ezra Jack Keats. 1967. Puffin Books.

Possum and the Peeper, by Anne Hunter. 1998. Houghton Mifflin.

Possum's Harvest Moon, by Anne Hunter. 1996. Houghton Mifflin.

The Puddle Pail, by Elisa Kleven. 1997. Puffin Books.

Rabbits and Raindrops, by Jim Arnosky. 1997. Puffin Books.

Raccoon on His Own, by Jim Arnosky. 2001. Puffin Books.

The Snowy Day, by Ezra Jack Keats. 1962. Viking.

Some Smug Slug, by Pamela Duncan Edwards. Illus. Henry Cole. 1996. HarperTrophy.

Stellaluna, by Janell Cannon. 1993. Harcourt.

Swimmy, by Leo Lionni. 1973. Dragonfly Books.

The Very Hungry Caterpillar, by Eric Carle. 1969. Philomel.

Whistle for Willie, by Ezra Jack Keats. 1964. Viking.

Chapter 4

A Is for Africa, by Ifeoma Onyefulu. 1993. Puffin Books.

About Hummingbirds: A Guide for Children, by Cathryn Sill. Illus. John Sill. 2011. Peachtree.

About Penguins: A Guide for Children, by Cathryn Sill. Illus. John Sill. 2009. Peachtree.

Bee, by Karen Hartley & Chris Macro. 2006. Heinemann Library.

Birds, by Kevin Henkes. Illus. Laura Dronzek. 2009. Greenwillow Books.

The Boat Alphabet Book, by Jerry Pallotta. Illus. David Biedrzycki. 1998. Charlesbridge.

Carry Me! Animal Babies on the Move, by Susan Stockdale. 2008. Peachtree.

Caterpillar, by Karen Hartley, Chris Macro, & Philip Taylor. 2006. Heinemann Library.

Chameleon, Chameleon, by Joy Cowley. Photography by Nic Bishop. 2005. Scholastic Press.

Chicks & Chickens, by Gail Gibbons. 2003. Holiday House.

Crayfish, by Lola M. Schaefer. 2002. Heinemann Library.

Daddy Longlegs, by Catherine Anderson. 2008. Heinemann Library.

Eating the Alphabet, by Lois Ehlert. 1989. Harcourt Brace.

Farfallina & Marcel, by Holly Keller. 2002. Greenwillow Books.

Fly, by Karen Hartley, Chris Macro, & Philip Taylor. 2008. Heinemann Library.

The Frog Alphabet Book, by Jerry Pallotta. Illus. Ralph Masiello. 1990. Charlesbridge.

From Wheat to Bread, by Stacy Taus-Bolstad. 2013. Lerner.

Magnetic and Nonmagnetic, by Angela Royston. 2008. Heinemann Library.

More, by I.C. Springman. Illus. Brian Lies. 2012. Houghton-Mifflin.

One Bean, by Anne Rockwell. Illus. Megan Halsey. 1998. Walker.

Owls, by Gail Gibbons. 2005. Holiday House.

P Is for Pakistan, by Shazia Razzak. Photography by Prodeepta Das. 2007. Frances Lincoln Children's Books.

Raccoon on His Own, by Jim Arnosky. 2001. Puffin Books.

See How They Grow: Butterfly, by Mary Ling. 2007. DK Publishing.

Snakes, by Gail Gibbons. 2007. Holiday House.

Unbeatable Beaks, by Stephen R. Swinburne. Illus. Joan Paley. 1999. Henry Holt.

The Yucky Reptile Alphabet Book, by Jerry Pallotta. Illus. Ralph Masiello. 1989. Charlesbridge.

Chapter 5

One Duck Stuck, by Phyllis Root. Illus. Jane Chapman. 1998. Candlewick.

Roadwork, by Sally Sutton. Illus. Brian Lovelock. 2008. Candlewick.

The Very Hungry Caterpillar, by Eric Carle. 1969. Philomel.

Chapter 8

Rain, by Manya Stojic. 2000. Crown Publishers.

Snakes: Long, Longer, Longest, by Jerry Pallotta & Van Wallach. Illus. Shennen Bersani. 2006. Scholastic.

Index

Subjects

Authors

128875